THE LOCAL SUPERIOR
CAPSTONE OF FORMATION

THE SISTER FORMATION SERIES

The Mind of the Church in the Formation of Sisters, Proceedings for 1954-1955, ed. Sister Ritamary, C.H.M., 1956.

Spiritual and Intellectual Elements in the Formation of Sisters, Proceedings for 1955-1956, ed. Sister Ritamary, C.H.M., 1957.

Planning for the Formation of Sisters, Proceedings for 1956-1957, ed. Sister Ritamary, C.H.M., 1958.

The Juniorate in Sister Formation, Proceedings for 1957-1958, ed. Sister Ritamary, C.H.M., 1960.

The Religious-Apostolic Formation of Sisters, Elio Gambari, S.M.M., 1964.

Program for Progress, Proceedings for 1965, ed. Sister Mary Hester Valentine, S.S.N.D., 1966.

Published by Fordham University Press

THE LOCAL SUPERIOR
CAPSTONE OF FORMATION

*Proceedings and Communications of Regional Meetings
of the Sister-Formation Conferences
1967*

Editor

Sister Mary Hester Valentine, S.S.N.D.
Mount Mary College
Milwaukee, Wisconsin

Foreword

Edwin A. Quain, S.J.
Fordham University
New York

FORDHAM UNIVERSITY PRESS

New York · 1968

© COPYRIGHT FORDHAM UNIVERSITY PRESS · 1968

Imprimatur ✠ TERENCE J. COOKE, D.D.
New York, March 27, 1968

LIBRARY OF CONGRESS CATALOG CARD NUMBER: 58-10465

Printed in the United States of America by
The Colonial Press Inc.
Clinton, Mass.

Table of Contents

Foreword

The title of this book: *The Local Superior: Capstone of Formation,* is, I suggest, no mere metaphor. If the religious life for women is to grow and develop under the impelling forces that were unleashed in seemingly casual fashion by John XXIII, the role of the local superior is of the utmost importance. It is important that local superiors themselves realize this, and not comfort themselves with the illusion that they are merely the channels that convey the directives of Provincials and Mothers General to the individuals who live in their communities. It is equally important that the function of the local superior be understood by *all* the people with whom they live: the older sisters, whether they be among those who view the current phenomena with some detachment and perspective, secure in their conviction of the power of divine grace and with an unshakable loyalty and love of the Master they chose, in their youth, to follow, or among those whose days are now lived in trepidation lest they somehow be robbed of the placidity they have, perhaps, too casually assumed would be their portion forever. Far more important is it, however, that the role and the responsibility of the local superior be understood and respected by the newest members of the community.

If these, perhaps of all concerned, the ones who view the way of life they have recently espoused with the greatest objectivity and a notable idealism, will exercise their not inconsiderable virtue of openness in *all* of its aspects—not merely openness in noting and expressing their reservations as to what they find uncongenial or irrelevant to their apostolic ideals, but rather by showing an *openness of mind* which will generate a willingness to appreciate the ideas and ideals of another person, a basic charity and love of others who walk the same path, then there is solid hope that they will come to realize the awesome responsibility that burdens one whose task it is to stand, immediately, as the representative of the divine will to other human beings.

The inspiring words of the decree of Vatican II on Renewal in

Religious Life and the manifold insights that have been formulated by various religious communities since the council will be of little effect, if they are not carried out *in the convent* in which a certain number of religious live and work and pray and spend themselves for the good of souls. "Living" is always "contact with other people" and it is in that restricted area, over which the superior has been given charge, that lives will develop and blossom, or they will wither and waste away, unless those high principles become daily reality in the lives of individual people.

Hence the task of the superior: to be the living embodiment of the particular spirit and ideal of the Community; to carry on her work with a deep realization of her responsibility to the individual souls with whom she deals, as people vowed to the service of God and whose human fulfillment and growth will often be the measure of their apostolic effectiveness. Great, indeed, are the gifts of nature and grace that will be required if she is to fulfill adequately such responsibilities. Needless to say, she cannot look upon her position as a testimony to her merits and as a reward for her former services to the Community—it is indeed a dubious "honor" to be burdened with the office of superior—but rather it should be her endless quest to come to know her sisters, their virtues and faults, their talents and weaknesses; she should be accurately aware of the extent of work and responsibility the individual is bearing and, very importantly, how *this* individual is bearing up under those tasks, and when the work-load is unevenly distributed, she should with justice and charity, right the balance; she must also be aware of the human relationships that exist within her house, knowing which personalities are likely to work most harmoniously together, and which are not; further, she should be constantly aware of what is often the hardest task for the individual religious, to wit, the possibility for *this* person to lead a life of prayer and recollection and nearness to God, in what is often, the maelstrom of the demands and duties that devolve upon the zealous religious. In a word, she should always be clear as to the distinction of means and ends: one does not enter the religious life to be so burdened in coping with the means of attaining the results desired, that it is morally impossible to achieve the purpose they had in mind—the salvation of their own souls and the salvation of others.

Apart from this burning *concern* for her sisters, she has, especially in these times, the delicate task of handling authority; not that this was ever easy of accomplishment but in the present climate of thought it will be doubly difficult. First of all, she must stand for what she knows of her Community and its aims and spirit; she must, in the light of her conscience, properly formed according to the law of the Church and the Rule of the founder, see that her house is truly a religious house of her specific Community. At the same time, she must respect the freedom of conscience of her sisters, which, incidentally, should be "formed" on the same basic principles; she must be aware of the varying behests of the Spirit as He works in the souls of her sisters, cooperating and helping them to find God and His will in all things; in a word, her authority should be a source of *strength* and not merely of *restraint*, of security and protection, not solely of domination. Rarely, indeed, will she find it necessary to issue any solemn commands in virtue of holy obedience—in fact, the religious who has received such will surely be rare—but she must, in conscience, find it possible to achieve compliance from her sisters with the directives she finds it desirable or necessary to convey to her community.

Now, it is precisely here that she must be very clear as to the machinery by which such compliance, desirable for the common good, will be achieved. To be sure, the "folklore" (and sometimes, unfortunately, the reality) of the religious life can dredge up horrible examples of direful and comminatory orders issued, but such conduct has never been justified, on any principles, old or new. It is the task of the superior, especially in these times, so to present such "orders" as she may give to her sisters, that they can, by reasonable people, be seen to be reasonable, rational and based on serious thought and reflective prayer. From the knowledge she has of her sisters, she will know how to motivate them toward the accomplishment of what, before God, she sees to be desirable. If her knowledge on a particular matter is deficient, she has an obligation to seek for advice and from whom better could she seek it than from those among her sisters who are themselves knowledgeable in a particular area? For, it goes without saying that, in receiving the *moral* authority of being a superior, she did not, by some mysterious process, thereby receive *knowledge*! Superiors are not automatically infallible and, in consulting with the members of her community, a superior is not abdicating her authority, but merely using it in a reasonable manner. This, naturally, does not mean that nothing can happen in a community unless every single member can be brought to agreement, nor does it mean that the "democratic process" should go so far that majority rule, irrespective of law or custom, must always prevail. A superior who sees her task as a spiritual function and who has a profound respect for the integrity and sincerity of her sisters, should not find her "authority" being whittled away, provided she approaches its exercise after prayerful consideration.

This process, however, by which authority is exercised in a religious community with consultation of the members with the superior, also places a serious obligation on the members of the community. These, in turn, must respect the sincerity and the freedom of conscience of the superior; "consultation" can never mean a general right to obstruction and there lies on the conscience of the individual the obligation of purification of motives, of prayerful consideration of the common good as well as of the spirit and Rule of the Community; after that, they not only may, but they should speak up, when the occasion arises. In the history of the democratic process since it was created in Athens, human nature being what it is, the tendency "to take sides" has often manifested itself. All too often, such "taking sides" has been motivated by personal liking and perhaps less laudable motives. Hence, the profound necessity of forming one's opinions on the basis of objective fact, avoiding at all costs (since, generally, the spiritual good of other souls will be involved!), any unworthy prejudice or, what might well be more harmful, any preconceived stand that, at its best, might have no more solid basis than a desire to have one's own way. If there is today in religious life a greater exercise of personal liberty, let no one deceive himself that this is a privilege without any concomitant responsibilities.

These, and many other considerations are given extended treatment in the papers that were presented at the regional meetings of the Sister Formation Conference of last year. The book will be of value to all religious and not merely to Local Superiors; any description of the function of a superior can profitably be read and prayerfully considered by those who live under her guidance. Few will read these pages without coming to a realization of the magnitude of the task of a superior in these times; no one should, without a resolution to pray fervently that all concerned, superiors and sisters alike, will be inspired by the Giver of all good gifts to labor constantly so that the guidance of the Holy Spirit that so obviously was at work at Vatican II, may be shared in abundance by all whose dedication to Christ Jesus, Our Lord has marked them for the special graces that are needed in their vocation.

EDWIN A. QUAIN, S.J.

Fordham University Press

THE LOCAL SUPERIOR
CAPSTONE OF FORMATION

PART
I
THEME

Renewal in Christ

MOST REV. EDWARD J. HERRMANN, D.D., V.G.
Washington, D. C.

I have noted that when this conference was formed in 1954 its purposes were stated to be "the advancement by formal and informal means of the spiritual and intellectual training of sisters on pre-service and in-service levels." The Second Vatican Council has made specific reference to conferences of this kind in the Decree on the Adaptation and Renewal of Religious Life which says:

This synod favors conferences or councils of major superiors, established by the Holy See. These can contribute very much to achievement of the purpose of each institute; to encourage more effective cooperation for the welfare of the Church; to ensure a more just distribution of ministers of the Gospel in a given area; and finally, to conduct affairs of interest to all religious (§23).

It is not your own communities alone with which you are concerned, but the welfare of the whole Church. The same council urges you to assist one another, sharing your experiences and your wisdom, for the total benefit of the Church. In the spirit of the council you are to have a sense of the universal Church in her missionary role, which means that the concern of one is the concern of all, so that the Mystical Body of Christ may be vigorous and healthy in all its members. We need a "sense of the Church as a whole."

In analyzing the conference, concerned as it is with the spiritual and intellectual training of sisters, we can see quite clearly that its aims are consonant with the needs of modern times, which indeed demand a blending of these two aspects of the sisterhood—the spiritual and intellectual. This might be said to be a modern and authentic development of that basic Benedictine ideal, work and prayer; or perhaps we might

3

put it into the current phraseology of love and service, for does not spiritual and intellectual development concern itself with these basic Christian commitments? The reason is essentially the effort to serve not two masters but one, through the love and service which is given to God and men through the vocation of the sisterhood.

Let no one ever presume to consider this vocation as irrelevant to our modern times. Who could be said to be more relevant than one who has given herself to teach, or nurse, or counsel, or care for the aged, the young, or for the poor in some tenement or inner city? All of these are equally relevant to the world, and the Lord who made it and its people.

There is a hazard in these days of renewal and reform, as someone has recently observed, in an excessive optimism. This hazard is no less present in your work. The problem lies in whether the action taken through such a body as yours is authentic Christian action, love and service, spiritual and intellectual development. It is if the course of action is ordered according to God's will, but the hazard is that even these apparently good objectives can become an excuse for self-indulgence. It may masquerade as an eschatological attitude when in reality it is purely pragmatic and utilitarian. The wedding of spiritual and intellectual development must be a true union of noble and truly Christian objectives.

No doubt there are specific areas of concern you are anxious to study, and these will be given careful consideration. The theme of the 1967 meeting is "The Role of the Local Superior in the Continuing Formation of Sisters." But before you take your steps into this work, it would be well to review, for a moment, the general guidelines set down for you by the Second Vatican Council.

The council has re-echoed the exhortation of Pope John XXIII, that renewal within the Church should first of all be an inner renewal, that mere external renewal should not replace inner renewal. It is false renewal, indeed, that does not rest solidly on a deep, inner faith in the unchanging Christ. For this reason the council points out that the first rule of every religious community must be the Gospel of Our Lord and Saviour Jesus Christ. It is the missionary spirit of this good news that must inspire the particular rules of every religious community.

As you concern yourselves with the updating of the rules of your communities, the council cautions you against departing from the original graces and the initial inspirations of your founders. As you re-

late your original purposes to contemporary culture, you may be sure
that the Holy Spirit will give the necessary increase to your efforts.
Each community, faithful to its initial purposes, must assume its full
share in the authentic, missionary life of the Church; so that, always
conscious of its original active or contemplative commitments, it will
nevertheless experience the missionary sense of the apostolic Church.

The council urges you to study the contemporary world and its
needs, and to devise means of serving these needs in terms of prayer
and good works, of spiritual and corporal works of mercy, depending
on the particular emphasis of the spirit of your founder. You will need,
specifically, to effect a balance between your original commitments and
the demands of contemporary society.

There is one master we all serve. When Jesus came He showed us that
the power to bear witness lies entirely in the love, the mutual self-giving, of the Father and the Son. Our witness to the supernatural reality
of the world to which we minister is only of value in so far as it is the
automatic, though conscious, expression of our child-like self-sur-
render to God and His purpose for us. You have chosen to serve Him
through the love and service of your vocation.

May the Holy Spirit guide you, may He enlighten your minds and
warm your hearts, that the Church of today may experience a renewed
vitality flowing from your sincere and generous efforts to provide for
the continuing spiritual and academic formation of the sisters. And
may St. John's vision of the Church as ever renewing herself become
a reality in your conferences:

And I saw a new heaven and a new earth, for the first heaven and the first
earth passed away, and the sea is no more. And I saw the Holy City, the
new Jerusalem, coming down out of heaven from God, made ready as a
bride adorned for her husband. And I heard a loud voice from the throne
saying: "Behold the dwelling of God with men and He will dwell with
them and they will be His people, and God, Himself, will be with them
as God." . . . And He who was sitting on the throne said: "Behold, I make
all things new" (Apoc. 21:1-5).

The Church Encourages Renewal

Most Rev. Vincent J. Hines, D.D., J.C.D.
Bishop of Norwich, Connecticut

It has been said that today, more than a year after the close of the Vatican Council, Catholics can be divided into three groups. First, there are those who have warm and nostalgic thoughts of the past, and who view the changes in the Church with alarm and dismay. The second group consists of those who wish to change everything as much and as soon as possible. And in between are the moderates, who recognize the signs of the times and who admit, sometimes with understandable reluctance, that adjustment is needed for progress and perhaps even for survival.

We find these three categories of Catholics among bishops, among priests, among the laity, and certainly among religious. And this should not be surprising; because the concerns of others must be the concern of religious. There is no wall so high that it would isolate religious from the concerns of the universal Church, and today the Church is interested in the welfare, spiritual and temporal, of the whole world. The Vatican Council's Dogmatic Constitution on the Church, which is the finest and most fundamental of the sixteen documents of the council, situated and focused on the life of religious in its relation to the universal character conferred on each by baptism. So the concern of the entire Church for renewal must be the concern especially of religious.

This is why you have gathered the papers of this conference, so that under the guidance of qualified directors you can review your present programs, and receive fresh ideas on how your programs can be improved. I am happy to see that formal essays have been implemented by "reaction panels" to further discuss the problems that exist and the possible solutions. It is in such informal but earnest exchange of ideas that you will be able to think your way to solutions, or at least to temporary reasonable adjustments that may lead to eventual solutions.

The American bishops are very anxious that you have conferences of this kind because no one knows better than the bishops the immense debt that the Church in America owes to the sisters. If the faith in America is so strong that it is the envy of and inspiration to the rest of the world, it is due primarily to the work of the sisters. This is true of your work in every field, primarily in education, but also in nursing, in hospital administration and in social work. Everywhere, success has depended on the sisters.

I say this with no purpose or pretense of empty flattery. I say it because I want to emphasize the importance which the bishops attach to the continuance of vibrant, up-to-date religious communities which will attract and challenge modern youth. Today's youth can find challenges in so many secular fields; they must be able to find a comparable challenge for their love and dedication in the religious field.

We all know that we are passing through difficult times. Today we have problems that five years ago we would not have believed possible. Renewal has brought with it headaches and heartaches. But this is no reason for leaders to lose heart; this is no time for superiors to lose confidence. Perhaps this is a time for necessary pruning of our ideas and our institutions. Perhaps it is a time for spiritual and physical checkups at all levels of the Church. Perhaps the readjustments that may have to be made will be a blessing in disguise; perhaps the retooling process will result in a better, more efficient, more up-to-date product.

At any rate, as Christians, we can be sure that nothing that happens, happens without God's knowledge and God's will. So to the delegates to this conference I say, *Sursum corda*—Lift up your hearts! Remember that to those who love God, all things, even the least promising, work together into good. I encourage you to begin this important conference in the confident Christian belief that adaptation, updating and renewal are the will of the council, the will of the Church, and the will of God. And in His will is our peace.

The Council and Continuing Formation

MOST REV. JOHN S. SPENCE, D.D.
Vicar General, Washington, D. C.

In the document on religious life emanating from Vatican Council II there is a single paragraph of eighteen lines dealing with the specific subject assigned me for explanation. That is not very much resource material to go on; but then all of the conciliar documentation is intended to be just a guideline, as well as a stimulus to further thought, development and legitimate experimentation in all the phases of renewal. Accordingly, with recourse to prayer and meditation, to advice and consultation, and finally to personal observation and experience, I shall proceed to render whatever contribution I can to the much-needed enlightenment on a topic of interest and concern to many—namely, "The Role of the Local Superior in the Continuing Formation of Sisters." Moreover I would point out right from the beginning that the Church did not begin with Vatican II; that there is a whole treasure chest of truth and wisdom of the past 1900 years to draw from, and that when all the Vatican II suggestions have been adopted there will still be constant need of individual and general renewal in every phase of the Church's life.

Few, if any, will contest the fact that the formation of a religious does and must carry on long after the subject emerges from the postulancy or the novitiate. Indeed most people will admit that during the entire pilgrimage of life a true follower of Christ of any rank must strive endlessly to learn more and more how to become the perfect image of the master. For religious women that bridal wreath worn on vow day as an aspiration and a pledge of devotion to the bridegroom is worn again in the casket as a proof that the vows have been fulfilled, and that it will designate the wearer as a true bride of Christ in the resurrection.

But the vital question before us is just how the local superior plays her definite part in the continuing formation of the sister assigned to her convent, no matter how many years she has been professed, no matter how much older or younger the subject is than the local superior.

The first injunction to the superior by the council is that she herself must be docile to the will of God, that she by her total example must grow in the observance of God's commandments, in the pursuit of the evangelical counsels, in the ministry to her subjects, always mindful that she, like the Son of Man, came not to be ministered unto, but to minister; that as God has been tolerant of her faults and forgiving of her trespasses, so she must be tolerant, forgiving and understanding of others' weaknesses, imperfections and lack of cooperation with spiritual opportunities. The law of charity must be her dominant characteristic, for charity is the bond of union and peace. She must see in all her subjects the daughters of God, and love them with as much of a divine love as she can supernaturally acquire. Such a manifestation of godlike charity will make it that much easier for her daughters to obey out of Godlike happy obedience than they would if they were rendering mere natural respect for, and compliance with, an earthly or legalistically appointed superior. This supernaturalized relationship of superior and sister causes the one to respect to the utmost degree the freedom of conscience in reference to the sacrament of penance and spiritual direction, and it prompts the other to be ever aware of the fact that she is part of a community with obligations toward all the members and above all to the head, without which it ceases to be a community.

In saying all this as is indicated in the Vatican decree, let us not jump to the conclusion that authority must never function, or that it must be overlooked. Charity does not remove the need for law and order; but in the atmosphere of charity, obedience to law and order is more joyfully given, *Ubi amatur, non laboratur*.

The question then arises: Given the truly Christian superior, operating in the climate and manner of charity, how does she go about achieving further growth in her subjects? The decree succinctly gives five general methods:

1. Have everyone learn Christ and His message directly and consistently from the New Testament;

2. In serving the interests of the Church the members of the community keep in mind and preserve the spirit of their particular

founder, and adhere as closely as possible to the traditions and goals for which their founder's community was ratified and blessed by the Church;

3. Do not allow the community to drift apart into isolation from the vital functions of the Church. On the contrary, insist that the members, while adhering to the special endeavor selected by the order's founder, nevertheless should master and foster in every possible way the enterprises and objectives of the Church in such fields as these: scriptural, liturgical, doctrinal, pastoral, ecumenical, missionary and social;

4. Insist that the members keep keenly aware of the needs of the people of their day and of their area, so that if the opportunity comes, they may more effectively come to the aid of their neighbors;

5. Above everything else keep the members constantly conscious that all external renewal comes to naught unless it begins and ends with a constant *metanoia* or renewal of self from within.

These five norms at first sound redundant and even contradictory, but upon reflection and analysis they are quite the opposite. They are simply broad directives for showing the sisters how to become total Christians, or, as St. Paul says, "all things to all men."

I think it might be well to expound a bit on a common specialized professional excellence in the temporal order and a basic, profound, spiritual formation in the supernatural qualities inherent in a religious vocation. This seems to be the focal point of the question. What can the superior do to fulfill the natural, normal desire of her subjects to become effective instruments in the history of their times by involving themselves in the techniques of the times, and reproducing the image of their times—the while they go about the all-important task of "putting on Christ," submerging their natural worldly ambitions of becoming champions of all the worthwhile causes of their times—without becoming victims of the pitfalls, heresies and totally humanitarian preoccupations of their times? How can she meld her daughters into the ideal combination of excellent teachers, activists, and social workers, while they remain growing representatives of the hidden God, Who redeemed the world by living and suffering and dying for it without ever being overcome by the evil in the world?

Our Blessed Lord Himself and the inspired writers of the New Testament had much to say about this double duty, and each of them placed primary importance upon personal sanctification first, and only after that upon involvement in the solution of the world's ills. The scriptural readings before meals should be carefully selected and planned in such a way as to inculcate repeatedly the necessity of becoming Christlike in thought, word, deed and outlook. From time to time, bible readings and enthronement of the scriptures could be held —all calculated to intensify the words of Our Lord about the preeminence of dying to self and living to Christ, before we can even approach proper dedication of self to neighbor and the world. New books from acclaimed modern authors as well as ancient writers should be made available, to provide ample opportunity and diversity of presentation to the sisters seeking perfection. No book which sells the notion of secular humanism as the essence of religion should be allowed on the library shelves. Beware of slogans and bywords that capture the imagination and fill the mind with false philosophy. Such phrases as "go where the action is" should be refuted by the sounder phrase "go where the chief Actor is." Daily visits to the Blessed Sacrament, private meditation and contemplation in the chapel should be encouraged by word and by example. A well-frequented chapel is a sure sign of a thoroughly Christian community.

Keeping the community spirit and the founder's goals seldom become meaningless or passé; after all, the basic needs of humanity remain much the same in almost every age. They may undergo external modification by taking on new forms in different centuries, but usually they are just the same old needs with new labels. As a consequence the sainted founders, were they to reappear in the society of today, would probably make a few adaptations in methods, but essentially they would strive after the same goals. There may be a few congregations that have completely lost their *raison d'être*; but the vast majority simply have to shift emphasis. I truly believe that the loss of so many vocations, particularly the secularization of so many religious, professed less than eight to ten years, is because their founder's purposes have not been properly interpreted in the community.

In the encouragement of the next conciliar recommendation, namely keeping the community in close contact with the vital functions of the Church of the day, there lies a special danger. In political science, before the air and space age, this was known as the danger of "foreign entanglements." But now that we have become one world in the realistic sense, the term no longer applies. It can be argued that no place on the globe is "foreign" anymore, but the fact remains that there are "entanglements." So with the Church. The Church is and always has been one, so in a real sense what is the Church's concern in one land is the Church's concern in every land. We are indeed our brothers' keepers. We must prepare ourselves to help our brothers and sisters everywhere, insofar as we can. However, because of the limitation of human nature, one person cannot become a *factotum* to everyone, everywhere else in the world.

Precisely because of this limitation of energy, ability, and time, of even the best intentioned and capable people, someone has to step in and set priorities, draw boundaries, and call halts. And in a community of religious women, the person to direct, channel and harness all these gifts and talents in the best interest of the individual sister as well as of the Church and of the order, is the local superior. Of course, it is also her duty to cause the individual to develop to the best of her ability in accordance with her own desires, if possible. But the nuns' lives do have to be ordered, lest illness, excess and chaos result. In encouraging extra study and specialization the superior must always keep in mind the particular objective of the community, whether it be praying, teaching, nursing or whatever the task at hand requires.

There are always those to whom the grass seems greener in the yard next door, and who would jump the fence to water and plant in the neighbor's bailiwick rather than in their own. Keeping these gentle souls happy, and making them aware that nearly all the soil in the area, if properly tended, will yield the same flowers or fruit, is no easy task; but it is one that falls to the lot of the local superior.

The fourth recommendation of the council is for the superior to help the sisters acquire a sense of civic community by becoming acquainted with people and their problems in the immediate environs. The purpose is twofold: first, to prepare them to exercise charity in whatever way lies open to them, and secondly, to make them aware of their own relative blessedness in being members of a religious community where peace, unity and contentment normally abound. However, both of these praiseworthy ends can be fraught with danger, if they are not engaged in in a temperate manner. I have seen a few religious sisters take their neighbors' burdens so to heart that they could not sleep for worrying about them; they could not work because of a compulsion to spend their time with the suffering, consoling them and trying to alleviate their burdens. Obviously then, if acquiring civic-community-mindedness interferes with religious-community-mindedness, the earthly association must yield to the supernatural one. Every religious must retain a valid sense of priorities in establishing her occupations and in utilizing her time. The superior must aid her in this task, reminding her kindly but firmly that she is not a social worker first, and a religious second, but rather that it is just the other way around. The inversion of this order can and does result sometimes in what has been referred to as "the heresy of involvement" which has been responsible for the departure from religious life of not a few noble and previously effective sisters.

We have reserved till last the most serious task devolving upon the local superior—that of fostering the *metanoia* or internal renewal of soul which comes only from the grace of God and the action of the Holy Spirit. First-hand experience with poverty, personal contact with disease and its terrifying effects tear at our hearts and are productive of sympathy, empathy and compassion. But all of these can be passing and surface sentiments only, which vanish with the change of scene or locale, unless they are rooted in solid, spiritual convictions based on the religious principle of love of God, and love of neighbor because of God. Before these two types of supernatural love can reign in a human heart, self-denial, sacrifice, penance and humble submission of the individual's will to the will of God must be practised, prayed for and heroically pursued.

The shrewd superior recognizes this internal attitude of soul just as an experienced appraiser of jewels is able to detect the artificial from the real. She will not base her judgments on mere words or deeds which bespeak understanding and Christian dedication to the relief of suffering; but she will look for consistency of Christian forbearance, earnestness in prayer, voluntary visits to the Blessed Sacrament, frequent spiritual communions, an across-the-board Christian reaction to correction, contradiction and humiliation. By example and exhortation she will supervise the development of Christian charity in each sister's relationships with her convent associates, with her pupils, with parents, with evaluators of classroom work, with comments and outlooks toward convent happenings, especially those of an adverse nature.

She will know that this *metanoia* is usually a long, drawn-out process, involving a slow death to self. She will not expect miracles overnight. A word of encouragement, an act of commendation, or praise of victory over selfishness will do much to give impetus to this gradual transformation.

In these days of transition and ferment, of youth demanding equality of consideration and expression with age and experience, it is not an easy job to be a superior, any more than it is to be a bishop. But superiors and bishops there must be. So let us pray for each other; let us learn from each other; let us help one another. Let us hold fast to the faith, the while we guide our charges safely through the turbulent currents of permissiveness on the one side, and the urge to exact rigid obedience on the other. There will come a day, when, God willing, those over whom God has placed us will bless us for having nurtured their growth, and will thank us for the very dynamic part we have played in bringing them to a state of mature religious responsibility and perfection.

Prudent Renewal and Self-Reform

MOST REV. KARL J. ALTER, D.D.
Archbishop of Cincinnati, Ohio

In reviewing your brief history as an organization and in examining your current program, it is clear that your goal is twofold: namely, to advance the spiritual formation of your members, and to improve at the same time their professional competence. The two purposes are inseparable, one from the other. Without a sound spiritual formation, you will fail to achieve the true goal of your religious life, and without a proper professional formation, your apostolate becomes ineffective. We heartily commend your purpose to develop the full potentiality of each individual member of your respective religious communities.

Turning my attention now to the liturgy of the day on which I write, I note that this is the feast of St. Matthias, an apostle like St. Paul, born out of due time. The event which St. Luke describes in today's scripture reading is concerned with the election of Matthias, chosen to fill the place made vacant by the defection of Judas. Certain things stand out in full relief from the text of the Acts of the Apostles. First, the existence of an apostolic college is clearly indicated; then the continuing nature of its function is established. Secondly, the primacy of Peter as head of this apostolic college is accepted as a matter of fact by the other apostles; Peter calls the meeting, announces its purpose and directs its action. Peter stands out as head of the apostolic group; he does not stand outside the apostolic college, but within it. The head cannot exist without a body, nor can the body without a head.

Here, in this first chapter of the Acts of the Apostles, the hierarchical principle on which the Church rests is already seen to be operative. It is this fundamental principle which the Second Vatican Council canonizes in its decree on the collegiality of the bishops. If there is any one decree which more than another needs to be emphasized in these

15

days of *aggiornamento*, it is this decree on the Constitution of the Church. Unless we understand the nature and structure of the Church, we will fail to appreciate the mystery of redemption. We will regard it as an event of the past, instead of seeing it as the continuing presence of Christ in the world. In the Church, it is Christ who continues to teach, to sanctify, and to govern the faithful by word and sacrament. We entertain the hope that the spirit of the Second Vatican Council will be your guiding star during these days of your deliberations. We ask, however, that you be on guard against certain arbitrary interpretations which reflect personal opinion rather than the mind of the Church. In an exaggerated effort to decentralize the authority of the Church, there is a growing tendency to substitute the principle of democracy for the hierarchical one, and thus it runs the risk of exposing the unity of the Church to the danger of confusion arising from conflicting opinion. The Church is a unique society, utterly distinct from any other known to man. It is the official medium of salvation established by Christ. It speaks authoritatively as Christ spoke; not in a spirit of domination, but in accents of love and persuasion. The true image of the Church is that of the Good Shepherd.

Now, in the gospel of today we have a reminder that salvation is achieved not by the high-sounding words of earthly wisdom, but by meekness and humility. St. Paul comments on the fact that he did not speak in words of human eloquence to his hearers, but he spoke of Christ and Him crucified. It would be a strange thing indeed if the great mass of mankind, who do not have access to esoteric knowledge and who are not familiar with scriptural exegesis and theological research, should be denied the benefits of the gospel. Salvation is for all mankind. The kingdom of God is a universal kingdom. It is not reserved to an elite of scholars only. I say this because of a growing tendency to subordinate the acquisition of virtue to a search for knowledge. The two indeed go hand in hand, but let us keep in mind the words of Christ: "Seek ye first the kingdom of God and His justice, and all things else will be added unto you."

The words recorded in today's gospel were spoken by Christ to the crowds that gathered round him, in order to illustrate this truth. He wished to disabuse the scribes and Pharisees in His audience of the notion that only the learned could grasp the truth of His message.

I praise thee, Father, Lord of heaven and earth, that thou didst hide these things from the wise and prudent and didst reveal them to little ones. Yes,

Father, for such was thy good pleasure. All things have been delivered to me by my Father; and no one knows the Son except the Father; nor does anyone know the Father except the Son, and him to whom the Son chooses to reveal him. (Matt. 11:25-27)

"Learn from me," says Our blessed Lord in conclusion, "for I am meek and humble of heart." We do not disparage any effort to make advances in human culture or grow in a knowledge of the truth; but we do seek to put first things first, in keeping with the admonition of our Lord.

The message of the gospel, moreover, is one of individual salvation. All reform must begin with self-reform. The whole can never be greater or better than its parts. Every man must save his own soul. He cannot delegate this responsibility to anyone else. "Unless a man be born again of water and the Spirit," said Christ to Nicodemus, "he cannot enter into the kingdom of God"; and in His farewell words to the apostles on the Mount of the Ascension, He repeated His admonition: "He who believes and is baptized shall be saved; but he who does not believe shall be condemned." When the Second Vatican Council therefore speaks of renewal and reform, it has in mind, first, the individual, and only as a sequence thereof, the social and cultural institutions of mankind, through which religion makes itself manifest. All social reform begins with individual reform.

Having said this much, let no man think that the gospel does not have far-reaching social implications. It would be an egregious error if we failed to appreciate the fact that the concept of redemption is a spacious one, involving all men and all creation. We are a pilgrim people indeed, but the kingdom of God does not embrace merely the world that is to come—it envisages also this present world. It wants to bring all human institutions into a right order, consistent with and subordinate to the will of its creator. The full measure of the gospel truth is emphasized for us in this latest decree of the Second Vatican Council in which it speaks specifically of the Church in the Modern World. The gospel is to be the "light of the world" and the "salt of the earth." The Church fulfills its mission by permeating all things with the light of its teaching and the gift of its sacred ministry. No human activity is to be regarded as alien to the Church or as a stranger to its interests and influence. It has no desire to dominate the life of mankind, but it does wish to impregnate public as well as private life with Christian ideals and principles, so that our legislation, public policy, and public opinion will advance the kingdom of God and thus bring about true peace and happiness for all mankind.

May the spirit of the Second Vatican Council be the criterion of values in all your work. Let me suggest that you be positive in your outlook on the world, rather than negative; that you cherish a generous appreciation of the past achievements of the Church, rather than assume an attitude of faultfinding and destructive criticism. Do not be afraid of change, but be sure that every change is for the better, not the worse. Not all changes mean progress. Precipitate and radical change, such as revolution, has frequently done more harm than good. Prudence is still queen of the moral virtues. But do not let the plea of prudence be an excuse for inaction or self-complacency.

The Second Vatican Council speaks of freedom, but it is a freedom that must be reconciled with good order. When the Scriptures speak of the freedom of the children of God, they speak of freedom from the ceremonial law of the Jews; freedom from the bondage of sin; freedom from the compulsion of man-made laws and human institutions— freedom, yes, in order to grow in grace and wisdom before God and man.

The Second Vatican Council speaks of the need of adjustment to the contemporary world, not in order to become like it, but in order to reform it from within. It speaks of a diversity of function, assigning to each member of the Church his own individual share in the apostolate. There is a priesthood of the laity; but it is not to be confused with the sacred priesthood established by Christ with its specific function to teach, sanctify, and govern the people of God. To the laity belongs the organization and guidance of the temporal order. To the official Church belongs the guidance of the spiritual order. While there is a distinction of function, there is no distinction with regard to the degree of merit which can be gained, nor the measure of the grace of God which makes us all alike and equal in the sight of God.

There are many self-appointed critics claiming special charismata, who are expounding their ideas for the building of a better world. They think that they are implementing the decrees of the Second Vatican Council. They are hurrying to set up at once the New Jerusalem; but it is always according to their own preconceived notions and individualistic patterns. We must recapture that sense of unity in the midst of diversity, with Christlike forbearance, which animated the fathers of the council. Without it, there can be no renewal and no reform. Each one has his own allotted task to perform according to the measure of his ability and training, but also according to the specific mission committed to him individually or collectively by the responsible authority of the Church. Recall the axiom of St. Augustine: "In sure things unity, in doubtful things liberty, in all things charity." St. Paul reminds us that God himself

gave some men as apostles, and some as prophets, others again as evangelists, and others as pastors and teachers, in order to perfect the saints for a work of ministry, for building up the body of Christ, until we all attain to the unity of the faith and of the deep knowledge of the Son of God, to perfect manhood, to the mature measure of the fullness of Christ (Eph 4:11-13).

Perspectives and Horizons

SISTER ROSE DOMINIC GABISCH, S.C.L.
Executive Secretary, Sister Formation Conference

"In the fifteenth century men in Italy attained an efficient knowledge of perspective. Painting achieved a new dimension, depth, and the impetus given to the art was like that given to literature by the invention of printing, to music by Bach's system of equal temperament enabling it to move freely in all keys, or to architecture by steel-skeleton construction." (*Encyclopaedia Britannica*, 1962. 2. 443b) One could now look *into* a picture.

The objective of this paper is to look *into* the setting of sister formation programs, to gain perspective on the heritage of the past, and to view a few emerging influences.

In drawing, the simplest way to attain perspective is to place a horizontal line across a paper where earth and sky meet; that is the horizon. What lies below and in part conceals the horizon creates an illusion of closeness. That which lies above the horizon creates an illusion of distance. The horizon, therefore, is seen as a continuous line between the observer and distant objects. Parallel lines appear to meet on the horizon at what is known as the vanishing point.

Obviously, to narrow the horizon by concentrating on the activities of a single community, or a single country, would be foreign to the spirit of the modern Church. Such narrow boundaries lead to vanishing points frustrating to those with a universal outlook on vocation. However, limitations of time for this paper permit a sampling only of many views.

Since it was my privilege to represent you at the *Pro Mundi Vita* Colloquium in Louvain, Belgium, in September, 1966, I intended to stress the perspectives found there. The *Pro Mundi Vita* theme was, "Women Religious and the Universal Apostolate." I would like to insert the English-speaking group's four-point program for effective participation in that apostolate:

1. *Systematic research* at the highest level, to identify obstacles to religious renewal and adaptation in the renewing Church.

2. *Experimentation* on the basis of the knowledge acquired through the above research, especially in developing attitudes for the "community without walls" where religious will work *with*, rather than *for* others.

3. *Preparation of specialists* in anthropology, sociology, economics, psychology, and political science who can direct sisters in acquiring an understanding of the world and of themselves.

4. Flexibility in *new forms of contact with the world*. Postulants need not be hermetically sealed; even canonical novices should not be completely separated; juniorate sisters definitely need experience outside their small circle; in-service sisters should have frequent, short tertianships.

These points stress the horizontal, incarnational level. *Pro Mundi Vita* participants also recognize the vertical, eschatological needs of sisters to become more and more closely united with God in imitation of Christ, loving, sacrificing, dying, and rising in the Paschal Mystery. With this as a background, let us return to perspectives.

The heritage of the religious life of sisters is a glorious tradition. To a degree, however, it is a roadblock, obscuring new demands on the horizon of "the Church *in* the modern world." A heavy ballast of outdated inheritances delays motion forward.

One of these entrenched inheritances, which in varying degree grip formation programs within old patterns, is a negative world-view. The "world" is seen as an evil to be shunned and the "good" religious is she who detaches herself from it. A spiritual wall of retirement and segregation surrounds the early years of religious formation, especially the canonical year. No one denies the inherent objectives of this withdrawal: spiritual depth and union with Christ. The persistent question on the horizon is whether such complete segregation prepares for a semi-cloistered rather than a twentieth-century active apostolate. Can a young woman suddenly step out of an enclave and begin, or perhaps —since many of the entrants were previously involved apostolically— renew an authentic apostolic dialogue with the world of Vatican II? Can she attain that end without meeting the requirements?

If the formation period is an apostolically static life, with personal contacts limited to a peer group and one older adult, the director, the transfer is difficult. Father Kierkoffe, secretary of *Pro Mundi Vita*, believes active orders will die out if they provide no dialogue for their young members. One cannot form sisters for a social apostolate in isolation. Bishop Martensen of Copenhagen says, "Even in the novices' seclusion, there should be found a happy and trustful openheartedness towards the world and the Church to which, by their unselfish dedication, they intend to render service."

American religious are not blind to the situation, but they do include the familiar "three classes of men." Most are in the second class, proceeding slowly, whereas Father Bernard Häring says some situations require "daring initiative" (*Canadian Relig. Conf. Proceedings*, 1966, p. 61), and Dean Samuel H. Miller of the Harvard Divinity School, in a similar vein, expresses a parallel concern about theological schools. He maintains that we may be smothering with small repairs and minor changes the basic need for a radical and thoroughgoing revolution in the whole system (*Higher Ed. and Natl. Affairs*, 15, No. 39 [Nov. 25, 1966], 4.). The radical (down to the roots) revision will take the best thinking of many minds. The national committee of the Sister Formation Conference appointed a special group to undertake such a study. Mother M. Thomas Aquinas, R.S.M., chairman, has a position paper "Everett Revisited" in the Autumn 1966 *Sister Formation Bulletin* (XIII, No. 1, 14-16).

Meantime small steps are not to be despised: limited apostolic contacts; relevant periodicals and books; periodic association with the professed community—especially with the retired sisters, eccentric or charming in their sanctity, who need the young as much as the latter need them; acquaintance with problem situations on the television; joint conferences with other groups, and similar devices.

A second inheritance from the past is a maternalistic spirit combined with authoritarian control, typified in the term mother-general, although the connotation never occurred to the older generation. Where "unthinking"—a better term than "blind"—obedience resulted, religious did not develop human dignity, nor attain responsible maturity. Vatican II, however, opened windows on a horizon of collegiality, subsidiarity, and shared responsibility, where the Holy Spirit works through *all* the members. In a patriarchal system, wisdom came with age. Modern specialization enables highly prepared sisters to make prudent judgments very early in their field. Hence, the best use of talent implies a horizontal relationship of shared responsibility; the superior listens before making decisions, decisions which she still must make.

Concurrently with *this* freedom, a self-sufficient secularism develops its own variety, seeking a greater fulfillment of humanity in a new creativeness in shaping society. This militant secularism resists anything imposed upon it; it ignores God, and hence His laws. It demands self-development, self-identity, a form of love different from paternalism, with greater regard for the dignity of the individual, based on purely secular values.

Within this secularistic freedom, the children of God exercise theirs. Hence "freedoms" circle the horizon, and seep into the most conservative religious houses. Some religious, lacking perspective, may never learn that not less, but more obedience, of the right kind, will bring maturity and genuine freedom under God; most will recognize the truth expressed by great modern theologians. Thus Karl Rahner says that "we grow to maturity not by doing what we like, but by doing what we should," and Hans Küng observes that "the *illusion* of freedom is to do what I want. The reality of freedom is to want what almighty God does" (*Freedom Today*. New York, 1966, p. 41).

The third restricting inheritance selected for this talk is a negative concept of virginity. Many writers of the past described virginal chastity as if sisters were angels and not human beings, and, furthermore, women, whose destiny, as Pope Pius XII said, is motherhood either in the physical sense or in a higher spiritual manner. Religious renounce married life and motherhood in the ordinary sense, but some authors overstressed the renunciation to the point where all natural love was suppressed, presumably to make room for supernatural love. This unnatural suppression led to aloofness and rigidity, for to love another supernaturally is equivalent to saying that she is not naturally lovable. Moreover, the misinterpreted adjective in the phrase, "particular friendship," often prevented the development of warm, loving relations such as Christ has in the Gospels, with each person a *particular* friend, loved deeply as an individual, but not to the exclusion of others or with jealous possessiveness.

Narrow attitudes viewed "the flesh" as if the body were divorced from the person. It (the flesh) became the principal object of mortification, and this view influenced attitudes also toward sex and toward the other sex. Sex was an unfortunate ballast from which religious should free themselves. The other sex was seen negatively as a proximate occasion of sin and every chance meeting a source of suspicion and mistrust.

A saner view is well above the horizon today. Without Christ-like friendships for fellow sisters and fellow men the love of God suffers. Religious virginity is a total, loving surrender of self to the love of Christ *and* to the love of His members. Such love is a prerequisite for apostolic contacts and for that genuine community life which is an eschatological sign. "How these Christians love one another!" was the astonished exclamation of pagan Rome. Should sisters love less? Experimentally, some are trying to make this love more manifest by living in small groups as part of the people.

Religious also recognize their right, and even their duty to be charming persons as well as saintly apostles. Mature association with adults of either sex is taken for granted. Some believe that dignified, friendly relationships are necessary for personal maturity; a certain polarity of masculine and feminine judgments and intuitions is a healthy tension for breadth of view. Even the Church added to revision of antiquated habits a timid acceptance of women at the council!

Twentieth-century religious women, then, seek perspective on widening horizons relative to their formation programs, their community life, and their apostolate. The resulting depth of view is both rewarding and disturbing. The classical regularity of Renaissance artistic perspective is gone; the panorama of the computer age is bizarre and tentative. Hence, sisters ground changes deep in history, unwilling to lose the treasured values of the past as they implement the results of self-examination and research.

PART
II
ELEMENTS OF COMMUNITY LIFE

The Local Superior and the Prayer Life of Her Sisters

Rev. Bernard Häring, C.Ss.R.
Visiting Professor, Yale Divinity School
New Haven, Connecticut

In this time of renewal, it must be very clear, very evident that everything depends on the renewal of prayer. If you renew everything else first and only afterwards do something about prayer, you come to prayer too late. Things will already have moved in the wrong direction. But if we endeavor to start with a deepening of our prayer, asking what prayer means; if all changes are turned in this direction so that we understand and realize better the truth and spirit of prayer, then we can be sure that renewal will really be what it was meant to be. If we know how to pray, our growing prayer life will give us the power of the Lord. We will be open to His grace and He will lead us.

How can the local superior help in this? Above all, by being herself a sister deeply convinced of the primacy of the prayer life. All other help is useless. The superior must be convinced that in her own life, as well as in the organization of the community, in the whole style of life of the community, prayer is the foundation. This is true of the entire Church because the Church is the mother of all the living only to the extent that she is the living bride of Christ. That means listening to the Lord in prayer, looking to Him, responding to Him. It is an outstanding way for religious because they too should manifest the true nature of the Church, the virginal bride of Christ.

Forty years ago Romano Guardini wrote that virginity as total openness to the Lord develops tremendous energies for the kingdom of God. But, he adds, the holiness of the spouse is taken away if the pattern of life and the organization of the day's activity prevails over prayer. Because virginity, the special witness of celibacy for the kingdom of God, means that we expect everything from the grace of God, let us be guided by His love. First of all we must be open toward Him; then and only then can we do anything of value. I cannot emphasize this enough; the local superior must know this, must be aware of this, must be convinced of this. But it does not suffice to have a hidden conviction. The way she distributes work, makes out the schedule of the day, must flow from this conviction. If a sister feels the need for more spiritual reading, more prayer, the local superior must find a way to help her instead of saying, "Really, we have to do our work." Words which express conviction are useless and even harmful if the daily order contradicts them.

What is prayer? We know, and yet we have to return to a fundamental understanding of prayer continually. The gospel defines prayer when it says that it is listening and responding to the Lord. The prayer of pagan religions sought only to speak to God, to try to convince Him, to make Him obedient. Sometimes even in religious communities you find this thinking; does not the sister pray to St. Joseph for a grant? The grant does not come and she turns St. Joseph's face to the wall. He was not obedient!

All Christian prayer depends on the word of God. The fundamental attitude is to know how to listen, to hear the word of God and then to act upon it. But first one must hear. We listen to the word of God in the Bible, in liturgy and in divine Providence, in the happenings of every day. The Holy Father in the first conciliar commission made it obligatory for all sisters to be introduced to the right understanding of the Bible, and this is to be done, not only to provide material for good explanations in the classroom, but also to strengthen prayer life.

Even for us theologians the primary goal in the study of the Bible is that we ourselves listen to the word of God and understand what He really meant to say. The Bible can only be studied and read prayerfully; the more we study the Bible in this manner, the more wonderfully it appears as the message coming from God. All good scholars, biblical scholars, desire to become men of prayer. One who has knowledge but is not a man of prayer does not yet obey the second commandment—"Thou shalt not invoke the name of the Lord in vain."

Plan so that your communities may study the Bible together. Sister Formation must encourage this. The Decree on the Renewal of the Religious Life emphasizes the fact that the Bible is the fundamental rule of every day. Our sister should be introduced to the right understanding of the Bible—how God speaks to men in the reality of their situation in the world, and in the culture of their time; how it touches their lives, how He appeals with his word for a lively response.

The whole Bible is to be seen in the perspective of prayer, because when God speaks to man He speaks in order to obtain a response, and this response is prayer. A prayer is not only service of the mouth but also a prayer of the heart and mind, a prayer that embraces the whole of our life.

Often the prayer of sisters fails because it has become monotonous, a monologue continually repeating the little wishes of the little world which grows smaller around the little ego. But if we learn to listen to the other things God intones in the Bible, our prayer responds to this expanding, varied world of God and our prayer life will not die, will not become monotonous.

How can the local superior help in this growth? One of the sisters, not necessarily the local superior, may have studied one part or one aspect of the Bible and the sisters may discuss this with her in the perspective of the prayer of each individual and of the community. Sisters should meet periodically not only to discuss school and hospital, but also to discuss the word of God and how to respond to it. This discussion is of great value as each sister brings to it her own charism, her own wisdom. The deepening of the dialogue with God should be the fundamental rule in such dialogue between the sisters.

However, we must be wary of biblical study that leads to a "God is dead" theory, a belief that God spoke once and then rested. God speaks to men always in their own language, and thus God continues to speak to us. Of course, there is only the one Bible, the inspired word of God, but God continues to act in His world, and where He acts He speaks because God's actions are words and all His words are deeds. Therefore, in the light of the Bible we must also listen to God in daily events. Through Church history we learn how He spoke, how He acted with His people in past times, how the saints found the right response, and how very many did not find Him. Only those who were men and women of prayer understood God's design which even today shows a most wonderful continuity. We learn that in the past many people, religious men and women, fell into formalism to such an extent that they did not recognize the signs of the times, did not recognize the work of God.

For instance, the people did not understand when John Bosco collected the beatniks of his time, the young criminals, and, building on respect, honoring every one of these young men as if he were his brother, daring, trusting in divine Providence, sought new Christian pedagogical methods. The Pharisees, the formalists, planned to take him to a mental asylum; his place was prepared, the director of the asylum was instructed to watch over him. The closed car arrived, and they invited Don Bosco to come for a visit. John Bosco not only revered the young men with whom he worked, he also revered these people, and said, "Please step in before me." Then he closed the door, and the driver drove off to the place arranged for Don Bosco. Don Bosco came behind, and after an hour smilingly liberated them. He realized the humor of the situation. There are always those who are conscientious about their prayers—formalists who do not recognize their real relation to God, who do not understand God.

Regularity at prayer, the routine recitation of this quantity of prayer that must be said, can lead to the "God is dead" approach. God is the living God, as Our Lord said, He is the God of Abraham, Isaac, and Jacob; therefore, He is not the God of the dead but the God of the living. He continues to speak to us in daily events. Each individual gift He bestows on us is a word coming from Him, everything that happens around us, the goodness, the kindness of our brothers and sisters, distress, worry, through that grace of the Holy Spirit become a word addressed to us personally, an appeal coming from God and making itself understood in a prayerful heart and mind.

We must realize that the living God is behind all things. We can enjoy nature in the deepest sense only if we admire Him, if we praise Him. The beauty of a flower or the beauty of the firmament is always, for a prayerful mind, a message from God. Joy is always an expression of joy and gratitude to God. This must be the goal of our education—that our whole life is understood in this great perspective of the gospel of St. John, "Through Him all things came to be." If they are made by Him, the Word of God, they mean something for us; for us created to the image and likeness of God. We see them only in this light if we bring them back in prayer, in praise, and in humble petition.

The unredeemed man even in religion—in all religions, in heathen religions, in the old Testament and the new Testament—tends to separate religious functions and life. Christ brought life and religion together. He has fulfilled the great perspective of the prophets who continually preached against those who separated life and religion, making of religion a collection of rubrics, of formulas, of duties. Christ's prayer was also prayer formulated in the psalms, the common prayer of the people of God. But in addition His prayer is spontaneous. "I praise

Thee, Father, Lord of heaven and earth, because Thou hast hidden this from the eyes of wise men and hast revealed it to the hearts of the humble." This is a spontaneous prayer, an expression of His heart. "Father, forgive them; they know not what they do"—that is a prayer.

The local superior's responsibility is to bring the sisters together so that they may help one another understand the signs of the times and their meaning. God's design is filled with meaning. God speaks through these events. Together in the spirit of prayer, in their revision of life, the sisters will help one another to bring prayerful reading and prayerful attention to God's marvelous deeds. They will bring professional earnestness to prayer, so that everything is received from God and returned to God through a prayerful mind.

Biblical theology shows that God speaks with great variety in the Bible despite the clear difference between the style in which Matthew proclaims the Gospel of Christ to the Hebrew Christians, and Luke preaches the same Gospel to the Hellenistic world. In Luke, the physician, you will find a special understanding of woman's psychology. It is really the living instrument of the living God speaking in a variety of modes because of those to whom He is speaking. You see a great variety even in the psalms. Biblical scholars justly make efforts to discover in which circumstances and time they were composed and what their most probable expression is. Effort must continually be made so that the word of God, the essential message of revelation, is understood. Theology is never completed. It is always to be done anew, translated for different environments, different cultures, that all, in their own way, their own language, their own culture, can understand the same message. This, of course, is only possible because of Pentecost, and to the extent that we are spiritual men. All depends upon the grace of the Holy Spirit. But the Holy Spirit does not dispense us from human effort, does not dispense us from studying modern psychology which helps us to understand modern men.

One of the greatest needs of the local superior today is that of understanding the very different psychological needs of the old sister, the middle-aged sister, the young. There are three generations under one roof. She may like the style of the old or the middle aged or the young, but she must show respect for all. And if a congregation does not wish to die out, the local superior must help the older and the middle-aged sisters to understand the needs of the young. They it is who are carrying on the tradition. It is a deadly decision to say that we shall continue in the old style which appeals to the good old sisters. Of course, we make concessions to the individual manner of prayer of the old sisters; we must not ridicule their ways. Nevertheless, sometimes a kind word will help them give up some of their individualistic devotions.

We must make them understand that we appreciate their style of prayer, but that they are obliged in charity not to demonstrate that which is not the image of the living Church, and which may disedify not only other older sisters, but the middle-aged and the young sisters, and especially the laity. The Lord warned us in the Sermon on the Mount not to pray in order to be seen, but we also have no right to be an example of an old-fashioned museum. Our intention must be in our prayer, to pray not only internally but also for the edification of our brothers and sisters that all those who see our deeds and our prayers may praise the God who is in heaven. If our common prayer is seen and heard by others it should be a help to them in the better understanding of the praise of God.

The local superior should take care that community prayers are worship, that every word is respected. Every word which is said to God or to the saints must be a word that can be understood, that can resound in our heart and mind, that can lead to an understanding of what we are saying, that expresses our deep respect. This is one of the great grievances of the young everywhere, that so often the older people who insist on tradition and on law and obedience betray themselves as "God is dead" people. God is dead for them. They treat Him as a means, an obligation, a duty, a function, as rubrics. The greatest virtue of the youth of today is that they are sincere; they wish for things to be meaningful.

The younger sisters must have the opportunity to express themselves and to make their contribution. This can be done in the revision of life, instead of the chapter of faults, that old session of accusations. Larger communities may divide into several groups to discuss together what must be improved in common prayers, and the means by which it can be done. After this discussion the younger sisters, especially in the houses of formation, but also when they come out from their houses of formation, should be given a chance to set up some common prayers, to seek prayers which appeal to them, and also in certain situations to compose the text. We ought not impose one formula rigidly, one set-up day by day.

In our individual prayer life it is a sign that something is wrong if we are confined almost totally to preformulated prayers. Our total prayer life must be predominantly spontaneous. Undoubtedly we have times when we are tired out, exhausted, and there is obviously less spontaneity. At such times we can be greatly helped by saying slowly, slowly, the *Our Father*, or another good prayer.

Even in common prayer there must be more spontaneity, more singing, more translation into life. There is a trend among sisters to adopt the divine office, the breviary as a part of the common prayer. This is right and good, but it is not necessarily progress; it can be a new formalism. There are several conditions, I think, under which the adaptation of the divine office, of parts—lauds, compline, or vespers—are a blessing. First, that the sisters be introduced into the meaning of the psalms and the lessons; it does not suffice that they have a translation. They must be introduced to what it meant at the time it was composed, how it expressed life. And even this does not suffice; there must be some variety. Why should a sister slavishly bind herself to this one text; why not on some days instead of the recitation of these psalms, or the official translation, take some of the Gelineau psalms and sing them? The wording of these is more than a translation, and the song makes it even more an event in our present time. It is an introduction into the very meaning of the psalms to take a paraphrase as it is given in the Gelineau version.

We must be aware of the tremendous danger of formalism which continually invades us. But if these experiments are made they must be explained. The local superior must not come in and say, "now we do this." The plan must be proposed, the arguments, the whys; only if the sisters understand what is meant, only if they cooperate will it become meaningful.

I have stressed the point that the local superior must be deeply, thoroughly convinced of the prime importance of prayer. But this must not be confused with the belief in certain forms of prayer, with a rigid imposition of times and quanitity. Nevertheless, as human beings are made we need a rhythm of time, we need the necessary time for prayer. On this point I continually examine my own conscience, and I appeal to all superiors not to diminish the time which our rules guarantee for us. It is not too much. I have looked through many rules and have heard many sisters, priests and brothers, and I am convinced that in general the time given to prayer is not too much. Many congregations, however, fill this time so completely with prayers that there is not time for prayer. We need time for prayer, not only for prayers.

The Holy Mass is not just a half hour when we express our individual affection to God, but a half hour when our togetherness before God is strengthened. But even during Mass there are necessary moments of silence, and the Mass should not be hurried. My brother told me yesterday that in Brazil the first word he learned was *paciência*, and the first word he learned when he took a job in New York was "hurry up, hurry up." Mass is a communal expression of prayer, a listening to the word of God, a common response; but there must also be some time when each individual can catch his breath, can express his own heart before God, otherwise it does not become a real response to God. It is most important that we have common prayer, especially that we have common singing to God which is a normal expression of prayer—pray to the Lord, sing to the Lord. But in addition to this we must have enough time for prayerful spiritual reading, for just being before the Lord in the tabernacle. And this is the chief task of the superior—to guarantee time. It would be wrong, however, if a local superior insisted (when a sister comes home in the evening exhausted), "you have to get in your prayers." Rather she should say, "Sit down for a quarter of an hour before the tabernacle and omit all your vocal prayers; you are too tired."

A fine old brother in our Bavarian monastery, Brother Stephen, was a tremendous worker; when he retired they had to hire four women. On work days he always came to prayer; he was always there, and I don't know how he made it. But on Sundays he was in the chapel the whole day. The day before he died, a brother speaking to him said, "You must be happy going to heaven, how much time you spent before the tabernacle!" "Oh, yes," said Brother, "I slept a great deal before the Lord." His intention was always to be before the Lord. But the sister ought not normally be so tired that she has no more energy for prayer. This is also the superior's duty. If a sister with twenty-five teaching hours is totally exhausted day after day so that she cannot pray, twenty-five hours are too much for her. Another sister who works forty hours teaching, and twenty hours in housekeeping may still be fresh and alive. But if the first sister has not the strength to pray, the superior is obliged to help her, to free her so that she may have, not only psychological, but moral strength.

I should like to say a word on the rosary. If I wished to abolish the rosary in the Church I would strongly emphasize the necessity for you to keep the fifty *Hail Marys*, to count them accurately, to get them in daily. I am sure that the younger generation would leave the rosary totally behind them. But as I wish to preserve the rosary I will try to explain how the young especially can say it. Remember that the 150 *Hail Marys* entered into life in the Church for those monks, those brothers who could not memorize the 150 psalms. So, instead of the 150 psalms which were to be said by the intelligent brothers, the less gifted had the privilege of saying 150 *Hail Marys*, with 15 *Our Fathers* and 15 *Glory be to the Fathers*. Today less gifted people can read the psalms. The rosary formerly was a fine family prayer for people who had no higher education and could not even read, and that was the majority. It conveyed a very essential message, the great mysteries of our faith. It emphasized how our Lady, the mother of faith, enters into this great mystery of the Church in the spirit of faith. There is great variety of method of saying the rosary. The children of Fatima in the custom learned partly from the vision of the Blessed Virgin, did not start with the *Hail Mary*, but began with a short meditation and then said the *Hail Marys*. In Cairo the mystery is mentioned after the name of Jesus. "He died for us" says the one side and the other responds, "which He did indeed for us." And then the *Hail Mary* is recited. There is always a strong affirmation of faith. I feel that what we must do is emphasize that numbers are not obligatory. The Council of Trent warned bishops to teach people not to trust in numbers—either of candles or of prayers.

One sister may read the account of one mystery from the Bible, or read from a good book (a meditation on it). She may then be caught by one great aspect of the mystery for ten or fifteen minutes, and may bring all this together in a single *Hail Mary* said slowly. No indulgence is lost if love, hope and charity increase, and no indulgence will be won if hope, faith and love are diminished. One may make a meditation on one mystery, another may go through five mysteries.

It is essential that throughout the year we meditate constantly on the great mysteries of the Lord in the faith and humility of the Blessed Virgin. Although you may recite the rosary in common, let the sisters make different preparation for different days. Perhaps in a Bible vigil they might choose readings on two mysteries and one of the sisters might give a two-minute meditation on it followed by silence and a song, perhaps the *Hail Mary* or the *Our Father*. With variety the rosary will be preserved.

St. Paul introduces all his letters with thanksgiving and praise, and I think that in the whole renewal of prayer life we must do it in this spirit of thanksgiving in the Eucharist. The very word expresses thanksgiving and praise, and in it we receive all the events, all the gifts of God, especially the gift of suffering in a spirit of gratitude. We will spontaneously express our gratitude to one another and our gratitude to God. Faith expresses itself before we have understood the word. Through faith we gratefully recognize a message from God. And only when we have expressed, strengthened, and deepened our gratitude, will the Holy Spirit guide us so that we understand what God really means, to bring forth a real response.

Prayer in the Bible

Rev. Sean Quinlan
Catholic University of America
Washington, D. C.

There is no definition of prayer, because there is no definition of love. Prayer is the voice of love. If you ask me how to pray, I will say, "I don't know." There was an old medieval saint who was asked, "Is it difficult to love Christ?" and he answered, "Not for those who do."

So, a first principle of finding prayer in the Bible is that it is not too helpful for the young. If you think you can hand the Bible to your novices and say "pray," you will succeed to a certain degree, but not fully, because they haven't had enough pain or enough time. Martin Luther has said very many good things, because he was a genius and a religious man, and one of the things he said was that only a man of fifty can read the psalms. I know what he means, because the Bible is sacred literature. It is a book in which mortality, birth and death, joy and sorrow, work and art, where all these things in our mortal shell meet the voice of God and the voice of Christ. There is no finding prayer in the Bible without human experience. You might say that at a certain age level the easiest key to the Bible would be *Hamlet*, or maybe *The Catcher in the Rye* because they tell us about this mortal flesh that Jesus Christ assumes and saves. The Bible is about people and a Person; it is not the action of a camera focused on a star. It is the voice of lonely pilgrims on their way to the resurrection. It is said that there is only one question: Is man absolutely alone in the universe? The Christian faith is that he has a brother and a kinsman called Jesus Christ. But when we pray, we are simply uttering our faith in Christ. Sometimes it may be a cry of despair; at other times a cry of gladness.

The second thing to observe in the Bible is what I shall call, for want of a better word, "atmosphere." Vatican II, as you know, speaks of the

power that is in the word of God, some kind of light and dynamism. If
you look at Robert Frost stopping by the woods on a snowy evening,
he says, "The woods are lovely, dark and deep," a light is going from
the woods to deeper things in the mind and the imagination, and he
adds, "And I have promises to keep and miles to go before I sleep." We
are taken from New Hampshire into all human destiny—the mystery
of life, along poetic lines. Now the Bible is that, plus one thing more.
It is words of poetry or prose that God wants us to know. You have to
take life into the Bible and remember that it is not about saints except incidentally. It is about people, the Jews. Some of them are thugs
like Samson; others, pre-St. Augustines like David, and there was beautiful Ruth, of course, the little immigrant girl.

Now to sense this power of the Bible to reach us, which is its paramount power, you don't have to be an exegete; that might be a disquali-
fication. Take my mother, for instance: she sings a lot, and she talks to
the neighbors, and about the neighbors, and she says the rosary a lot;
the "jewels of the poor," Sean O'Casey called it. I saw her looking
out the window one day and she said, "I will go into the hills of Sion."

So, I said to her, "Where did you hear that?"

She said, "On television." Then she said to me, "What is Sion?"

I said, "That is Jerusalem."

"Isn't that beautiful?" she said.

I didn't ask what she meant, because that is the spirit speaking. And,
there's a priest I used to know, who is externally a businessman as most
people have to be, but he had a secret kind of a mind. And on his grave-
stone there is written "Thy laws are my song," and I never know whether he chose it or whether someone gave it, who was trying to divine
his secrets. So prayer is faith taking voice in the heart of the human
condition.

When I was a seminarian and they were unsuccessfully trying to
teach me how to pray, we used to fix our rational minds on the supreme
Being. If you try to do it, you won't succeed for long; the world record
may be a fraction of a second. And that, of course, was a philosophizing
of prayer, or, if you like, it was a kind of a mathematicizing of prayer.
But, the Bible really is a memory book, and, as you know, our lives are
held together by memory. When you get older, you remember more.
So, when Jesus Christ says, "Do this in commemoration of me," (the
word "commemoration" for us has a very slight kind of meaning:
Fourth of July, St. Patrick's day, things like that) but when Christ said
"commemoration," he meant going back on a living journey to a su-

preme event. If you look at the Hebrew, when the Hebrew mind wants to say what we would say in this way, "I accept a tradition," the Hebrew mind says, "I repeat it." So, instead of accepting tradition, he repeats it again in an action, and that is what we call liturgy. Liturgy is the repetition of the intensity of a sacred memory.

Jesus Christ on Holy Thursday, if you look back on what He said, echoes remembered words and remembered events—the new and eternal testament. He is thinking of Jeremiah: "I shall write a new law in your heart." Then he speaks about the division of flesh and blood, thinking of Sinai when some of the blood went on the altar and some on the people to signify union between God and the people. So, Jesus Christ that night weds an immensely new life with sacred memory. If you want to pray from the Bible, you have to know it fairly well in some of the great memories of the Jewish people, which they live and relive again and again.

The next thing about the Bible is that you have to accept the emotion in the Bible, holy emotion. We are very sober as you know, but the Bible people were not; they were Jews, a Mediterranean people. Take Hosea, the great Hosea, who makes his unhappy marriage into a symbol of the love of God for his people. He sings a bridal song or he has God sing a bridal song, and God says:

I will betroth you to myself forever. I will betroth you to myself in righteousness and justice and in kindness and mercy; and I will betroth you to myself in all faithfulness and you should know the Lord. . . . The earth should answer the grain, and the wine should answer the oil, and they should all answer Israel and I will sow her for myself in my land and I should say, "You are my people," and they should say, "You are my God."

And I will say that without an intense emotion at times, we are wasting our time in what they call the aridity of prayer. On the famous night when Jesus Christ is going away St. John, the beloved evangelist, remembers that He said, "I leave you peace; I give you my own peace. I do not give it to you as the world gives," and He says, "Your mind should not be troubled nor afraid."

Notice that the Mass always tells a story. We are approaching Lent, the theme is sad; because, sometimes, the theme has to be sad, but at other times it is joyful. If you read your Mass tomorrow, you will find echoes of Genesis and echoes of Christ's healing. You will see the misery and the promises of healing. You can trace a very intelligent theme through the Mass, because when they first composed the Mass, they had a kind of rough and ready genius which was quite intuitive, and knew all the themes pretty well. I hope that when we put them together we will be equally ready and simple.

Now, if you look at the Mass itself, you will notice that it tells a story. There is always the Introit, the ascent to the holy mountain; then there is the act of contrition, the *mea culpa;* and then, the songs of praise; the psychological variation in the Mass. You are never saddened too long; you quickly become joyful. Then you have the Christian gospel, which comes from the tremendous life of the history of Israel—the mighty acts of God in the old, and the mighty acts of God in the new. Then you move on to the Canon, which is the place of peace. I would imagine the best way you could teach the Bible would be to take all the Sunday Masses and track down each section in a scholarly fashion.

Looking at the Bible itself there is a significant thing that can be said. Whenever there is a great moment in the Bible, there is a prayer moment, which is to say that someone calls out or someone praises. A very significant place in the Bible, Exodus 33:12 tells us of the famous conversation between God and Moses. It is so very familiar that you might even think it was ourselves, which of course it is. And in the nicest possible way, God said to Moses, "I will go along with you myself from Egypt," and he said to him, "If thou ought not go along thyself, do not make us go from here." A touching thing. And Moses said, "If you won't come with us, we are afraid to move. For how then can it be known that I and my people have found favor with you? Is it not by Thy will alone that we may be known?" And then the Lord said, "I will carry you like a baby. I know you by name." And Moses said to the Lord, "Show me Your glory." Prayer is best that has the simplicity of a conversation.

Then we come to the time of Solomon which is more sophisticated. Solomon is about the only success story in the Bible and he had his troubles too. Here in a beautiful temple, Solomon stands up, "O Lord, the God of Israel, there is no God like Thee in the heavens above or upon the earth beneath who keeps loving faith with all Thy people, who walks before with all Thy heart." Faith in the promises is primary in prayer.

Now another thing about the Bible is that you rarely, if ever, get a personal prayer in the Bible; they are all "we" prayers. They are all community prayers. And you notice that when Jesus Christ, our Lord, prays alone in the Bible, he goes aside; especially in St. Luke, "He went aside to pray." We never know what He said. This is the secret of the individual and God. The Bible always makes allowance for that. Not even the Bible itself can go into the individual recess of the heart. The psalms in general are all community prayers; it is the cry of the race.

In the New Testament there is revealed to us the Incarnation. "He is God amongst us." Jesus Christ, if you see him in the New Testament, is placed right in the center of man's incessant appeal. He becomes like us in all things except sin; but He also becomes like us in prayer. He prays as a pilgrim or as a traveler. Mark 1:37 says: "Early in the morning long before daylight, He got up and left the house and went to a lonely spot and He prayed there." "And Simon and the companions sought him out and found him and said, 'They are all looking for you.'" So it is interesting that even when the whole world wants him, he will go aside. But most powerful of all I think is the passion night, which again is Mark 14:36, when Jesus Christ said, "My heart is almost breaking." And he said, "Abba, take this cup away from me." Jesus was plainly terrified. God knows, for all I know, that maybe half of you are praying with breaking hearts; but then, if that is the case, you are in supreme company. And that leads to the Epistle to the Hebrews. "Jesus in his life cried aloud with tears to him who was able to save him from death, and because of his piety, his prayer was heard." That is no formal prayer. That is a cry of anguish. We too at times may know only the prayer of anguish.

Now look at the early Church. It always prayed at the great moments. In the Acts of the Apostles, when they were going to elect a new member of the twelve, they pray; this is simply the belief that they are in the hands of some greater power, and they ask for guidance.

Let me close with the words of St. Paul (Romans 8:26-7):

The Spirit too comes to help us in our weakness. For when we cannot choose words in order to pray properly, the Spirit himself expresses our plea in a way that could never be put into words, and God who knows everything in our hearts knows perfectly well what he means, and that the pleas of the saints expressed by the Spirit are according to the mind of God.

The Eucharist: Experience of Community

REV. BERNARD HÄRING, C.Ss.R.
Yale Divinity School
New Haven, Connecticut

The farewell discourse of Our Lord at the Last Supper (John, Chs. 13-17) synthesizes the whole Christian life: "This is my law: love one another as I have loved you"—in the experience of the Eucharist, the experience of community. There we experience anew the truths of the Sermon on the Mount introduced by the Word, when with His disciples gathered close around Him He "opened His mouth and taught them." During the farewell discourse we see the disciples gathered again around the Lord at the table where He, as father of the family, washed their feet. This is His way of teaching them, of correcting them, of "controlling" them and keeping down the "old man" in them. "You call me Master and Lord; this I am. But if I, the Master and Lord, have washed your feet, you are expected to do the same." There is no accessibility to the Eucharist without this experience of washing the feet.

There will never be a building up of a community of true disciples of Christ if the superior does not really seek the most humble service, if she does not sometimes expect to be humbled by the greater experience or the greater wisdom of some of the sisters, if she does not dare to acknowledge humbly that she makes mistakes. "This did not work out well. Let us try to do better." We all have to learn at the Eucharistic table that we are to wash each other's feet; we must all perform the most humble services, and do them in reality, not merely symbolically. It was not merely a symbol in Christ's day. The slave girl washed the dusty feet of the man who came in from the dusty street. The superior, as well as every one of us, has to share with others this experience learned from the Lord. There is no love where one does not offer the most needed, the most humble service to one's brethren. Humility is

42

the first step to the altar. "I confess to almighty God and to you, brethren." This is the initial experience of the Eucharist, and this experience must be embodied in our communities.

Let us give more reality to our chapter of faults. If we wish to rid ourselves of unreality, then let us not continue to confess throughout a lifetime that we broke a glass or silence. Let there be a revision of life in which we face our shortcomings in community life, our imprudence, our rushing into activity, or our lack of judgment. Let us encourage one another through humble confession.

Last year I had an unexpected experience of which I would not have approved had I been asked beforehand. The professors of the Academia Alfonsiana offered a four-week course for the clergy, religious, and laity of Mexico City. Six hundred attended the course which ended with concelebration. I was a concelebrant, and was a little surprised, therefore, when, at the beginning of Mass, the monsignor who was the director of the Pastoral Center, told us that we would introduce this Eucharist with a penitential rite—the concelebrants would confess the sins of their pastoral life and conduct. He began with striking humility, and was followed by the concelebrants who likewise evidenced a real depth of humility in confessing their misbehavior, their impatience, their arrogance, their routine in the performance of pastoral duties and in their attitudes toward their brethren. All the other participants at the Mass were led into a deep personal examination of conscience. Such an experience may disturb the peace of many; but they may be encouraged to similar simplicity and openness when they see how everyone expresses his shortcomings humbly. This is the first step to the altar; this is also a decisive step into the new era. The old era reflects pride; Adam and Eve accused each other. "This wife thou has given me, she has seduced me!" Should not Adam have confessed, "I, too, am guilty?"

Let us learn from the Eucharistic sacrifice to acknowledge our faults to each other. The Eucharist teaches us to pay the price of our discipleship. It is always the glory of the Lord which we celebrate in the Mass, but we must also recall the price our Master paid and expects us to pay —real self-denial rather than the little mortifications, the no-meat-on-Fridays type. Real mortification is the death of our selfishness, our pride, our closed minds, our impatience. It should always be practiced with the real needs of brothers, sisters, and community in mind.

The Eucharist is the mystery of faith which builds up a community of faith. But the celebration is not an event circumscribed by itself; it is the proclamation, the humble and joyous acceptance of that faith which should transform the whole world. In the Eucharist we acquire the light of the Lord, that we may let that light shine before men so that they may thereby praise the Father in heaven. Only if we are hidden with the Lord, if we are paying the price of our discipleship, if we no longer seek our own light or our own glory, will our light shine as the light of Christ. Only then will men praise the Father in heaven.

The Church is a community of faith. As we listen to the Word of God, we not only listen to a book written centuries ago, but to Christ Himself who proclaims the gospel. All words receive their meaning from the essential message: "This is my body, sacrificed for you. This is my blood, shed for you." What is read in the gospel and what is said in the homily receives meaning from the essential message: "I died for you. I live for you." The acceptance of this essential message is an awesome experience. Woe to us if we accept it as a "normal" thing. The Lord, the only-begotten Son of God, the perfect man has shed His blood for us. If we really believe this, we are shaken, and we ask ourselves, "Did [we] in our struggle against the sin of self-centeredness resist to the point of shedding blood?" (Cf. Hebr. 12:4.) Do we respond with a faith which is fitting response for this message of faith: "I died for you. I live for you"? We will not dare to profane the blood of the covenant by which it was consecrated (cf. Hebr. 10:29).

In faith it is essential that we listen not only to words, but also to the one who *is* the Word, the messenger, the person who is the loving presence of God. We look to him, and this gives meaning to all words. We are aware of his presence. This knowledge must be learned here in the Eucharist: then we listen not only to the words and thoughts of our sisters; we listen to them as persons. We listen to an individual. We look into her eyes, into her soul with deep sympathy; we really feel how this person is suffering, how this unique person is appealing to us as a person.

Faith brings one face-to-face with a living Person and demands the surrender of oneself as a person to this Person. If we celebrate the Eucharist as the great mystery of faith, where God makes visible the full extent of His love, where we surrender ourselves to Him in this mystery of faith, we will learn to look into the real needs of our communities, and to look in the right way at our individual gifts as links to the community. This community will not be considered only as an abstract institution, but rather as this *We*, which is composed of Thou and I, of persons who meet others in their uniqueness.

If you read the farewell discourse at the Last Supper, you can see this personal way of talking. Christ is speaking about the Eucharist, the Paschal Mystery. He is seated at the table listening to Philip, to Thomas, to Peter. Everyone receives his responses. To Philip who has so naïvely asked, "Show us the Father. We don't know the way," Our Lord, astonished, replies: "Philip, such a long time I have been with you, and have you not realized that I am the Way; he who sees me sees the Father?" Philip understood: "Now he speaks plainly; now we understand." There is kindness and goodness in Christ's reply, as well as firmness and frankness with Peter who boastfully tells the Lord, "If all these people here betray you, I will not. I am the rock. I am appointed superior. I know it." The Lord is frank, but good to him; He tells him, "If you will be converted, then give strength to your brethren." Does not the Eucharistic Christ sometimes tell sister superior, "If you will be converted to greater humility, converted not to look down on other people but rather to look to me and to others, to find others in me, if you will be converted to full humility, you will give strength to your sisters"?

The Eucharist is the celebration of the mystery of faith and joy. Was it not a joyous experience today? The joy of each one sustained the joy of the others! All our joy and gratitude for the message of joy grew together in one hymn of praise! Take care that the Eucharist is always the joyous hour. Be humble but, nevertheless, dare in humility to discuss the issue with your chaplain if he rushes through the Mass too hurriedly. Be courageous enough to tell him, "We are not such impatient people; we are not so hard-pressed. We have time; we have time for the Eucharist. We have time to listen to Christ's words." Then help him by taking your part in the reading and singing, in dignity— it is the word you can offer to the one who is the Word, the Incarnate Word. And sing, sing joyfully to the Lord, because faith is the source of joy. Where there is neither joy nor an expression of joy, faith is weak and love will be weak. At the Eucharistic table in the Cenacle, the Lord introduced his great command, "Love one another as I have loved you" with these words, "This I tell you, that my joy may be in you, and your joy complete. This then is my command, love one another as I have loved you." We can celebrate the Eucharist joyously if we have prepared ourselves by bringing joy to our brothers and sisters, by being attentive to how we can foster joy, joy in the Lord, fully human and Christian joy. We keep ourselves open to the joy of discipleship through the necessary cost of self-denial. Where our attitude is not that of openness to others, we do not pave the way for joy.

Thus we should learn from the Eucharist to promote a joyous approach to life, and this not only in spite of, but even through difficulties, for Christ has paved the way for joy by suffering. This must be our trust.

I was happy this morning that Mother Angelita emphasized strongly that the superior as a genuine Christian will always show trust in the Lord. We look forward to turmoil, and trust in the Lord that, if we accept difficulties by offering them on the altar, they will be a source of joy. This we learn from the great mystery of faith. The Eucharist confirms what St. Paul writes in his letter to the Ephesians: "There is one hope held out in God's call to you" (4:4). Our hope will be firm when we realize that it is the rallying call of Christ assuring us that things are going well, that they will bear rich fruit to the extent that we accept and honor his solidarity. He did not come to please himself. Neither does he leave us with the anguished question: "How do I find the merciful God? How do I save my soul?" If we understand the mystery of·hope, we realize that Christ died for all, and, therefore, no one is allowed to live for himself. Hope is in solidarity.

Modern psychology and sociology show us the tremendous power of environment; our environment shapes us to a great extent. A bad environment, group division, a climate of competition, a contentious temper—all too easily shape us. But how can we be liberated; how can we escape from this shaping power of our culture? Many seek the answer in selfishness, in a philosophy of self-fulfillment. There is so much restlessness, so much superficiality in this tense business of self-fulfillment! It is never possible to find liberation as isolated individuals. The Eucharist shows us that Christ has transformed the shaping power of history by His solidarity; He took upon Himself the burden of the whole world. We can reshape whatever is formalistic, legalistic, superficial, selfish; whatever is a burden and a handicap, we can reshape to the extent that our solidarity implies cooperation rather than distinct separation. In each of our sisters, in the most old-fashioned, conservative sister we can find something precious—a deep desire for continuity. We find something in the most impatient, restless people; it is life they are seeking, true life, though they may not realize that it is in continuity. Every one of us is old-fashioned and stubborn in at least one aspect; in other aspects we are quite adaptable. Let us cooperate in our differences, and let us not break the community into two groups, the goats and the sheep.

In solidarity and hope we are gathered around the altar, around Christ in His solidarity. Therefore every celebration of light gives us

His attitude which is found at the beginning of the Pastoral Constitution on the Church in the Modern World: "The joys and the hopes, the sorrows and worries of the men of our time are ours." And indeed the joys can be ours only if the sorrows are also ours. We can rejoice with our brother only if we can weep with him. Hope is in patience, in gentleness. "How blessed are those of a gentle spirit! They will possess the earth." In your patience you will possess your soul. It is true that many changes are long overdue; they should have happened years ago, and now many impatiently urge change. But the solution cannot now be in a complete break with the past. The solution can only be in patience, patience as realized in the collected energies of Christ on the mount of the beatitudes, on the Mount of Olives, and on the cross; in the collected energies of John who, outrunning Peter, waits for him.

One of the sisters asked in the question box, "But what does St. John do if Peter never arrives?" The solution is clear: "Love hopes for everything." Have enough love, and you will have enough hope that he will arrive; but also let him know that you trust that he will arrive. Let us trust each other, and let us trust in the power of the Spirit.

The Eucharist is a community of love and adoration. We can praise God only in our unity. This, however, does not mean that we have no time for explicit praise in songs and hymns. Before St. Paul extols love in marriage—that is, before he exhorts the husband to love his wife as Christ loves the Church—he exhorts the whole family of God to sing hymns and songs constantly, to praise the Lord always (Eph. 5:18-33). The more we learn to praise God, and the more we are aware that our whole life is to be a shining light exhorting the people to praise the Father in heaven, the more will we also find that our oneness, our loving kindness, our patience, and our love constitute the praise which God desires. The Epistle to the Hebrews (13:16) exhorts the Christian to "offer continually to God through Jesus Christ a sacrifice of praise, that is, tribute of lips acknowledging His name. And never forget to show kindness, and to share what you have with others, for such are the sacrifices which God approves." God approves our kindness and generosity in sharing everything with others; this, however, is not possible without sacrifices.

In order to assure this charity, Paul admonishes us to offer to God the tribute of our lips, as more than mere lip service. We must acknowledge His name. Name here refers to His countenance, His face turned toward us. His name is Father, Savior, Redeemer. Such tribute we give only if we pray *"Our* Father." If we have included our sisters

and all suffering people in our prayer, and if in our praise we have included not only ourselves but all who rejoice in the Lord, we praise
God worthily. Only if we train our voices for singing (and this not
only in formalistic training), only if we are willing to pay the cost of
discipleship in oneness can we praise God with our lives.

St. Paul, in reference to racing and boxing, says: "I am like a boxer
who does not beat the air; I bruise my body and make it know its master in order not to be useless while I am preaching to others" (1 Cor.
9:26-27). In our asceticism, our exercises have often been marginal to
our life. There were rules, and one could fulfill all the exercises without ever "hitting the point." We must be watchful in order to understand clearly where we need humiliation, where we need sacrifice to
keep us free, where we need renunciation in order to be free for
prayer, to be free and watchful of the needs of our neighbors. Every
one must undertake an examination with the eyes of love, and under
the eyes of the Lord. Often we find the wrong solution for our problems because we treat them only with an abstract principle in mind,
with the rule alone instead of before the face of the living Lord. "Keep
in mind that Christ died for you and rose for you." In the problems of
the day, the problems of the community, remember that Christ died
for you. Ask Him, "Lord, can I offer this solution, this desire to You in
gratitude for what You did for me?" This is what is meant by paying
the cost of discipleship. It is easy at times to conform to an abstract rule
while forgetting the more urgent rules, the precepts of the gospel. But
if we face Christ, we learn to discern the spirit. We learn the criteria
of true love, not abstractly, but by facing Him in prayer where He
will show us what can and must be sacrificed to build up this adoring
community which, with one mind and voice, can praise God the Father of our Lord Jesus Christ.

The Eucharist makes us truly a "fellowship in the Holy Spirit."
(2 Cor. 13:13). Christ the High Priest is not a man of routine; He is
not a functionary. He does not even belong to the tribe of Levi, of
Aaron. His whole priesthood is to be anointed by the Spirit in order
that He might sacrifice Himself. "Thou hast prepared a body for me.
. . . Behold, O Lord, I come to fulfill thy will" (Hebr. 10:5-7). Only
because the fullness of the Holy Spirit has come upon Him can He
extend His hands to all and offer His life: "Father, into thy hands I
commend my spirit." We must pray to the Holy Spirit for all the things
we expect from Him. When Our Lord promised the Eucharist, many
were scandalized. Many even left Him. His final words, His final re-

sponse is simply: "The Spirit alone gives life. The flesh is of no avail. The words which I have spoken to you are both spirit and life" (John, 6:63). Only if we trust in the Spirit, if we implore His help, if we ask Him over and over again to make us docile, if we learn this docility from the Spirit in docility to our sisters and to our superiors, then and only then will the Holy Spirit open our eyes in faith by opening our hearts to the Word of the Lord in the Eucharist: "I died for you." The Spirit leads us thus to the life-giving Word.

We must also sustain each other. Perhaps religious congregations will have less control over prayer life in the future. We can renounce these controls of prayer life only if each individual sister sustains the others with her prayer, that is, with the witness she gives to prayer and listening to the word of God. Before the Lord gathered His disciples around Him in the Cenacle prior to the Paschal Mystery, He entered the temple to throw out the distracted, the buyers and sellers. He then said, "My house is a house of prayer."

The Eucharist reminds us day by day that the whole Church is to be "a house of prayer." On several occasions, I have suggested that larger communities, realizing the danger of their community members' becoming exhausted by too many activities, open a house of prayer. Since then I have received letters from sisters who have told me, "Father, it's a fine idea, but it's wrong. If some sisters are taken away from the active life for a year to renew their prayer life, those who remain will have to bear even greater burdens and will become more distracted. We cannot afford this; it is just not practical." But it is easy to discuss this problem and its answer with American sisters, especially with the group here at Sister Formation. Eight to ten years ago many said that it was not possible to release sisters for study for a period of one, two or three years. Today all are convinced that you have become more effective because you have given enough time to permit your sisters to receive an appropriate formation. If we believe in the "fellowship of the Holy Spirit," and if we believe that we are to be "a house of prayer," we can afford it. If a sister, realizing that she is exhausted and empty, asks for a year to return to a house where the one and only concern is to listen to the Lord, to study spiritual theology, and to ponder the Word of God, she will come out filled with the joy of the Lord, and will do more in one year than an "empty" sister can do in ten years.

Day by day we bring our whole life to the Eucharist, but we must also bring the Eucharist to life, our life must be permeated with the spirit of prayer. One of the questions asked was: "How much prayer?" My response is always: "Fewer prayers and more prayer!" Some communities have too many prayers, "duties of prayers." Perhaps some sisters face the same hard experience I did when I entered the novitiate. Without proper preparation, we were obliged to say the whole Office. Each day I was so glad when it was over because I could once more start praying. Perhaps it would be better if very busy sisters could just put their troubled hearts to rest and sit quietly for a half-hour before the tabernacle rather than rush through the Office. There would thus be more time for prayer in listening to the Lord, pondering upon His words, and expressing our deepest being to Him. Let us not forget that the half-hour during the Mass, which was formerly a time for individual, private prayer, has now become common worship once more. It is right that it is so, but time must now be found for another half-hour of private prayer. Only if we have enough time for personal prayer during which we can present our brothers and sisters to God, can we express ourselves to Him and listen to Him. Only then can we sustain common worship in the Eucharist and the spirit of faith and prayer in daily community living.

Authority and Mature Obedience

Rev. Bennet Kelley, C.P.
St. Ann Passionist Monastery
Scranton, Pennsylvania

The topic I am going to discuss is one about which a great deal has been written and one for which the Vatican Council has provided brief but significant guidelines: we shall try to consider just what mature and responsible obedience really means.

It is significant that in the document of the Dogmatic Constitution on the Church—the most fundamental of the documents—referring to benefits that accrue to religious following the counsels of Christ, the first reference to obedience is in a rather strange statement: "These religious families give their members . . . liberty strengthened by obedience" (§43). Put in an oblique way, the first thing mentioned is liberty and then, "strengthened by obedience."

There are further statements in the decree on Religious Life. The whole of §14 is dedicated to obedience, more precisely to the point we are here considering, namely, maturity. I quote:

Realizing that they are giving service to the upbuilding of Christ's body according to God's design, let them bring to the execution of commands and to the discharge of assignments entrusted to them the resources of their minds and wills, and their gifts of nature and grace. Lived in this manner, religious obedience will not diminish the dignity of the human person but will rather lead it to *maturity in consequence of that enlarged freedom* which belongs to the sons of God. [Emphasis added.]

In that same section, speaking of the type of leadership to be given by superiors, the decree states:

Let him [the superior] give the kind of leadership which will encourage religious to bring an *active and responsible* obedience to the offices they shoulder and the activities they undertake. [Emphasis added.]

These two ideas must be the starting points of our discussion.

Connected with the general idea of obedience are three topics the council gives us: freedom, maturity, responsibility. And these are ideas we have not been accustomed to put together. The general idea of obedience, yes, that goes back to the very foundations of religious life itself. But obedience was basically: do as you are told. However, we now see that that does not fit in with *freedom*. And where does *maturity* come in? and *responsibility*—in the sense of full responsibility?— since we are never fully responsible for an action unless we ourselves have made the decision to perform that action. For example, if a sister in a classroom decides to use pink chalk instead of white and the youngsters at the back of the room cannot read what she has written because it is not clear enough, it is her responsibility to act appropriately in this situation. She is responsible for her action because she is free.

If, however, a sister is teaching the second grade and is not qualified to teach that grade, and is not doing a good job because of that, that is *not* her responsibility but the responsibility of the person who assigned her to that post. In other words, responsibility comes, as the document points out, only in consequence of freedom. We must, therefore, take these ideas and, since they are so basic, find out just what they do mean.

Freedom means that we are able to make a particular decision at our own choosing. We may make it from our own whims, or we may make it from the light the Holy Spirit gives us, but, as long as there is no interference with our choice, we are free. If we are not allowed to make our own choice in this particular area, then we are not free.

We understand maturity as paralleling the maturing process of anyone growing up in a natural life-situation. A child begins by being given everything he needs: care, shelter, protection. Gradually, more and more is expected of him; certainly, more is expected of a six-year-old than of a six-month-old. Yet, we don't call a six-year-old really mature, because we're always looking for something further. Ordinarily, we speak of maturity as a comparison after a peak has been reached, even though, strictly speaking, there is no one real peak or point of maturity; it should be a continuing process all one's life. We do, of course, reach a point where bodily energies diminish, and there does tend to be a period of physical decline, but, at least during the greater part of life, there is a gradual growth.

Let us look at maturity from an emotional point of view. An emotionally mature person is one who is able to do what he knows he should under one given set of circumstances, to fulfill the purpose he needs to achieve. He is not pulled along by his whims. A child is completely a slave to his feelings; he can do only what he feels like doing. The process of maturing emotionally is a gradual one whereby we are able to act at the direction of our minds, and by which we become able to think and act creatively, developing the resources that are within us. A mature adult is one who is able to act from his own mind, his own will.

Even here, maturity admits of further degrees. It is not as if we ever reach a certain point beyond which there can be no improvement. In one sense, the only full maturity is perfect sanctity, and God does not ordinarily leave us around much after that! But, I repeat, the process of maturing should be a progressive one, constantly continuing until we are able to act as our minds tell us to act. If we ever say to ourselves, "I know I should do this but I cannot bring myself to do it," in that area at least we admit to immaturity.

For the maturing process, a growing freedom is needed. That is why a child is given a growing freedom, why parents will ordinarily assign responsibilities to a six-, eight- or nine-year-old; sometimes, for example, allow a child to help out with the cooking. If a nine-year-old girl is taught how to make a cake she must be allowed the freedom to make it, even to make mistakes and to learn by them to do better the next time. An adolescent is allowed still greater freedom, and if the process goes on properly his degree of freedom will continue to be increased until he reaches adulthood. Obviously, all of the intervening steps must be taken. Freedom to make decisions of growing importance must be allowed. Overprotection on the part of parents, denying the child the opportunity to make necessary decisions, seriously handicaps the maturing process. Frequently, in such situations, the adolescent reaches a point of rebellion against undue limitations on freedom, against the prevention of what the youngster considers necessary in his development to adult maturity. At other times, the reaction is one of withdrawal, with the result that there is no naturally developed initiative or creativity. Rarely can they truly mature who are overprotected or prevented from making decisions on their own.

One of the chief consequences of freedom is responsibility. If we are free, then we are responsible for our free actions. Children learn by degrees that responsibility attaches to every freedom. Very often it is only after freedom has been abused a few times that a sense of responsibility gradually grows. But the freedom has to come first. We can never wait for a sense of responsibility to develop in someone before we give him freedom; the simple fact is that the sense of responsibility will never develop without experience. Freedom has to come first and responsibility will follow.

Sacred Scripture frequently speaks of freedom; the freedom of the children of God. St. Paul speaks of freedom that all Christians are given when he says, "But do not use this freedom as an occasion for self-indulgence." Freedom is not given that we might simply satisfy ourselves, but so that we can act to follow the voice of the Spirit leading us to follow in the footsteps of Christ, to fulfil the particular purpose given us, to develop the gifts of nature and of grace in a creative way with true Christian initiative.

Now, these are ideas that we are not used to considering when we think of religious obedience. The maturing process is not something confined to the individual; it goes on in society as well. There has been a growing freedom in civil society, and even though there have been, and still are, many abuses, there is far more capacity or opportunity to develop one's personal talents and initiative. This is probably much more obvious with women than with men.

Think of the average woman of a century or two ago. She lived at home with her father who had all the authority. Practically all decisions of any importance were made for her by him. She worked in the house, under direction, being told exactly what to do and how to do it. All of her associations with anyone outside of the house were strictly supervised. She was never allowed to go out and work for society on her own. The modern idea of the business woman, or the career woman, was entirely unknown. Even a girl's marriage partner was chosen for her by her parents. Certainly she could have no voice in civil government, no voice in the moulding of society except indirectly by moulding characters. Today, even teenage girls are trusted; their contacts are not strictly supervised. They are allowed to choose their own marriage partners, and they have a voice in civil society. They may choose a career, and it is presumed that they will make the choice. These are all areas of growing freedom, a freedom which can be and often is abused, but there is no great threat to society as a result.

With time, a new and changing concept of society has grown, one of progress, of developing the material and cultural world. The Church, too, has caught the idea: The Vatican Council is definitely a council of progress looking toward the future, giving men a picture of the Church as dynamic, progressive, a pilgrim Church on the march.

Like the Church, religious life has many structures. We are human beings and we live the counsels of Christ in a human way. There are many conventions in our dealings with one another. What we say and what we do or how we greet each other, the type of work we do—all of these are conditioned in large measure by the society in which we live. We eat the food that is customary in the society in which we live; we greet each other as is customary in the society in which we live; we engage in the type of work that our society understands.

Religious life developed its outward structures in the early ages of the Church, reaching a high point in medieval society. In that medieval society, a girl who entered the convent found most of the structures similar to those she had known at home. She was cloistered, but she would have been cloistered at home too. At home, she accepted the fact that practically all of her decisions were made for her. Even if she were married there would have been very few decisions that she could make, so conventual life was not anything very different. The convent was a home to her similar in its structure to the home she had left.

Society has changed, hence we are now at a point in religious life where we are re-evaluating structures. We are asking why we do the things that we do. And when we are faced with answering that question, we find that many of the things that we do are being done because they have always been done that way, and nobody really knows or remembers why! As intelligent human beings, as intelligent Christians who must constantly ask the reason for things, we have discovered that we do not have proportionate reasons for the structures in our society. Presumably they fitted in very well in the society in which they originated. But they do not fit in with our society today.

The postulant is told that she will find a new home, and a new family in the convent. Does she find proportionately the same structures that she had in her own home? Often, she finds things very different indeed. She does not have free access to all the rooms in the convent; she is not free to use all of the stairways. At home, she made her own decisions as to when and to whom she might speak, or when she would remain silent. Now she is told when she may speak and when she may not speak.

At home, she wrote a letter when she wanted to. Now, she is told when she may write, and the letter must be given to someone else who will tell her whether she has written what she should have written! And then, when she receives a letter someone else will read it first to find out if this is something she should be allowed to read! If she has a headache, someone else decides whether she needs an aspirin! If she needs to do something so extraordinary as to use the telephone, this requires an unusual permission!

In other words, now that she has entered the convent, a girl finds that she is expected to take a step backwards; that all the decisions she had learned to make even as an adolescent now have to be made for her. Why? Because someone made them for the girl in medieval society! As a result, instead of helping the continuing process of maturity, convent structures are holding it back. This has been realized for quite some time; it was not the Vatican Council that first made it evident. But there was a general principle used to justify these structures, namely, "holy obedience." Rather vaguely it was understood that if you asked a permission and received it, you had the "blessing of holy obedience." This was true enough but there was in it an implication which, viewed in the light of our re-evaluation, does not stand the test. It was sometimes imagined that to get this blessing of holy obedience one had to have explicit permission for every detail.

When assigned a task or a function, the individual who uses her gifts of nature and of grace, and makes decisions on how to act within that function, still has the blessing of obedience, even though explicit permission is not asked for each time for each separate thing that has to be done.

In our re-evaluation we have come to see that the essence of obedience is not absolute regimentation, that all decisions need not be already made and handed down by rule or custom, by the actual directive of a particular superior, or in some other way. And seeing this, we ask: what particular structures do we need?

We know that we need obedience. Christ Himself was obedient and obedience is essential to any society, even such a small society as a marriage. There has to be at least—or rather at most—one head. There has to be someone to make the final decision in anything affecting the society. Every individual retains a private life in a society, and every individual in a society ought to be able to make those decisions that relate to that person as an individual.

In religious life there are personal decisions and there are community decisions. Decisions that affect an individual as an individual should be made by that individual. Help in making the decision must be given while the person is still immature, but an adult religious woman should be able to make personal decisions that any adult in her society would be expected to make. This has not always been practiced, due to the many structures in religious life that prevent the making of such decisions.

There are multiple permissions required in the structures of religious life before a sister may do the things that any one should be able to do with the simple light the Holy Spirit gives. Religious should have the freedom of the children of God. In matters that affect the community in any way whatever there is something else to be considered, but in her own personal life—in her prayer life, in the choosing of her friends —she should be able to make decisions on her own.

In a family there should be normal freedom to perform normal functions, and even a child is allowed to make decisions unless they are detrimental to the very purpose of the family. In religious life the numerous permissions to be sought militate against normal freedom in many cases. We are not accustomed to thinking of this kind of freedom in the religious life. In fact, we think of permissions as the normal thing, freedom as the exception, a sort of privilege. In the Christian life freedom is the normal thing, and the light of the Holy Spirit given to each individual adult Christian is amply sufficient for the things that need to be done personally.

There is also another area to be considered, that of community decisions. A community decision affects either the whole community or the individual as a member of the community. Here is where we need authority. To make a personal decision authority is not needed, but for a community decision it is. When we enter a society we automatically accept the authority within that society. As the decree points out, it is always the superior who has the final voice, the decision in all community matters. Anything that pertains to the community as such, for example, the ordering of the schedule, the doing of things together, the use of community equipment, is ultimately the superior's decision.

In this regard, the council uses another term—a word used frequently in the Vatican Council documents. We notice it first used in reference to bishops in dealing with the principle of collegiality; the word is *listen*. Here it is not used primarily in the sense of listening to the personal problems (although that is a tremendous function of every superior); it means listening on a decision level. Every superior who has authority to make a final decision in any matter relating to that particular community, the local community if she is a local superior, the province or congregation if she be a major superior—needs to listen to the members of the community. Why? Because the Holy Spirit speaks to each.

This is not something we are just finding out. Even St. Benedict incorporated it into his rule. He says, "Let him [the superior] listen even to the youngest brother lest, perhaps, the Holy Spirit may have said something or be saying something through him." In other words, everyone receives lights from the Holy Spirit, a truth based on the indwelling of the Holy Spirit in everyone. Here is where there is a great need for re-evaluation, because in decision-making all adults should be heard. This does not mean that the opinion of every individual, nor even of the majority, is necessarily to be followed. The final decision rests with the person in authority, and if that authority is to be used responsibly, the one using it must know the lights God is giving those under that authority. She needs to know those as part of the material that will be used in making the final decision.

Now, in light of all that has been said thus far, we ask the practical question: how do we treat sisters as adults? My own personal opinion is that the sooner we can re-evaluate the customs, practices, and traditions that we have right now, the better off we will be, for we have not only to remove the present structures which prohibit an individual from acting as an adult, but we must go further still. Already, the Holy See and the norms emerging from the council have given considerable leeway to major superiors for experimentation with ideas contrary to present customs, rules, and even canon law. That is progress. That is why before experimenting we must remove obstacles that treat the sisters immaturely, because only mature sisters are capable of experimentation. There is so much more we need to do to develop creatively all the potential there is in our religious life in order to meet the challenge of the needs of our times.

There are many practices in religious life that have no real sanction of a rule; even an individual may change them. In many cases, these practices seem to be more sacrosanct than the written rule. It is well to remember one principle that has always existed but which sisters have been much more afraid of than male religious, or priests in general, and that is the principle of exception. The fact that something is a general law does not mean that it is universal, that there can never be any exception. Because the rule specifies that a meal, for example, or a choir observance is to be at a particular time does not mean that there could not be reasons to have it at another time. Even a local superior has the power to make exceptions when there is a reason for them; there must be a certain amount of flexibility. The rule must be something that can be lived, because the rule is for the sake of the sisters, not the sisters for the sake of the rule. Persons come first, not rules. Unfortunately, we have tended to look at this the wrong way round.

How do we treat sisters as mature adults? They must be given all the freedom possible at present with a view to giving even more. Freedom will inevitably result in certain abuses. Christ Himself did not demand that there should be no abuses: He gave freedom to the Apostles even though they abused it at times—even though Judas abused it seriously. A certain amount of caution is unquestionably needed but we must not hope to stop every abuse. And we must beware of imposing extra restrictions after each abuse.

When a group works together, reactions come. If, working together, we ask ourselves: how can we improve our customs? how can we improve what we are doing now? what can we do to leave the sisters free to really grow up?—the answers will come. Where there is good will the majority will use freedom properly. For the sake of the few that won't, we should not restrict so great a good. We cannot follow the Holy Spirit, Who leads and guides us, unless we are free.

The Church is encouraging the use of freedom in all areas. Lay people are being given more of a voice in the affairs of the Church. This recognition of mature adulthood is a growing thing; it won't happen overnight. If everyone recognizes freedom as the good the Church holds up, knowing that when it is there responsibility will come gradually, and that maturity will develop too, there will be far more free, happy religious who will work well and attract vocations. Happy religious don't leave, and you need freedom to be happy.

Humanizing Community Relations:
The Convent as a Living Center of Love

VERY REV. MSGR. CHESTER MICHAEL
Holy Comforter Church
Charlottesville, Virginia

Every convent should be a living center of love radiating to all those who come into contact with it. This means, first of all, that the superior herself must leave no stone unturned to become an example of sincere, unselfish concern for everyone in the community. Regardless of the situation, she must keep going out in love to all those around her. She must strive never to think of herself first, but, like Christ on the cross, sacrifice her own desires and pleasure in order to please God and to please others. Love begets love—love is contagious. The other sisters will learn love primarily from the example of heroic and unselfish love they see in the superior. This atmosphere of love will not be accomplished overnight, especially if there are nuns who have had experiences in the past of the lack of love from parents, superiors and other sisters. The example of love in the superior will not necessarily produce love in everyone else in the community, just as the love of Christ did not always result in love among those He encountered. Sometimes it may cause just the opposite reaction, but this should be the exception and not the general rule.

In order to be a true center of love, the superior must seek to identify herself with each person in the community and try to see and feel things as others would. In order to project herself into the place of others, the superior must be filled with great inner security and peace of soul. The more balanced and settled she is in her own mind, the more unselfish she can be in handling the problems of others. This constant going out to others in their needs takes a tremendous toll of energy from the superior, but by allowing herself to be stretched thin for the sake of the community she will become truly another Christ and saviour of her brethren. Like Christ at the Last Supper, she must be willing to stoop to the lowliest tasks in the convent, and never ask another nun to do something she is unwilling to do. She will radiate love to those around her to the extent that she thinks of herself as truly the servant of all those over whom she has been placed as superior.

Each nun in the community will become another living center of love to the extent that she is convinced, first of all, of her own worth and lovableness and, secondly, of her ability and the worthwhileness of loving others. It is the task of the superior to convince each member of the community that she is truly lovable and worthwhile by showing a sincere and wholehearted love for each of them. For some of them this experience of being loved in a mature, adult way may well be the first opportunity they have had in their whole life to receive such love. As a religious the nun is deprived of the experience of an adult love from a husband. So often there has been such a fuss made in the novitiate about particular friendships that the nun is likewise deprived of any experience of love from another nun or adult. Therefore, if she does not receive a deep love from the superior, she may well be a person without any real experience of love. When the faculty to love has been allowed to stagnate over the years, it will require heroic, superhuman efforts to strike the needed spark to re-ignite the powers of human love that are present in every person. Regardless of the cost, no price is too high to pay to bring about such an activation of human love in the heart of a person.

Every superior carries many unconscious images or projections as far as the rest of the community is concerned. The more unconscious the others are of these powerful projections at work in their relationships with the superior, the greater is their influence either for good or evil. First of all, the superior carries the projection of all the experiences each nun has had with her parents and all other superiors and teachers, especially those of childhood, but also later experiences continuing right up to the present. If the past has been at all traumatic, then the present superior will be looked upon with suspicion, fear, dread, even hatred and contempt. Unpleasant memories, especially of childhood, are usually repressed and not consciously remembered. Nevertheless, they are powerful in forming one's present attitude toward the superior. A sister may not like you without knowing why she so strongly dislikes; or she may attribute it to some reason that is not the real cause for her hostility. This makes it all the more difficult for either party to straighten out the hostility that has arisen. Superiors must realize all this, and be exceedingly tolerant of those who have such problems.

To each of the nuns under her a superior represents all authority, including the authority of God and the Church. Very often the reaction to the superior is not to the person of the superior but to the person of God, or general rebellion against anyone who attempts to limit freedom. Our generation has been given new appreciation of the value of freedom insofar as it is essential to maturity and the practice of mature love for God or our fellow-man.

Often the opposition to the exercise of authority by a superior is unconscious. The more unconscious the hostility is, the stronger and deeper it will be. Because the superior is the unconscious carrier of so many projections, images and archetypes for the nuns under her, they expect at least unconsciously that she be superhuman in her strength of personality, maturity, goodness of character, her unselfish love and willingness to sacrifice for others. With patience and much instruction, the members of the community can be gradually educated to appreciate these facts of unconscious projection. However, even in the most mature and well-educated community, the superior must try in every possible way to be truly another Christ to each member of the community and to the community as a whole. Christ was superhuman and every superior is likewise expected to be superhuman. This, actually, is not asking the impossible because it is made possible by the grace of God and the Sacraments, especially the daily Eucharist. Every Christian by the fact of Baptism is called upon to be truly heroic in living a Christ-like life. Being placed in the position of superior simply emphasizes this need of living up to the heroism that is expected of every Christian, religious or lay.

The head of any group of people, especially a group living as closely knit and interdependent lives as those of nuns in a convent, has a tremendous responsibility. Much of the success of community relations depends upon the personality, character, heroism, love, attitude and reactions of the superior. Because of the present and past structure of the religious life of most nuns, the superior's importance is considerably increased. There is a long tradition in religious life that presumes that the superior does all or nearly all the thinking and decision-making for the rest of the community. Many of the older nuns have grown accustomed not to do any thinking or decision-making for themselves, but to depend entirely in a childlike way upon the superior to make up their mind or will. Even though the younger nuns and the stronger-willed ones among the middle-aged and older nuns may deeply and bitterly resent this situation, nevertheless, they are still caught in the system. Old habits and ways of acting have a tendency to perpetuate themselves without anyone's being consciously aware of it. Even those who most strongly rebel against being treated as children in the convent, without realizing it, will expect the superior to do most of the difficult work for them as far as the making of decisions is concerned. The new breed of nun in her new-found freedom usually fails to realize the tremendous responsibility and work that go into exercising this freedom in a reasonable and proper way. They would like the privilege of freedom of choice, especially when it concerns themselves, but they are either not equipped or are unwilling to do the background work of thought and study to prepare for this decision. A good superior today will be willing to do humbly this necessary preliminary study, and then find some way of bringing the other nuns into the picture to help make the final decision in activities that concern them.

Nuns must not be forced, or indeed, may not even be allowed to live all of their life in a hothouse environment, closely guarded and protected from the slightest danger of contamination. They must be treated as adults, not as children, and encouraged to act in an adult, mature way. Great patience will have to be shown to those who have lived so long under the old pattern, and are unable or unwilling to forsake their childish ways of dependence. Patience must also be shown to the new breed of nuns who want to change the old ways too quickly, and to allow too much freedom of choice for the individual. To change a firmly established tradition too quickly could easily do more harm than good. Great wisdom, prudence, and intuition are needed by modern superiors to steer a clear course between the Scylla of the *status quo* group and the Charybdis of the "new breed" of instant change.

The religious vow of obedience must never be construed to mean the denial of that basic freedom needed by every person to develop the peculiar maturity and sanctity for which she has been destined from all eternity by God. An atmosphere of freedom should be present in every community, so that each nun is able to be the individual she desires to be, rather than to feel constantly constrained and pressed into some kind of a straitjacket where all nuns are exactly alike in their actions and reactions. A superior should not demand something under obedience unless she is reasonably convinced that it is necessary for the welfare of the community and the individual religious. The general principle should always be "as few rules as necessary," not a multiplication of rules to be obeyed for which there is no good or obvious reason. Local superiors should be reluctant to make permanent changes even of rules that seem manifestly unjust or unnecessary; however, the need of such changes should be presented to the higher superiors, and a serious effort made throughout the whole chain of authority to make the entire rule both reasonable and of definite value to the needs of today. Unless the nun of today is aware that such a serious effort is being made by those in authority, it is asking the impossible of her to accept the rule at its face value. This was possible for the nun of another generation, but not in the atmosphere of freedom that is present throughout the world today. Nuns as well as everyone else are children of their own generation, and it is impossible for them to escape from the tremendous modern emphasis on the value of freedom.

Room must be found in every religious community for the expression of the individuality of each nun. Freedom must be given first of all for the particular development of the spiritual life of each person. This spiritual life includes both the natural psychological development of maturity or wholeness, as well as the supernatural development of the life of grace. Ways and means must be found to develop the peculiar talents, graces, and mission in life that God has given each person. This means freedom to consult those confessors, spiritual directors or other persons needed for growth in maturity and sanctity. Censorship of incoming or outgoing mail and phone calls would seem to be completely contradictory to the adult maturity we assume any religious needs in order to take the religious vows validly.

The convent should never be thought of as a refuge for childish, immature women who refuse or are unable to become responsible adults. In most instances we should assume that the person who chose a religious vocation and its vows is capable of greater maturity and responsibility than the average normal woman in the world. There will be exceptions to this, but if we expect a nun to be a leader and teacher in preparing the next generation for maturity, then she should be sufficiently mature herself to make the right decisions about her friends, her contacts, and the disposal of her time. Unless nuns are given the opportunity to develop initiative, responsibility, adult mature behavior, it can be expected that nuns will be lacking in the maturity necessary to their vocation. There is obviously real danger in giving so much freedom, especially when it has been denied in the past; however, there are even more serious dangers for religious life in the denial of the most basic freedoms that are taken for granted by even immature people in the world. Like anyone else, nuns have the right to make mistakes. Unless they are given the opportunity to risk themselves, they will never learn maturity either for themselves or for those whom they are teaching.

It is the duty of superiors to treat each nun in the community differently, according to the individuality of each person's needs and mission in life. This is especially necessary in any situation where all members of a group wear the same uniform and live as closely together as do nuns. In such cases it is very easy for a mask to develop (the *persona* of C. G. Jung). This destroys the authenticity of the person wearing the mask; instead of being herself, she strives to live up to some artificial image of the ideal nun. This ideal very clearly loses those peculiar attributes necessary for any authentic human life. The nun who tries to surrender herself completely to this artificial image of the ideal nun will lose many of the human traits necessary in reaching the full development of her person as expected by God and society.

To prevent the formation of the mask, it is necessary that every nun have as large an area of privacy as possible without seriously interfering with the common good of the community and the apostolic work to which she has dedicated herself. Each member of the community should be encouraged to develop her own special talents in a creative way and be a true individual.

Because of the advantages of living together in a community, certain basic and necessary rules must be observed by all. Otherwise an individual's freedom of action would seriously hinder the exercise of freedom of the other members of the community. For example, if her arising awakens the others who are sleeping, a nun should not be allowed to rise earlier in the morning than the rest of the community. But, if she can quietly do her work in her room without disturbing the others of the community, it would seem that a nun should be treated with the same respect as might be shown to an adult woman of the world. Likewise, in the matter of recreation and use of free time, a nun should be given as much freedom as possible without doing harm to the rest of the community. Different people have different ways of relaxing and recreating. Watching television might be quite relaxing to one group of nuns but exceedingly boring and a waste of time to others. No nun should ever be forced to sit with the community and watch a TV program. Opportunity should be given for those who en-

joy good music to have access to a record player or an FM radio. If it
helps a nun to relax or even to work, it would certainly not be contrary to the spirit of poverty to allow her to have a record player or
FM radio in her room and to use it even during working hours, provided that she does not seriously interfere with the freedom of others
in the house.

Superiors especially, but other members of the community as well,
should endeavor to practice strict justice, fairness and honesty to all
others in the community. Any lack of this virtue will be disastrous to
community relations. Even the most just superior will at times be accused by another nun of being unfair to her, or of giving special privileges to another nun. This is to be expected because every person, even
a nun, is prejudiced in his or her own regard. As long as the superior
sincerely tries to exercise care in dispensing justice in the community,
she need not be upset by their occasional accusations. However, it
would be well for her to check with some more objective third party
to make sure she is not deceiving herself about her own fairness and
honesty. On the other hand, she should not be afraid to treat different
individuals in a different way, according to their own peculiar needs.
Some members of the community need more attention than others,
but scrupulous care needs to be used by superiors as well as others in
any position of authority that they do not have one or two pets who
are specially favored with friendship and special privileges. It is almost
impossible for a superior who is also a human being to exist for very
long without developing these "pets" among the members of the community. Therefore, every year she should make serious efforts at time
of retreat to identify her mistakes in this regard and attempt to correct
them. There is no reason for discouragement here but rather of challenge. It goes without saying that those members of the community
who are mentally sick or emotionally disturbed need special love and
care not only from the superior but from the whole community. However, the rest of the community should not be made to suffer seriously
because of the peculiarities of personality in one nun.

A superior should be most careful not to betray the confidences
placed with her by the other members of the community. Not only
should she not reveal to other members of the community what she
knows about a particular nun, but if something is told to her in confidence it should ordinarily not be revealed to her own superiors unless
the nun is told that the superior is obliged by her office to do this.

There will be real conflicts of conscience at times as to what is the proper course to follow. In case of doubt, the confidence should be kept; otherwise, the members of the community will lose trust in the superior.

Mental Health in Religious Life

ALEXANDER A. SCHNEIDERS, PH.D.
Boston College
Chestnut Hill, Massachusetts

There are many persons today—psychologists, psychiatrists, vocation directors, priest-psychologists, and religious superiors—who are anxious to come to grips with the relationship between religious life and mental health. This desire has its origin in several different sources, not the least of which is the storm and stress so characteristic of religious life today. Not all of these turbulences are related to mental health or to mental illness, but certainly there is an important relationship between the upheavals we are witnessing in religious life and the mental condition of many priests, sisters, and brothers. Particularly since Vatican II, there have been many, and sometimes very disturbing, changes in the structure and character of religious life; at the same time there has been a disturbingly large number of defections from vocational commitments that extend as far back as ten, twenty, and even thirty years.

Perhaps even more disturbing, but not as closely related to the problem of mental health in religious life, is the falling off of decisions for this type of vocational commitment. It is not improbable that these tendencies are related to each other, but whether they are or not, it is important for everyone involved in religious vocations to understand the relation between religious life and mental health. As Father Vaughan says so pointedly (1962):

Contrary to public opinion, among all the walks of life there is probably no other in which a neurotic or psychotic condition can be more handicapping than that of a religious. It is not unusual for a lay person to believe that the place for a neurotic young man or woman who finds any kind of social contact with others intolerable is the religious life. A successful religious,

68

whether he or she is engaged in the active apostolate of preaching and teaching or devoted to contemplative prayer, must have a strength and stability of personality that is beyond the ordinary. The absence of these characteristics seriously hinders spiritual growth, adjustment to community life, and achievement in the apostolate.

The seriousness of this position is pointed up by a recent article in the *American Journal of Psychiatry* by Sister M. William Kelley, I.H.M., with the title "The Incidence of Hospitalized Mental Illness among Religious Sisters in the United States" (1958-1959). This study, conducted in 1957, covered the hospital year from January 1, 1956 to December 31, 1956, and is described as a replication of the 1936 study by Thomas Verner Moore. In the current study a total of 378 private and public hospitals with psychiatric facilities was contacted, and usable responses were received from 357 hospitals for a total of 94.4 percent. Without going too far into all of the data amassed by Sister Kelley, we would like to point out a few trends indicated in her study. First of all, by far the highest incidence of disorders among sisters of all types were psychotic disorders, with a percentage of 80.3. Of this number 61 percent were classified as schizophrenic. Nine percent of the psychotic cases indicated disturbances of affective reactions, and 5.25 percent of all of the cases were classified as psychoneurotic reactions. Sister Kelley points out that, although the rate of mental illness was lower among sisters than among women generally, both in Moore's earlier study and in the present one, the discrepancy between the two rates is not as great now as at the time of the earlier study. Moreover, the rate of hospitalization for the 1956 population, compared with the 1935 population, increased significantly per 100,000 from 485.19 to 594.81.

Another significant fact brought out by this study is that the difference which Moore found to exist between the incidence of mental disorder among cloistered and "active" religious has also decreased considerably. On the basis of these data Sister Kelley suggests that since the rate of increase has been so much greater, relatively, among "active" religious, it can be tentatively hypothesized that the strain associated with modern conditions, such as overcrowded classrooms, accreditation demands, and adjuncts of the professional life of today's sisters, may well constitute insupportable burdens for a number of sisters who find the demands of daily life too great. As Sister Kelley says, "The apparent increase in mental disorder among active religious, however, suggests that factors of stress may be contributing more to eventual breakdowns than was previously supposed" (1958-1959, p. 75).

This increase of stress in everyday life should be related to the changing pattern of religious life in today's world. Take, for example, the phenomenon of ecumenism itself. There are many sisters who find it difficult to relinquish the older ways of fulfilling their commitment to God or to community, and find the stress of change and of newer demands hard to bear. In addition, the old, familiar pattern of values, of family life, of the priestly character, etc., are changing to a noticeable degree, and these changes can also have a disturbing effect on mental equanimity.

Nor can we afford to overlook the rapidly changing concepts of freedom, authority, religion, and sexuality in contemporary society. It is not as easy today for a young girl entering religious life to commit herself to its demands, regulations, and denials as it would have been twenty-five or fifty years ago. Obviously, this type of situation is much more productive of the kind of frustration and conflict that often precede mental difficulties. I think, too, we may safely assume that many of the defections from religious commitment that we see today have their origins in these changing concepts and their impact on the minds of many religious, both young and old.

Nor should we overlook the influence of the radically altered concepts of feminism that have become prevalent during the past fifty years. Contemporary ideas of feminism are firmly rooted in equality, freedom, and opportunism; and these qualities are not particularly conducive to either the formation or the stability of a religious commitment. Add to these powerful influences the enticements of materialism, affluence, and libertinism, not to mention the insidious influences of existentialism and allied concepts, and it is not difficult to understand why so many young women find religious life too difficult and too conflictual, and why countless others do not find it as attractive as they would have in a previous era.

The implications of all these value changes, and of alterations in basic attitudes, for a life in religion need hardly be emphasized for anyone who is aware of what is going on in the world today. It is a psychological truism that personality and mental life cannot be divorced from the social and cultural matrix in which both of them develop and have their being. It is impossible that persons in religion should remain aloof from the swirling eddies of life all around them, although the majority will be able to maintain their spiritual commitment as well as their mental integrity.

These same factors that characterize the contemporary world have equally serious implications for mental health, as evidenced clearly in the increasing incidence of maladjustment and mental disorder in contemporary society. Both of these implications are important for the life of the spirit. As Vaughan says (1962, pp. 9-10):

> Growth in the spiritual life is dependent upon cooperation with Divine Grace. The individual who is so occupied with himself and who abounds in numerous personality defects, such as one often finds among the neurotic and psychotic, has considerable difficulty co-operating with God and His Grace. His purely natural limitations stand in the way of his spiritual growth. Whereas other religious can concentrate their efforts upon corresponding with Divine Graces, the mentally ill religious is often so absorbed in his own inner struggle that he has little time or energy left for the pursuit of perfection.

Having thus set the stage for a discussion of mental health in religious life, let us now try to determine exactly what mental health is so that we can know what to strive for. This is not an easy task, because mental health is many things. It has to do with feelings and attitudes, family traits and bodily condition, maturity and integration, and a host of other qualities that make it hard to pinpoint and to define. In place of a definition that would necessarily leave a lot unsaid, let us consider instead four different but closely related facets of mental health: (1) the conditions of mental health, (2) the determinants of mental health, (3) the qualities of mental health, and (4) the outcomes of mental health. In this way we should get a broad and yet precise perspective of this somewhat elusive quality of the personality.

In a paper of this length we can do little more than indicate what these various factors are, since to discuss each one of them would lead to a volume of considerable size. By *conditions* we mean those characteristics of the human personality without which it is difficult and sometimes even impossible to achieve or to maintain mental health. Here we would include sound physical health, recreation, healthy attitudes, a redeeming sense of humor, good interpersonal relations, integration and control, and an enduring capacity for reality thinking. Reflection on these several characteristics will indicate quickly that in the absence of any one of them, mental health is likely to slow down and even come to a complete halt. The religious in poor health, or who cannot get along with her fellow sisters or superiors, or who lacks a sense of humor, or who substitutes fantasy thinking for reality thinking, and so on, is not likely to enjoy robust mental health.

The category of *determinants* of mental health is obviously closely related to the conditions, but can be better understood if studied by themselves. Here we would include basic temperamental qualities, family background, social structure, adequate need-gratification, and healthy feelings and emotions. What this category implies is that mental health is to an important extent determined by the basic temperament or emotional disposition of the personality. This characteristic has genetic overtones, but it is certainly clear on the basis of empirical and clinical evidence that personalities vary a great deal in their basic temperamental makeup, and that this makeup contributes to a quality of mental health. Along with this factor is the quality of healthy feelings and emotions, one of the most basic and important determinants of mental health at every level of development. The religious who is plagued by feelings of hostility, guilt, self-rejection, feelings of worthlessness, shame, rebellion, scrupulosity, obsessive fears, or extreme anxiety is a poor candidate for mental health. It is well known that at the core of every mental illness there is emotional inadequacy, disruption, or excess; therefore healthy feelings are a *sine qua non* of mental health.

Closely allied to this quality of healthy feelings is the process of need-gratification. Deep within the structure of the human personality there are certain dynamic tendencies (needs) that must be gratified if the personality is to maintain mental equilibrium. Briefly, these needs include affection and love, a sense of belonging, self-love and self-esteem, security, independence, self-identity, and love of others, including some form of sex gratification. When we refer to sex gratification in this connection we are obviously not referring to concrete sexual relationships, since this would be impossible under the rule of chastity. It would also be impossible morally for many persons not in religion. Nevertheless, as a need and as a drive, sex cannot be simply ignored or denied, for this can only lead to chronic frustration which is one of the immediate determinants of psychological disturbance or maladjustment. Even sex must follow the rule of need-gratification, even if this is accomplished only indirectly through love, sublimation, or creative effort. If we are going to accept need-gratification as a determinant of mental health, we cannot then exclude sexual satisfaction on the grounds that sex is somehow immoral. This is an issue to which vocation directors and religious superiors should give the most careful attention.

We must note also that mental health is determined to an important extent by external factors, particularly the family and the social structure of which the person is a part. It is well known that family characteristics and relationships have a great deal to do with the mental health and the adjustment of the growing child; and by the same rule social structure, including the structure of religious life, have an important bearing on the mental health of its constituents. This is an area that requires careful study by those in charge of religious. It must always be borne in mind that the more highly structured and the more rigid the situation in which a person functions, the less room is there for growth, maturation, personal expression, need-gratification, affective relationships, and personal adjustment. Both productivity and creativity can be seriously limited in a situation that leaves little room for freedom of expression. And where there is little or no freedom of expression, there is apt to develop the most serious and crippling frustration.

In this connection we should mention briefly several of the more immediate determinants of mental difficulties often encountered in the religious life. There are four of particular importance here: frustration and conflict, stress and threat. Of these four factors, threat probably plays the least important role, although it should not be excluded from consideration. But it is obvious that the religious life provides numerous opportunities for both frustration and conflict, and, as we saw when citing the article by Sister Kelley, it may well be that stress has assumed considerably larger importance in recent years. The important point is that no one of these four determining factors can be tolerated indefinitely—not at least by some personalities—without the development of symptomatic responses that seek to relieve the stressful situation, the frustrating condition, or the intolerable conflict. It is this process of symptom formation that is the forerunner of mental breakdown.

Let us turn now, briefly, to the qualities that distinguish the mentally healthy from the mentally unhealthy person. Actually, of course, there are many such qualities because mental health is a many-faceted thing, but we can pick out several that are of particular significance for sound mental health. These are: maturity, independence, responsibility, self-esteem, self-reliance, sex-identity, self-identity, and goal-direction. We cannot comment on the relevance of each one of these qualities to religious life; but even a small amount of reflection will indicate quickly how difficult it may be for some persons to develop these qualities within the framework of the religious life.

Let us emphasize this point with a few questions. Is religious life conducive to maturity or to independence? Are the various spiritual emphases of this mode of life conducive to self-esteem? Does the rule of obedience promote self-reliance or responsibility? Does the rule of chastity or the style of dress of religious promote either sex-identity or self-identity? Are the roles assumed in religious life clearly enough defined for goal-direction? I am not qualified to answer these questions, certainly not as well as those who have had years of experience as vocation directors or religious superiors; but I do feel qualified to raise questions that should be given serious consideration by vocation directors, especially in view of the alarming attrition that is occurring at the present time. As a psychologist I cannot ignore or deny my own conviction, based on years of study, research, and counseling of religious and former religious, that these several qualities are essential to the achievement and to the maintenance of mental health. I would be traitor to my own profession if I took a lesser stand. But the questions are put to you not as a surreptitious means of evaluating religious life, but as a challenge—a challenge to examine carefully age-old traditions and concepts, rules and practices, institutes and institutions that may be out of kilter with a rapidly changing and expanding world of ideas, goals, values, beliefs, and practices. The world we live in is a changing world that refuses to stand still, and we must move with it, or we will find ourselves left behind. Let us at least give the matter serious thought.

To complete the picture of mental health as we conceive it, we must consider also its several outcomes, because it is these outcomes that make the pursuit of mental health worthwhile. Here again we cannot study each one in detail, but their significance is obvious in itself. Listed in an order of importance, they are: 1) energy, 2) productivity, 3) freedom, 4) spontaneity, 5) capacity for love, 6) adjustment, 7) sense of well-being, 8) equanimity, 9) serenity, 10) happiness. Anyone may of course quarrel with the order of these different outcomes of mental health, but he cannot quarrel with their significance for psychological effectiveness. Nor do we pretend that all of them are dissociated from psychological disturbance or maladjustment. It is not uncommon to see a highly neurotic person who, because of his need to excel and thus to deny his own inferiority, exhibits considerable productivity. But on the whole, mental disorder and maladjustment militate strongly against these characteristics, whereas the condition of mental health strongly supports them.

Now that we have studied religious life and mental health, and the nature of mental health itself, we should consider briefly the implications of religion for mental health, since it is obvious that religion is the core of religious life. What does this type of commitment mean? Where does it come from? What does it require? What does religion do for the personality? What does it do *to* the personality? Is religious life—for some persons at least—inimical to a life in religion? This is an extremely complex and a very deep problem that requires the most astute analysis which we could not attempt in so brief a presentation. However, there are some basic relationships that can be described briefly, and that bear directly on the problem of mental health in religious life.

Perhaps the simplest way to approach this problem is to distinguish the positive effects of religion from its negative effects. From a positive point of view, one cannot quarrel with the conclusion that religion is salutary to mental health when it is able to furnish perdurable values that promote the process of personal growth and integration. As Moore has said (1944, pp. 244-245), "If religion has become an essential element of one's mental equipment, if it constitutes a plan of life that the individual has made a real part of his daily existence, if it is a practical ideal that he has adopted with enthusiasm, then it becomes a powerful inhibitory force in the development of unwholesome mental conditions." As I have pointed out elsewhere (1965, p. 433), if this concept means anything, it means primarily that religion is something more than an emotional tranquilizer to which we have recourse when we encounter serious difficulties. If religion is nothing more than a personal subjective experience, it will fail miserably as a tool for mental health. Religion to be meaningful must be an objective system of values that gives meaning and stability to daily life, and that should preclude the development of deep-seated conflicts and frustrations that work toward the destruction of personality. This it often does, especially when the basic and stable values of religion are integrated into the totality of a person's daily life.

Nevertheless, we must note that religion, with its other-world orientation, and its highly imaginative symbolism, lures many potentially neurotic or emotionally confused persons into an unrealistic attitude toward life and life's problems. For the insecure person, the frustrated person, the pathologically inferior person, or the one who cannot cope effectively with moral conflict or guilt, the concepts of original sin, human depravity, personal weakness, and other ideas associated with certain religious beliefs have a particular attraction. Wrongdoing is typically rationalized as the result of original sin; neurotic suffering is a cross one must bear for having incurred God's displeasure, and the frustrations, conflicts, and difficulties of daily life as inevitable stumbling blocks on the road to eternal salvation.

For such persons there is a strong tendency to interpret every difficulty as divine punishment and every personal failure as a lack of divine grace. For them, prayer is a demand for personal assistance rather than an act of love. For neurotic and emotionally confused persons, therefore, religion is truly an opiate. It is an escape from reality rather than a means of coming to grips with the demands and problems of their daily lives. For the religious neurotic, religion is a mixture of fear, threat, shame, guilt, or vague promises that are supposedly realized through prayer or the possibility of a future life. This attitude is essentially escapist and unrealistic since it precludes a direct, straightforward approach to everyday problems and conflicts (Schneiders, 1965, p. 432).

As you well know, this description fits many persons in religious life, especially those whose commitment ends in a flight from their vocation, or worse still, in mental breakdown. In attempting, therefore, to evaluate the relationship between mental health and religious life, we must take into account the meaning of religion for the member of the religious community. Without this type of evaluation, the vocation director or the religious superior will fail to understand the many difficulties and defections that occur in religious life. Because of these facts, it is of primary importance for directors of religious vocations, and for all those involved in the Sister Formation Conference, to take a close look at the dynamics of religious vocations, prior to or immediately following the commitment to religious life. Before a candidate enters religious life there should be the most careful scrutiny of the dynamic factors and the personality characteristics that led to the decision. While it is a pious thought that a religious vocation reflects the gift of divine grace or a special calling, the attrition rate in convents and seminaries, and the incidence of psychological disorders, forces us to the hard-headed position that candidates for the religious life must be screened and evaluated most carefully for the good of the community and for the good of the individual. Only when a concerted effort is made in this direction will there be real headway in the solving of the problem of mental health in the religious life.

References

Carrier, H. *Sociology of religious belonging.* New York: Herder & Herder, 1965.

Dondero, A. *No borrowed light.* Milwaukee: Bruce, 1965.

Evoy, J. J. & Christoph, P. F. *Maturity in religious life.* New York: Sheed & Ward, 1965.

Kelley, Sister M. William. The incidence of hospitalized mental illness among religious sisters in the United States. *Amer. J. Psychiat.,* 1958-1959, 115, 72-75.

Moore, T. V. *Personal mental hygiene.* New York: Grune & Stratton, 1944.

Schneiders, A. A. *Personality dynamics and mental health.* New York: Holt, Rinehart and Winston, 1965.

Vaughan, R. E. *Mental illness and the religious life.* Milwaukee: Bruce, 1962.

Person and Community

REV. CARLO A. WEBER, S.J.
Loyola University
Los Angeles, California

Before I begin with what I have prepared for this talk on the person in the community, I feel that I would be a lot less than candid and honest if I didn't share with you a feeling that has been rather persistent while I prepared these two talks. And in view of the fact that when we talk about the superior as a counselor we shall speak a good deal about the necessity for honesty and openness, I feel that I would be less than honest with you if I didn't share this feeling. I am not the least bit convinced that this particular Sister Formation Convention will amount to anything at all in terms of the lives of the sisters in your hospitals and your schools.

I really have not too much confidence in the power of a particular lecture or particular speaker or particular group discussion. It is entirely up to you whether or not the movements that we discuss, the problems which are real, are honestly faced, and your doubts, your concern, your confusion, your care, are honestly communicated to your sisters. I do talk to a lot of sisters, and what is perhaps a great deal more important, I listen to a lot of sisters in my office. And there I listen to their loneliness, to their unrest, to their often critical feelings of hypocrisy, to their feelings of jealousy. This listening is, of course, taken from a very restricted, and perhaps prejudiced sample; but I would suggest that it is a growing sample.

These are enormously critical times for anyone involved in religious life. The comfortable structures which we have known for a great number of years are threatened. We need only cite as instance of this the number of defections. Not all of these are due to a loss of faith by any means. Many are saying that the communities have nothing further to offer to the Christian world. I instance also the decreasing number of vocations to religious communities, which certainly may not be any kind of tragedy at all; but for many people, for many young people particularly, religious life today seems to be in danger because it seems to them to be inauthentic. It is not truthful.

The Church, as Hans Küng has so notably remarked, has the truth. That does not necessarily make it truthful. It is inauthentic or seems inauthentic to many young people because of a growing feeling that there is hypocrisy involved in the religious communities. We say one thing; we talk of the charity and the universality of Christ, and within our communities we live something else. We live a life that is often characterized by petty jealousies, by frustrated desires, by bickering. Religious life is accused today of being complacent. In the novitiates we are still telling ourselves that we are, after all, the elect; that we have the truth. What truth? The truth of physics, of sociology? We are also accused of being irrelevant; that we have lost sight of the essential apostolic qualities of our vocation, and that we have substituted for the essentials a growing mass of historical accretions which we call religious life.

Here let us remark upon the vow of poverty. In what sense do you think that we now have a vow of poverty? Have we simply subsumed it under the vow of obedience? All of these are critical problems.

I should like to focus a little bit more directly upon this point of the individual and personalism, and share with you my great concern about our growing personalism. It was released by the Congregation of Religious not too long ago that approximately 75 per cent of the religious who applied for dispensations from vows did so on the grounds that they were unable to attain personal fulfillment in the religious life. We are not altogether sure what they individually might mean by "personal fulfillment," and what sort of self-deception might be involved in this statement of personal fulfillment, but that was the statement. We are, therefore, I would submit, at a kind of crossroads in the history of religious and ascetical life.

We are in the process of substituting a person-centered religious life and ascetical ethic for the traditional community-centered religious life and ethic. And in our self-examination it is important to ask ourselves to what extent this emphasis on personalism—the importance of the individual person—has, first of all, contributed to the number of defections, has undermined the traditional structures, has been responsible for the decreasing number of vocations, and then to ask ourselves the more graphic and gripping question, to what extent are these—that is to say, the number of defections, the undermining of traditional structures, and the decreasing number of vocations—to what extent are these really undesirable? We have spent, after all, a great deal of time in the last number of years in religious communities counting heads—counting the number of people who entered our novitiate, and again perhaps congratulating ourselves that we in one community had more this year than another community, and that therefore we were, somehow, closer to the body of Christ. In doing this, of course, we have imposed upon a great number of young people counsels which were not intended for them. The evangelical counsels were counsels, they were not mandates, and we have been so insistent in our urgency to draw people, to draw laborers to the harvest, that we drew many who were perhaps not ready, and have done great injury to the Church, to us, and to themselves.

I would like to study then, something of the transition from the community-centered concept of religious life to this more person-centered concept which I would suggest as the new ascetical dimension to religious life. By way of preface, I don't want to make this a discussion of the philosophical implications of the relationship of the individual to society, or to the body politic, or to the body social or to the body ecclesiastical, or to whatever other body may be concerned. This is not a disquisition on the relationship of society and the individual, the sociological relationship of the individual and the group, nor one on the political scientist relationship of the individual to the political society. I want to describe, first of all, the development of the community-centered asceticism in religious life—a history which I will do very briefly.

The dawn of the religious life for women began in about the second century with the practice of the consecrated virgins and deaconesses who for the most part remained in their family homes. This, of course, proved to be somewhat ineffectual, and as a result the cenobitic or monastic life developed. As early as the fourth century, St. Augustine and St. Pachomius, who wrote the first legislation about community life, formulated and framed the context of religious community or communal life in which we still live. The Rules of St. Basil, St. Benedict, and for women, of St. Scholastica, are still operative in many of our communities, and this way of life has been sanctified by fifteen centuries of rules of life. The legal sanction for this became most emphatic in the year 1283 with the decree of Boniface VIII, *Periculosa*, in which the establishment of enclosure for nuns was ratified. And coming rapidly upon the heels of the imposition of the legal tradition of the western rite upon the entire western church, and with it the Roman legal tradition, the concept of legality of community structure was established and stratified and pretty well formulated. We have therefore a tradition of fifteen centuries of a rule of life in various ways; fifteen centuries of regulated common life. This is not to be taken lightly; it forms the outward appearance of the conventual life. At the time of the Reformation a certain change in the dimension was required—a switch in the emphasis because of the need for some almost polemic activity, the need for a certain warfare, and the growth therefore of the specifically apostolic rather than the specifically monastic communities. We are, and I say this facetiously, indebted to St. Ignatius for the structure which we now find somewhat difficult. In hospitals and in schools the emphasis was upon the apostolic life, while preserving as much as possible the structure of the monastic life. This, I think, is the background for most contemporary apostolic communities.

Now the result is that we have fifteen centuries of this established way of perfection. We have fifteen centuries of the development of rules, constitutions, customs, local customs, procedures in common life, and, I would submit, we have identified sanctity with the observance of the established common life. There are personal advantages involved in this. To identify oneself with the common life, to do what these fifteen centuries of regulations require of us, to follow it out with a certain amount of literalism, provides for the individual these advantages: it is a reliable system; there is no great personal risk—one simply identifies with the established mode of common life. It is expressed in the axiom which we have all heard and perhaps repeated: you keep the rule and the rule will keep you. It has the advantage of being sure; because it has ecclesiastical approval—indeed, fifteen centuries of it—and because it rejoices in the ecclesiastical approval, in some kind of divine approbation as well. It has the advantage of making us feel strong. We gain a certain power, omnipotence, by identification with the community, with God, with the Church; we "can do all things in Him Who strengthens us"; we can do all things in the community that bolsters us. We gain certain power by identification with this structure and a certain security in resting on it. Some of the structure is derived from Scripture and from Tradition, but by far the great bulk of the structure which we rely upon is drawn from historical additions and accretions in local customs. The danger, of course, is that we can accept all of this structure as though it had the same scriptural origin. All of this has the spurious advantage of creating a kind of automatic sanctity. One enters the novitiate, one places herself at the disposal of the mistress of novices, one is dissected and put together again in two years of the novitiate. She is then subject to the established community process, and is turned out at the end of this automatic process a formed sister.

The dangers of this structural life, and I surely would like to allege some of them, are, I think, these. The structured sanctified life can easily lead to the sanctity of the long black line where my individual responsibility in gaining sanctity, and my individual responsibility in general, is subsumed into being part of the long black line, and therefore of destroying my individuality. There is a certain security, obviously, a certain comfort in belonging, in taking part, in the long black line. One has in the long black line the strength of many, and if there is a dependency need in the individual person, that dependency need will be strengthened, will be reinforced; the individual gains the almost womb-like security of the long black line. One is no longer Jane Addams but a Sister of Charity.

The structured life can lead to a self-concept which is nothing other than the concept of the community, of the ideal sister, of what sister is expected to be, what we would call normally the "expectancy image." I live exactly what others expect me to live; I am what they want and expect me to be. I gain approval, I gain substantiation personally by identifying with their expectations of me. So you might have a young sister, and I am thinking of one, who has shown great promise throughout her entire religious life, who is appointed a superior at a fairly young age, who does everything precisely as is expected of her, and then confronts personal failure which she cannot tolerate, cannot live with because the community expects her to succeed, not to fail. The personal confrontation with failure is overwhelming, and this particular sister fell into a very profound depressive reaction. There is no self in this person; there is only the reflected self of what others want.

The structured life can also lead to what I should like to call the security lull. I find a certain comfort in the community life; there is no individual responsibility; I can preserve myself in something resembling a fetal position. If I am the superior, I find comfort in the fact that I can rule by the custom and by the law, by the code. All I need do in my individual responsibility as superior is to cite the passage and place in the epitome, or in the constitution, or in some other equally ratified document. This, of course, takes all the responsibility off me as the superior. I simply say, "After all, Sister, I am not telling you or I am not asking you to do this, the Rule is . . ."—which is, I would submit, an enormously obvious bit of deception. It can lead to a structured consciousness which in our lives can very profoundly affect our work consciousness.

In the apostolic, evangelical counsels, each of the vows was recommended for a purpose, not for itself. The scriptural basis for the vow of chastity runs this way: "there are some who are eunuchs by birth, and eunuchs by choice, . . . there are others who are eunuchs for the kingdom of heaven." They are not eunuchs because this is a good thing to be. Christ did not recommend virginity, chastity, for anyone because it was an end in itself. It is there for an apostolic purpose. The counsel to poverty: "Go sell what you have, and come be my disciple." So in each instance the purpose of the counsel is not the counsel itself; not virginity for its own sake, not poverty for its own sake. Our structured consciousness and the protection of these vows can rise to such a pitch that they become the end in themselves. I recall hearing an exhortation by a fairly renowned asceticist who remarked to a group of religious that you could give nothing except your chastity to God. If this is all I have got to give to God, I think I shall leave. These are not ends and objectives in themselves; they are means to an end and when we become enormously structure conscious we make them ends, we idolatrize them, we apotheosize the vows themselves and make them the god. And we are guilty of a form of idolatry.

Structure consciousness can also lead to a certain kind of omnipotence. My need for infantile power, which of course is the primitive condition of the child (the omnipotence of perfect helplessness is the most omnipotent of all omnipotence)—this need to sustain my omnipotence can be gratified by the identification with the structure. I may be nothing, but as a sister I can do all things, because I have the community sustaining me. This in a sense is regressive. Just as the child gains its strength at the point of satellization and identification with the mother at the age of three, and gains its first self-concept by identifying with the strength of the mother, so we as religious can gain our individual strength by identifying with the strength of the community, and by this way preserve our power, preserve our omnipotence. Just as the child satellizes around the mother, we can satellize around the community to retain the sense of infantile omnipotence—an omnipotence that is geared to a kind of spurious helplessness. This, of course, can lead also to a sort of self-debasement—the community is everything; I am nothing. And the greatest emphasis in community life is on humility, which of course means in most instances playing the game of self-debasement reasonably well. There is an asceticism of self-annihilation, of self-sacrifice, that approaches a kind of self-punitive masochism involved in the concept of self-debasement. I am nothing. I am only of value insofar as I identify by rule with the community.

At the other extreme it can lead to a certain righteousness. We have chosen the better way because it is the way that has been established by fifteen centuries of tradition, and therefore we are somewhat more elite, somewhat better than others. The righteousness that can lead to what a friend of mine has facetiously described as the teaching sister, or teaching brother, or teaching priest, who has never violated a single clause of the Holy Rule and never taken an extra class. It can also lead to a ritualistic, game-playing type of spirituality. Everything is all right so long as within the confines of the community we play the game properly. Poverty has become such a game, I think, and again we can attribute this to my founder in his concept of poverty of dependence. Obedience also leads to a certain game-playing mechanical ritualism. Everything is all right in the community if the superior is giving the orders and the subject is obeying, and if the school burns down while the superior is giving orders and the subject is obeying, what difference does it make? The Church does not need the school. The community is carrying itself along in the proper procedure.

This, I suspect, is harking back to the axiom of the Abbot Cassian as provided for us in the annals of Rodriguez about the monk who dutifully planted the cabbages upside-down. But we are not planting cabbages; we are doing the work of Christ. He cares about that work, and we must too. And the work is the purpose for the community; the community is not the purpose of the work. Christ did care about the work, and was willing to relinquish structures for the work. If He did not, what was He doing when he wept over Jerusalem? What was He doing when He cut down the scribes and the Pharisees? What was He doing when He told us that what we did to the least of our brethren we did to Him? He cared. He did not play games; we can never be a witness of His authenticity, if we do.

Perhaps the greatest danger to the individual, of the structure-centered or community-centered religious life, is the loss of individual creative potential. The process of identifying with the structure, with the community, can produce an obviously stylized behavior, can produce stereotyped behavior. This is the way that sister walks; this is the way that sister talks; this is the way that sister suppresses her emotions;

this is the way that sister represents the community when she goes abroad. What happens to the individual in this context? What happens to his own creative potential? Ernst Krist, a rather noted ego psychologist, defines creativity as regression in the service of the ego, which means a dipping down into the primitive individual forces, largely emotional, in order to draw out from there the potential to impose some new order outside. The willingness to live without order, without structure, has been established empirically as one of the characteristics of the creative person. The tolerance, for example (and this has been discovered by studies of Frank Barron and others at the University of California at Berkeley), the tolerance for disorder, the tolerance for atonality in music, the tolerance for asymmetry in design and art, all of these willingnesses to live with non-structure seems to be one of the prevailing characteristics of creativity. To be able to go back into the primitive sources, the emotional sources, in order to come back out again as an individual person; the ability, for example, to regress temporarily into perhaps a depressive reaction; to feel oneself suffering, perhaps, and hurt, and individually lost, and to work through the feeling, a very primitive and regressive feeling indeed, a childlike feeling, to go through it and to come back out with the confidence of knowing that you could go through that fog and still survive, with a greater potential than one had before; to do this one must relinquish a certain amount of structure, at least temporarily. Just as a woman in any context must relax her propriety in order to be creative—otherwise she is frigid and cannot create—so all of us to be creative must relax our structure, must reduce ourselves into a fairly primitive conscience, must get below the ego-control level, the level of how I have learned to respond to certain situations, my patterns of response, my sets, my defenses, all that is part of my ego-mechanism; these must momentarily, at least, be diminished so that I can dip into the wellsprings of myself in order to be truly creative.

The transition from the community-centered or structure-centered religious experience to the person-centered religious experience has come upon us with a great crash. We are in it whether we like it or not. The common life has been blown wide open by a number of factors, all occurring, perhaps, in the last twenty-five years. First of all, there is the loss of structure in society in general. The man in the Middle Ages, in the thirteenth century, the man in the nineteenth century, knew where his boundaries were, his social boundaries, his geographical boundaries, his religious, moral boundaries; he may not have cared for them, but he knew where they were. Within the last twenty-five years most of these boundaries have virtually disappeared; the boundaries of class society are crumbling to a certain degree, to be followed by another kind of boundary, of course, or another kind of structure, a somewhat more subtle one. The boundaries, geographically, have disappeared; whereas the Upper Volta was a place that you and I read about in geography, it is now, for the young person, just next door. The young person can no longer confine himself to his block, or his street, or his neighborhood; he is a citizen of the world and the usual structures which impinged upon us in our sub-groups, in our childhood, in our youth, are no longer the same. So, society by-and-large has lost a lot of structure. The moral boundaries are changing rapidly and as theologians investigate a more personalized morality I suspect this trend will continue.

Common life has been blown wide open by this change in structure in which the young people are raised. It has been changed considerably by the advent of modern psychology and psychiatry. The former impersonal emphasis was always on the communal aspects of the person. Yesterday had many answers to the question, "What am I?" The philosopher can say, "I am a rational animal," which is something that all of us have in common; the theologian can say, "I am a creature of God," which is something which all of us have in common; the physiologist can say, "I am an individual who is made up of an intricate network of physiological systems," which is common to all of us; the psychologists can say, "I am a person whose average reaction time is 'xx,' " which is common to all of us—"the statistical average concept of psychology." All of this had to do with the individual in terms of his communality with others.

Today the emphasis in psychology and psychiatry is not on the communal aspects but upon the individual and his unique aspects. The answers to the question, "Who am I?" (not "What am I?") are in terms of what I do not share with others, what I do not have in common with others, what my individual differences are. For this the vehicles for self-discovery in contemporary psychology are largely the self-awareness experiments, the attempt to dip into oneself by one means or another, to find who is there; in sensitivity groups the same process is involved. All these stress the emphasis upon the individual as a unique person, different from others; the "who" that I am.

I also suggest that I think the traditional structures of community life have been somewhat shattered in the last twenty-five years by the advent of Vatican II, which has reaffirmed in a most dramatic way the central position of the doctrine of the Incarnation which has been so long neglected. So long in our dualistic ascetical tradition have we separated the divine from the human, for so long have we been unable to accept the fact that God really became a man; for so long have we separated the spiritual from the material, in our Manichaean dualistic tradition, that we were unable to accept the person of Christ. We as Christians emphasized the divinity of Christ. It has been remarked that the Jews were unable to accept the divinity of Christ, and that Christians by-and-large have been unable to accept the humanity of Christ. Of course, the emphasis upon the humanity of Christ places the great impact upon the value of the self, the value of the individual person, Christ as an individual unique person. We are scandalized by Christ in many respects because we cannot accept what He could so readily accept—our humanity. In the acceptance of our humanity we become persons, and yet we still see ourselves in something of the Pauline tradition as being imprisoned, in chains, spirit encrusted with an unwanted body, pulled down to the lower level of the passions by a body which we must somehow or other control; because we do not accept the Incarnation, we do not accept the value of the humanity of Christ. In Vatican II there was the reaffirmation of our faith in the person of Christ and in doing so our respect for humanity, for the fact that God created us free and does not treat us like puppets, or pawns on a chessboard, that providence is a much more subtle thing than a chess game in which we are moved by the benevolent hand of the divinity. And the man who did this, of course, was a man who himself was fully a person, John XXIII.

Now all of this means that in this experience of change—from a community-centered religious ethic to a person-centered religious ethic—we can no longer rely simply on the structure, on the legal paraphernalia. We no longer can rely on something outside of ourselves from which to take our bearings. We must go into ourselves, we must rely on ourselves more, and this, of course, is the emphasis of the new moral theology. On the other hand, the characteristics of person-centered religious asceticism are based on the emphasis upon personal individual growth—the growth of the self, the total awareness of "me" as one apart, and dipping into that inner core of myself which requires two things: a balanced view of myself as a person who is at the same time both dependent and independent, and out of this the capacity to love.

And, as the psychologists constantly remark, the criteria for this self-discovery, this self-development, are perhaps the following: first of all, the sense of one's independence. I can now take a certain comfort in my uniqueness, where in the structure-centered community life I took comfort in the identification with the group. This follows the analogy of the purpose of growth. The primary physiological analogy for the growth process, and the individualized growth process, is the expulsion of the fetus. The fetus in the mother's womb is a parasite. If it remains there parasitically attached to the mother, neither the mother nor the child will survive. In order for there to be growth, the fetus must be expelled. Of course this sets the basic physiological paradigm, for all the growth processes; the purpose of growth is separation at whatever level one confronts it. This is an enormously difficult thing for parents, teachers, superiors, or counselors to accept. The parents' job is done when the child can leave; the teacher's job is done when the child, or the young student, can stand and say, "I disagree with you," providing there are good reasons for doing so. That the superior can tolerate the separation of the individual, that the counselor, the therapist, can tolerate the separation of the patient, can rejoice in that moment when the patient says, "I don't need you anymore"—that is the purpose of the whole therapeutic process.

This independence requires, of course, an acceptance of oneself. Self-acceptance can easily be confused with what I like to call symptom-acceptance. An individual says, "Look, I am a very irascible, intolerably impatient man—that's what I am. You must accept me that way; I do. And therefore I enjoy a certain amount of self-acceptance." This of course is not self-acceptance; it is symptom-acceptance, characterized very strongly by the young college student who told me the other day, "Well, what do you expect of me, I am an only son?" Now whatever effect his being an only son had on his present behavior, it wasn't anywhere nearly as great as his desire to exploit the fact that he was an only son. This is not self-acceptance; it is symptom-acceptance, and there is a great difference.

Self-acceptance is a long, painful process of discovery behind the mask that I make even for myself. This, I think, is important in our dealings with our sisters, that in their cry for self-acceptance let us be sure that that is what they are talking about, and not a very deceptive form of symptom-acceptance. But self-acceptance, however arrived at, must be there. We cannot accept Christ's self unless we accept our own self. If there is not self-acceptance there can be no love, because if I think I am an absolutely unworthy individual, if I am unacceptable, then what I give in a loving relationship with another is an extremely paltry thing and I can't give it. There must be a certain self-acceptance and self-esteem for there to be love, for me to say, "Look, I give me to you." In order to do this there must be an acceptance of the "me." For a long while, it seems to me, community life has militated against this acceptance in some ways. Maturity on this level, or the discovery of oneself, also requires the opposite of this—the sense of dependence. The adolescent enjoys the myth of independence for a while but his myth is quickly shattered. I must realize, too, that I am a needer. I must accept my creatureliness, my dependence, my needing of others.

And finally, there must be what Freud called a growth out of primary narcissism. The infant, of course, is totally narcissistic, according to the Freudian concept, at least the later one, after Carl Abraham managed to dissuade him from some of his earlier opinions. The infant is born in a state of primary narcissism; the world is his body as he discovers it. He is body-centered. The process of growth is a gradual cathexis, an affectionate response to the world outside, the moving of one's affective preoccupation from the self gradually to the world outside, to the mother. If this growth process, the growth out of the primary narcissistic condition, is frustrated, then the natural tendency is to go back into a condition of narcissism, and this Freud calls secondary narcissism, a characteristic, he said, of all the neurotic conditions. The growth out of this narcissism, the growth into what the existentialists call a "being in the world" is characteristic of self-discovery, "being" meaning a self, a one, but not a one that is irrevocably apart, but a one who has chosen voluntarily to recommit himself to the world. There are any number of ways, or modes of self-discovery, going through this. I think the goal of individual self-discovery which I am trying to describe in some modest way here, actually has been stated by One who was certainly not a psychologist; He didn't have to be. But He said very simply, "unless a man lose his soul he will not find it." This paradox, I think, perfectly frames the process of growth into being a person.

There are several modes of this growth. The first, as we have already suggested, is the interaction with the world and this describes the normal development of the child. The infant begins to distinguish his self, by distinguishing first from what is not self; he brings into himself, into his mouth, his foot, his finger, his body wherever he can find it, his mother's breast, the spokes of the cradle, his blankets, anything that is within his reach, and gradually he distinguishes between what is him and what is not him. Then as he walks, the world of what is not him and what is him grows more distinct and broader and he can think about things, he objectifies them. He interiorizes objects in a different way. The process of ego development in this sense is largely a discovery of the self in the experience of the world outside. And the paradox of the growth process is precisely that the self-discovery is accomplished by not digging into the self so much as by reaching outside of the self.

The second mode of discovery, which is perhaps the conscious mode for adults, is not interactive. When I come to a point in my life when I realize that this process of development has not taken place in the absolutely ideal fashion and that there are parts of me that are unknown to me, I then enter into a second mode of self-discovery, a mode of self-awareness in my personal meditation, in my solitude, and this is also necessary; for the religious today in a person-centered ethic, there is an absolute necessity for this kind of self-discovery. For the moving into oneself in solitude, just as Christ had His desert, as Ignatius had his Manresa, has always been the prelude to a genuine personal religious experience. If religious communities are to survive in a person-centered rather than a community-centered life, this process of self-discovery through individual meditation is absolutely necessary.

What do we make of our meditations? How comical it is to soothe ourselves by saying, as we have all been told, that at the point of meditation it doesn't really make any difference what is happening, that you are kneeling in the chapel is in itself a gift of God and what is happening inside you is immaterial, and thus the very fact that you are there is itself a gift. This is structural nonsense. It does matter what is happening in the moment of meditation, and I would submit that if you are not doing anything in that moment in the chapel that you had better leave the chapel at that moment. We are not making what we can of the moments of solitude and meditation, the moments when we can dip into ourselves and find somewhere in the core of ourselves what may very well be the genuine image of God, and the communion with God which in this person-centered religious ethic is utterly essential. Silence is always the prelude to communication. There can be no communication with others on the adult level without the prefacing silence. Communication is a matter of both sending and receiving, and I cannot receive, I cannot hear, I cannot listen to the soft voice of Christ within me, unless there is silence. Christ cannot come unless there is silence. If my meditations, and if the sisters' meditations, become the purely ritualistic presence in which nothing is happening within, it seems to me that there is a great need for the search for God within ourselves.

In this meditation in the self, one is in pursuit of a genuine self-awareness and this can be for all of us an enormously revealing process: to find in myself the things that get in the way, that get in the way of my creativeness, that get in the way of my relationships with others, that stand and block my genuine communication with others, the defenses that appear, the degrees to which I have identified myself with some ideal so that I am no longer a real person, or the degree to which I have identified myself with my job, or the degree to which I am perpetually distracted and driven. Why must I work? Is it because I am convinced of the importance of the work, or because I am driven? I must reach that elusive self which requires a painful journey through the host of defenses which I have learned to construct. This, I think, is essential in the person-centered religious life. Of course, I am afraid to do this, and this is why Christ always came to the apostles at the moment of their anguish with the words "Fear not." I must not be afraid of my loneliness. Thomas Merton says "to live with God, to live alone with God, one must really be able to live alone." One cannot live alone if one cannot stand loneliness, if the desire for solitude is based on the frustrated need for human affection. One has to be able to disregard the whole issue and simply love the whole world in God. The loneliness of self-discovery, which may be done in a crowd at any point, the loneliness of dipping into oneself, of finding who is really there, is the prelude to a total person-centered religious life.

There is a danger in this transition from the community-centered religious life to the person-centered religious life, and I should like to draw upon perhaps an author whom one might not normally think of in this context, Erich Fromm. In the transition of his books, beginning with *Escape from Freedom* through *The Art of Loving*, he describes I think, this process. There is first of all in the growth process of this society the escape from structure. In the 13th century, he says, there was the ecclesiastical community with which one could identify and upon which one could depend; man knew his boundaries, he was not apart. From the 16th to the 20th century, there was a gradual growth away, an emancipation, if you will, a freedom from that medieval structure. But with that emancipation, with that freedom, came the estrangement and the alienation that is so common now, the feeling that one is alienated from the world because the structure is gone. And there is, he says, a great need as the result of that, for an estranged man, an alienated man, to recommit himself, voluntarily, to once again lose that freedom. And in this sense we mean freedom of choice, of course. There may be a far deeper meaning for freedom, but that is another matter. To be free from structures, precisely in order to be free to some one, some thing, some cause, some work—this, of course, is the process of coming in to the act of love, as described in the last of those books, *The Art of Loving*.

There can be extremes on either side. Should the community-centered ethic lead to a kind of dependency, we can have the tragic picture of the scrupulous, indecisive sister, who can make no decisions for herself because there is no process by which to make them, who can only rely on the structure, whose individual self is debased in favor of the community. This, I think, has been largely the history of our asceticism, the emphasis on the fact that before God and others I am nothing. We are fond of recalling the words of St. John the Baptist, "He must increase and I must decrease," which we take entirely out of its prophetic stance and make it a psychological aphorism, which, of course, it was never intended to be. And so, therefore, the purpose of the individual in community is to decrease somehow, and this can lead to the self-debasement that is characteristic of practically all neurotic behavior—I am nothing, consequently I cannot love, I cannot give myself, I can only become preoccupied with my unworthiness; I can only be preoccupied with my own unlovability. This is the most common element among all of the disturbed sisters whom I see, one of whom once said to me: "You don't really like me, you only like me because you have to." If you take that statement apart it says worlds about the neurotic's suffering.

On the other hand, a person-centered condition, a person-centered life, can lead to its own abuses. There is the danger of individual anarchy, of a kind of megalomania, passing under the need for self-fulfillment. How (and this is a point that must aggravate most superiors) and to what extent can the community be sacrificed for the needs of one, to what extent can the community be allowed to suffer because of one outspoken, aggressive, demanding subject?—who, of course, has not discovered herself either. Can we allow the exaltation of the individual over the community? Can we allow the community to suffer, to be sacrificed for the needs of one? What is the balance?

I would like to take at least the general outline for the balance between the person in the community in these two traditions, one very,

very recent and one very, very old, from the analogy of human development. My development and yours is framed in its early years as individual growing persons by the oscillation between extreme dependence and extreme independence. The physical dependence of the fetus from the embryonic stage to the fetal stage—that total dependence upon the mother for sustenance is broken by the independence of birth, the fetus is expelled and now one is independent of the mother's physical sustenance; that is the first movement into independence. But that independence is never final and it is quickly supplanted by the symbiotic dependence of the infant with the mother, the infant at the mother's breast, the life-together concept, the helplessness of the infant who cries to announce its helplessness and its needs to its mother. This symbiotic identification with the mother is then broken, that being again a kind of independence that is broken by the strong independence of the toddler who from the age of one-a-half to two-and-a-half is absolutely independent, who can get into everything, who can do all things, who can move and bump and grab and hit everything and is absolutely nativistically independent. But he fails in this, as he must, and that independence is quickly supplanted by the dependence upon the mother once again, at the point of identification of around three or four years of age, when the child becomes mother's little helper. This again is the dependent phase, and this dependence once again having gained the strength of identifying with the mother and having her accepting response, this dependence of identification becomes quickly the executive competence of the preschooler, who with the others around him can once again do all things, who can now pick flowers, and run bicycles, and make things and do everything. That independence is supplanted by, once again, the dependence of a school satellizer, who in the first grade is utterly dependent upon the first or second grade teacher to the point where mother, who previously was infallible, now knows nothing, because the first grade teacher knows everything. And once again there is this dependence with some exceptions. As the process goes along, of course, the exceptions, because of individual differences, grow larger; but the early stages of growth are characterized by this oscillation between dependence and independence, and it goes on.

Maturity is characterized by the balanced view of the self as one who is a needer, who is dependent, and one who is separated, and this is the purpose of growth. I think the Christian statement of this has been perfectly expressed in the Magnificat when Mary says precisely this, "He has seen the lowliness of his handmaid, but He that is mighty has done great things in me." Both aspects, the dependence and the independence, are juxtaposed perfectly in that statement. This, I think, is the model. Practical problems involved in the growth into the person-centered religious ethic, as away from the community-centered religious ethic, are enormous. I can't possibly deal with too many of them at this point, but I would like to draw the outline at this stage, and I should like to make one quotation as a statement of what well might be something characteristic of the relationship of the superior to the subject in the person-centered religious life. This is also taken from a rather unlikely source which I will not state.

Your children are not your children. They are the sons and daughters of life longing for itself. They come through you but not from you, and though they are with you, yet they belong not to you. You may give them your love, but not your thoughts. For they have their own thoughts. You may house their bodies, but not their souls, for their souls dwell in the house of tomorrow, which you cannot visit, not even in your dreams. You may strive to be like them, but seek not to make them like you, for life goes not backward nor tarries with yesterday. You are the bows from which your children as living arrows are sent forth.

The Development of Personality in Community

REV. MICHAEL McHUGH, S.J.
St. Ignatius Parish, Portland, Oregon

My topic is "person and community," and I am going to base my treatment upon what we find in the Vatican Council and upon what we find in Scriptures. I base my notion of person, and the development of personality, on the two good references, among others, in the Vatican Council which I will offer to you for your study later on. One is a statement made in §8 of the Decree on Education where it tells us what we as educators are supposed to be doing for our pupils. The statement is that we are to make sure that their human personality receives adequate development and nurture along with, and at the same time as, we make sure their baptismal character and personality receives its development. The council, therefore, in its statement on education makes it very clear that the development of the person's humanity, his human personality, is a valid idea.

Another statement that the council makes on personality is pertinent to us as religious. This is found in the chapter on religious in the magnificent document, Constitution on the Church. It states that we are to understand that our living our religious vows is not in any way meant to be detrimental to the development of our human personality. The strong positive affirmation, therefore, is made that the human personality is not something meant to lie dormant, or to go into a deep freeze or to be killed, when a person has committed himself to religious life. The person's humanity—his human nature, his character and personality— is not only to find help, aid and nourishment in religious life, but our committal to the religious vows lived in community can be a magnficent help to the development of our personality.

With regard to community, I am going to base my ideas on §15 of the council's Decree on the Appropriate Renewal of Religious Life. There, in speaking of the common life or community, the council fathers bring together a number of scriptural references from the Acts of the Apostles, the fourth chapter, then the second chapter; from St. Paul, Romans 12, Colossians 6, Romans 5, then from Matthew 18, and finally a collection of all the statements, mostly from St. John, that have to do with the relevance and the necessity of love in our life. These references you may find quite easily in the text of Vatican Council II.

I talk now to people who are superiors and I have focused the point of my talk to you as superiors. It seemed to me that the best results would be achieved in this talk if I addressed myself to you, hoping that the way you live your personal fulfillment in your community would be an example to the members of your community to find their own personal fulfillment with you, under you, in the community which you govern. I am not addressing myself to you merely as a superior who is interested in the formation of her junior religious or young religious. My whole premise on the development of personality in community is that all of us are persons and equally persons, and that all of us are members of a community.

To implement that, let me begin now with the reference to the fourth chapter of the Acts of the Apostles. This is a description of community life as it was, and as it ought always to be. The statement is made that the multitude of believers were united in one heart and one mind. Because of that unison of heart and mind, because of their belief and faith, they decided that they ought to live in common, and that no one should possess anything by himself; that they should have everything in common. There you have the basic motive for community life. It is not a mere matter of efficiency. It is not merely a method of having celibates or virgins live together for protection. It *is* efficiency and it *is* a matter of protection, as it is a lot of other things. But the basic reason for living in community is a unity of mind and heart. This unity is not a matter of our agreeing that it is nice to live together, or that it is nice to live as celibates under one roof. The unity has to be deep, and the depth of our motive of unity is found in our union with Christ. We believe that Christ as he is today is the Christ present in a mystical manner; a Christ whose members we are. Because Christ is one, one heart and one mind, and because we are Christ's, therefore, we are one in heart and mind. It is not merely a matter of our free choice deciding that we prefer community life. It is a matter of our being incorporated in Christ in accepting the fact that belonging to Christ we are to have that mind in us, as Paul says, which was in Christ Jesus. Because we possess Christ in common, because we not only have Christ in common, but because we are Christ in common, we decide, therefore, that it does make sense, according to our faith, to possess nothing as our own, but to have all of us and each of us fully possess whatever all of us possess, because our basic possession is Christ.

Fundamental to this notion of the unity of mind and heart which comes from the possession of Christ is a principle that underlies the whole religious life, and that is the eschatological idea that we are by our living doing our best to give witness to a kind of life we are all going to have after the parousia. We are now giving a witness to our glorified life in Christ which we will all have in heaven. There, you see, will be this common possession of Christ had by all the people of God. We are attempting now to demonstrate by our lives, by our actions, that this common possession of Christ, and the possession of all things in Christ, is a valid way to live.

Consequent upon this principle of the common possession of Christ come all of the ideas which we have developed with regard to common life, with regard to divisions or distinctions that are made in community life. It is my sincere conviction that we have in our religious communities no room at all, no basis at all, and no reason at all, for any kind of a caste system. There is no room for the haves and the have-nots. There must not be any divisive distinction among the members of our community. The council, of course, has pointed out that we ought to make sure that there is one class of religious in a given community, and that this one class of religious should have equal opportunity to enjoy the rights and the obligations of religious life. Now let me make it very clear that I recognize the obligation we have to take care of those who are old and ailing. But our obligation to give them special preference is not merely because they are old, but because with old age may come infirmity, or the need for preferential treatment. The sick, therefore, do need more, but I do not see any justification for distinction in community life whereby we say that because someone has worked hard, and has gone through a period of training, she is therefore to be given more of the "good things" that are found in community life; and that consequently the young people, those who have not been with us, who have not worked, who have not borne the burden of the day and the heat do not deserve special preferential treatment. I say that we who are united in Christ are to continue as long as we can, as long as our health holds up, to keep that common possession of Christ. I do not see any room for special treatment given to people because they have an education. I certainly see no room at all for preferential treatment given to people because of entrenched positions, because they have succeeded in feathering their nest, or because they have a peculiarly sharp tongue and are to be feared unless they get preferential treatment. I say that there must be living in common based upon the fact that we, united, have Christ in common.

In the second chapter of the Acts of the Apostles the point is made that this religious community which was founded in the early Church nourished itself upon the teaching of the Gospels, upon Scripture, upon the Liturgy and especially the Eucharist. Let me refer you to a very magnificent part of Vatican II. It is in the Decree on the Appropriate Renewal of Religious Life, §2. There the blueprint is given for the renewal of a religious community. There it is said that renwal is a constant process, a movement that must always be going on. And renewal is always made by continually going back to the source of religious life, Jesus Christ, as found in the revealed word of God, the Gospels, the Scriptures. The point is also made that we must continually go back to the original inspiration of our founders. Now going back is one movement we must be doing continually, but at the same time we must adapt these principles and these inspirations to the present conditions in which our community lives in the Church and in the world around us. I refer now to the chapter of the Acts of the Apostles, in which the need to go back continually to the message of Jesus Christ is emphasized.

We must always make sure that our motives are right. We must return to the original sources to find out what was, what is, the call of Christ to us as religious. I have indicated that this call concerns the need for some in the mystical body of Christ to give witness to the kind of life all of us, the people of God, will live in Christ forever.

I ask you to make your own references now, to the message that Christ has made to you, to your community, to your foundress. I say that it is important for you as superiors, for you as religious, continually to go back and renew your sources of inspiration. You must always go back to the message of Christ by which you chose freely to sell, to give to the poor, to come and to follow Him. You must always go back to the original inspiration whereby Christ tells you that you must be lifted up as He was lifted up if you are to draw all men to you. You must go back to find that inspiration which brought you to the foot of the cross, so that by dying with Christ you might live with him in anticipation of the risen state of glory. You must go back to find and renew the original inspiration by which you chose to be empty, and to be poor for

Christ and in Christ. You must always, of course, go back to the Liturgy, to the Eucharist, and find there in your daily communication and communion with Christ the sources of that unity. Unity in Christ is the basis, therefore, of community. We are united in Him.

You are well aware, of course, of the union we are meant to have with Christ in Holy Communion. The nourishment your community is to get from the Eucharist, from the Mass, is paramount and must never be disregarded. The union to be had among us in prayer is of absolute importance. There must be in your community, and therefore in you, a realization that *we* give to God in prayer and *we* receive from God. It must never degenerate into the idea that *I* pray to God and that God takes care of *me*. It must always be the notion that *we* are united in Christ.

I want to go on now to three references to Saint Paul. One is to the twelfth chapter of Romans, the other is Colossians 6 and then Romans 5. The reference in the twelfth chapter of Romans is an exhortation by Paul to us—an exhortation reminding us that we are supposed to outdo one another, to excel each other in showing respect, in showing honor, to each other. Now, the council makes it clear that the motive for this honor and respect is because we are members of Christ. As members of Christ, it says, living fraternally together, let them—that's us—show, or outdo each other in showing, honor and respect to the other person. The motive has to be that the other person, the rest of the people in the community, belong to Christ. They are, therefore, to be reverenced; they are to be respected; they are to be honored because God has chosen them to live this life of witness. Therefore, respect and honor and reverence for that reason is due to everyone in the community no matter how young she may be, no matter how difficult she may be to get along with. Because she belongs to Christ, because she is a member of Christ and, therefore, because Christ is in her (which really means that she is in Christ), we owe her respect. This is why the notion of responsibility has real validity. When I use the word responsibility I mean responsibility as seen in this way, that I as a person am aware of my responsibility to other persons. Because I respect them and honor them and reverence them I am aware of my obligations, my responsibilities, to do unto them as I want to do unto Christ.

This notion of responsibility is something that is receiving a great deal of emphasis in all treatments of religious life, especially concerning the treatment of the young religious. Now I certainly say that responsibility must be given, and it must be shared, but I should like to emphasize the fact that responsibility is not primarily something which is given to somebody, like the right to drive the car, or the right to invade the refrigerator whenever you want. Responsibility is an obligation which I have to do to others as they have a right to receive from me.

This notion about doing to one another in respect or in reverence also has a great deal to do with the notion of honesty. I believe that there must be an honest communication between persons in religious life, I mean a delicate, Christ-like honesty based upon respect, based upon reverence, an honesty which is truly honorable toward the other person. I feel, too, that some applications of this notion of respect and honor as due to the other person have real immediate application in this matter of the acceptance of other people as they are, and the appreciation of other people as they are.

There is a great pitfall that we superiors are in danger of falling into; it is the great temptation to want to take young people and make them over to our image and likeness. Now, these people are made to the image and likeness of God. They are incorporated into His mystical body as we are, but they are incorporated into His mystical body as *they are* from God. God took them as the human persons they are, and invited them to belong to this life of witness that we have in community life. Christ wants them to remain the human personalities that they are. He wants them to be divinized; He wants them purified. He wants them to live intensely this life of poverty, chastity and obedience in community love. But He wants them to do it as they are. Therefore, we must learn to accept them as they are, to help them to become what they ought to be. We must never make the mistake of thinking that what they ought to be is what we are or think we ought to be. This notion of acceptance of the other, and the basic appreciation of the personality of other people is fundamental to good religious living. It means that when a person enters into the community of Christ, into this membership in Christ, that she must become Christ. We, as superiors, must help her to become what Christ wants her to be.

The next section is based on the scriptural reference in Colossians, which states that, because we are members of Christ, because we belong to Him, we ought to carry each other's burdens. This notion of respect or honor or reverence can be called an attitude that we have, and carrying another person's burden is the attitude put into action. We ought to try, because we belong to Christ, to carry or to help another person to carry her burden.

I do not intend to talk about such an obvious burden as housework, and yet I am well aware that housework has become, in the last ten or twenty years, a great bone of contention among religious. Older religious say that the young ones do not do the housework well; the stairs are not kept dusted. And the young ones say, "Well, I couldn't care less about housework! Let's get out and save some souls and quit worrying about whether there is dust under the piano or not." I don't intend to get into that, but I do suggest to you that this matter of housework, the sharing of burdens in the material fashion, is something that does need clear thinking. Perhaps it needs correction in our contemporary communities. I do not propose at all to have any solution to the problem. But it is a problem. It strikes me as being a rather small problem, honestly, but I know that for you, religious women, who do not have people coming in and cleaning up your house the way I do, it is a real problem. So I suggest it to you as one application, and a very practical one, of this carrying another person's burden. I certainly give as a principle for the solution of this problem that there must be justice and there must be equality.

There is, however, a more delicate and a more tenuous and less easily grasped problem and burden, and that is the burden we all have of loneliness. I am going to give you a reference now from the Vatican Council which is addressed to priests. It is beautiful because it is true— although it is a painful description of the burden that priests carry in our contemporary society. I feel that it is equally true or applicable to religious. At the very end of the Decree on Priestly Ministry it says that priests in our time suffer the great danger of disillusionment because they feel like strangers in the world. They feel that there are tremendous obstacles to the faith in our modern-day society. They feel that their past labors have been sterile. They feel a bitter loneliness in their lives. Because of that, they—we priests—are, according to the council fathers, subject to disillusionment, to discouragement and frustration, and I say, "Amen! We are!" But I say also that many religious are subject to the same disillusionment, discouragement, and frustration. This is not to say that ordinary people are not subject to the same loneliness, to the same frustration, to the same feeling of sterility in their labors. This is not to say that no one else has problems with faith. But it is to say that we in our life of community, celibates, perhaps, are more subject to these temptations.

These, then, are burdens that we carry. These, then, are burdens that the religious in your community carry, the feeling of a loss of faith, the fear that faith is fading out, the inability to find God as she once found God, or felt she was finding God, the frustration that comes from looking at her past labors and feeling that all has been for nothing. The frustration that comes to so many religious when they look at the turnover in religious life—and I do not mean merely people leaving, I mean the changing of traditions, the rooting up of tried and true methods, of tried methods that perhaps have not worked out so truly. This can be a great burden of frustration to many religious. I speak also of the frustration that comes to young religious or old religious who think like young religious, who feel that the past labors, the past apostolate of the community have been rather sterile and worthless, and just treading water. I speak of that frustration that comes from the need that some religious have to get more elbow-room, to get involved, to do for the people of God in a way that the community apparently has not been doing. I speak also of the great frustration that comes from this loneliness that settles in on a person when she feels that she is not understood, when she feels that she is not appreciated, when she feels she is not loved. These are burdens.

Whatever you can do to help your fellow sisters carry these burdens will be a tremendous gift that you give to the Mystical Body of Christ. To do this, however, you have to be able to hear the other person; you have really to be able to listen to the other person. This is not easy. You have to do your delicate best to intrude cautiously and carefully into the thinking and the feeling of your fellow sisters so that you really, sensitively hear what they are feeling. It may not be what they are saying. You have delicately to make yourself available to them, to attune yourselves to them so that you really know and sense and feel what they feel, and sense the difficulty they have in hearing you. You have to be willing to take that positive step to go out of yourself and make it possible for someone else to really get what you are trying to communicate to her. This is a delicate matter. But this is, in my opinion, so much more of a burden and a problem than a mere matter of dust on the staircase. St. Paul tells us that because Christ's love has been poured out into our hearts, therefore, we have a firm foundation for hope. Now this hope that we have, this hope that we live on is something that you must have and must communicate to your community. This hope that we have is a hope in Christ, a hope in Christ's love for us, a hope in the fact that Christ's presence among us will work its way out in us. This hope is the solution to the burdens, to the frustration, to the feeling of despair of the people of your community. This hope is based upon our faith, our belief in the fact that Christ does love us, that Christ has not forgotten us, that Christ is still communicating with us, that we are to find Christ in our contemporary lives, that we are in Jesus Christ today as we were yesterday, as we will be tomorrow. Because of this great hope that we have, based upon our faith in the fact that Christ has and does pour His love out upon us, the council tells us that we, the community, are a real family. We are a real family because we are members of Christ.

This notion of family is another item that is bandied about a great deal in contemporary talk on religious life. The council says we are a family. Many young religious today don't use the word; we don't like the idea of mother-daughter relationship. I do know that we are a group, an association. You are an association of women gathered together at the foot of the cross to do the purposes of Jesus Christ. And that, for want of a better word, is what I call a family. If you say you are a family in the sense that there is a mother and the rest are daughters, I should like respectfully to back away from the particular connotations. But if you are a family in the sense that you are united under Christ, with Christ, for the purposes of Christ, much like the group of women standing at the foot of the cross, then, I say, that is a family. I say it is a family of adults, I say it is a family of adults who are willing to take and who are given adult responsibilities. I say it is a family of adults each of whom as person is willing to stand and to be judged on what she says, what she feels, what she thinks.

I say that we religious are a family. I say we are an association, not of individuals going our own selfish individualistic way to God, but a group united for Christ, in Christ, needing the strength and support that we can give to each other. I say that we are a family in the same sense that the Holy Trinity is a family, and our community life is based upon the example, the prime example, of community living that is the Holy Trinity, where there is a distinction of persons, where personalities are not melted together, although there are distinct personalities; where there is equality, where there is love, where there is responsibility, where there is a sharing of burdens, where there is an attempt to outdo each other in giving respect and reverence to the other, where there is unity. Now, everything that can be said about community living can be said, allowing for differences that have to be made, about the Holy Trinity.

The final part of the section on Vatican II is a series of references to all the magnificent sections that St. John gives us on love. Paul has it too, with love the bond of perfection. Love is the fulfillment of the law. Love is that which proves to us that Christ is with us. Love is the proof to anybody who wishes to look and to see that we are Christ.

I realize that I have said what has been said before, with more clarity, with more vision. But I know this too, that somebody has to start putting all these magnificent theories into practice. And if all you do, as a result of hearing me, and as a result of our hearing each other, if all you do is go back with the determination to be a person in your community, then, believe me, we will have come a long way toward achieving this fullness of personality in the fullness of community living that is meant to be our life of witness here on earth.

Communication as Charity

Rev. Trafford P. Maher, S.J.
Department of Education
Human Relations Center for Training and Research
St. Louis University

Thurston N. Davis, S.J., recently stated:

Revolutions are never altogether pleasant, orderly or controllable events. No one can say just how far this revolution will go on or when we shall again come out upon some plateau of relative stability. But we are in it, and we cannot get out of it. We are on the way to a better Church in a new age of freedom and openness.[1]

The idea of democracy has literally leapt from civil structures into the Church. It is influencing every phase of the Church: government, worship, interpersonal and intergroup relationships. And let there be no mistake: while this revolution with its piercing idea is challenging the traditional manifestations of authority, it is not threatening the *basic principle of authority!*

As Davis indicates, the democratic revolution is threatening only to those who think in terms of authority and its predemocratic functioning. Authority today is thought of as a fresh and creative tool.

It is an instrument of service and inspiration in a more and more democratic world of the human spirit. This is a world in which love suffuses but *does not replace law*, where greater pluralism finds a home, where order and discipline learn to live harmoniously with spontaneity, pragmatism, debate and a measure of unrest and much heightened emphasis on the dignity of the human person.

1. *America*, November 5, 1966, p. 526.

When we face the reality of religious community life today, we find that the science of organization is prompting us to sound out in full Mozartian tones a death, a *requiem* for traditional bureaucracy. Herein lies the full, the new witness to today's word wherever authority functions for apostolic purposes.

Up until now, the predominant form of human organization and authority has been bureaucracy. It was perfected in the Industrial Revolution to organize and direct the activities of various institutions and agencies. It has reigned since that time wherever people direct concerted effort to achieve the goal.

Bureaucracy is a social invention which relies exclusively on power to influence through rules enforced from a centralized power position, through reason and through law. It was created by Max Weber and came to the United States around 1900. It was developed as a reaction against personal subjugation, nepotism, cruelty, capricious and subjective judgments. This was management prior to the Industrial Revolution.

It was a broad system based on such devices as:
a) a division of labor based on functional specialization;
b) a well defined hierarchy of authority;
c) a system of procedures and rules for all phases of work;
d) an approach which officially sponsored the impersonality of personal relations;
e) a regulated plan of promotion and selection based on technical competence and often on convenience;
f) an organizational chart presenting the familiar pyramid.

For its time in the evolution of knowledge and skills, it was an improvement, more humane and more Christian, but it has run its course. Its day is over. It must now give way to new insights, more creative knowledges and more appropriate skills. Bureaucracy as a manifestation of authority does not fit contemporary realities. There are new shapes, new patterns, and new models emerging. These more appropriately fit today's realities and more efficiently produce a witness for Christ in current religious life.

Some new and fresh realizations have helped to shape the more appropriate and creative forms of the "authority-witness":

a) a new operative concept of man as a *unit* human being endowed with immeasurable resources, dignity and freedom;

b) a new concept of power based on collaboration and reason with the elimination of coercion and fear;

c) a new concept of organizational values rooted in humanistic democratic ideals which so admirably flow from Christianity's most basic tenets as set forward in the gospels, replacing the depersonalized and mechanized values of a bureaucratic type of authority.

These new and fresh realizations look to power and efficiency as *ennobling behaviors* eliciting these behaviors from: consensus; from the power of people in the organizational structure who are part of policy- and decision-making; from the process of collaboration with its factors of conflict, clarification and commitment.

An apostolate is any area of the human effort wherein persons, singly or collectively in a specialized profession, attempt specifically, formally and officially to present Christ by living His values and demonstrating His behaviors for the temporal and eternal salvation of man. Our best view of the apostolate of religious life today comes to us from the Decree on the Adaptation and Renewal of Religious Life from the Second Vatican Council. This decree, fewer than 3,000 words, is the fruit of immense labor. Each sentence and each section must be read very carefully in order to understand thoroughly their implications. It must also be read in connection with the implications and the spirit of every other council document.

The roots of the decree on the renewal and adaptation of religious life are in the dogmatic Constitution on the Church, promoted on the closing day of the third session of the council. There the permanent value of religious life is emphasized and its particular forms attributed to the Holy Spirit Who distributes His manifold gifts in the Church. But because there clearly remained a need for a special declaration about the participation of religious institutes in the grace of renewal that is being given to the whole Church, *Perfectae caritatis* was structured and promulgated.

In the context of this decree the word "renewal" means first a return to the early Christian sources of spirituality, the gospels above all, but also means a return to the original inspiration of the Holy Spirit given to the founder of each particular institute. "Renewal" also means the necessity for an adaptation to the demands of the twentieth century.

At no time in the decree do the words "renewal and adaptation" mean a break with the past, nor do they mean something merely formal and nominal. They mean a real renewal, with a number of practical and external changes, with a true conversion of heart by way of an organic development that gives new life to the whole body. The council carefully lays down some basic principles to be followed in this renewal and adaptation:

1. To live the life of Christ should be the supreme rule for every religious. To live the life of Christ means to take part in the mysterious process of His Incarnation.
2. Each institute should remain faithful to the spirit of its founder and to its own authentic traditions. The council wants every religious institute to preserve its own personality. The diversity of religious orders and congregations is something highly to be desired within the Church.
3. All religious should take their full share in the authentic life of the Church. This means that each individual religious should be aware of the great initiatives that enrich the life of the Church, and each one should take part in the great movements of our days. The council particularly mentions the Biblical, liturgical, theological, pastoral, ecumenical, and social movements.
4. Religious institutes should promote among their members an adequate knowledge of the state of the world and of the needs of the Church. Apostolic work demands factual knowledge of the circumstances in which men live today. This knowledge points up the possibilities that are open to the Church in our day. Natural knowledge joined with the vision of faith will lead institutes to new endeavors and to more efficient action.
5. The source of all adaptation of the religious and the apostolates to the needs of our age should be in a renewal of the internal spirit of the community and of its members. The primacy of the spiritual life is asserted several times in vigorous terms in the decree. The council, however, warns us that internal renewal will not be enough. The new spirit is to be expressed practically in the everyday life of religious communities.

It is clear that the Church expects each institute to hold a practical inventory to see if its way of life, devotions, and actions correspond to the psychological, physical, social, and economic conditions of the particular areas where the members live and work; to see whether its spirit and mode of living and government fit contemporary realities.

The decree states that such development is not possible unless each and every member of an institute makes his contribution toward the desired development. Superiors must not neglect or exclude this contribution.

Religious are taught from their earliest years in religion that one of their most significant characteristics is that they are "to think with the Church." In our day, the living teaching voice of the Church comes to us through the council. This means practically that we have no choice but to back the council's documents enthusiastically.

Let us take history to be an account of the events or occurrences which relate to man, together with an interpretation which gives these events meaning according to some human dimension. Then salvation history is an account of the events of the human race interpreted according to the salvific intent of God, and is, particularly, an account of God's salvific intervention in human history. The Bible is, therefore, salvation history par excellence and the original source of all religious life. But salvation history continues as the history of the people of God under the guidance of the Holy Spirit. Now, it seems to me that the Catholic view is that God not only guides human history by a sort of general salvific providence, but that He continues to intervene by special and original actions.

Such is the case with many of the saints, especially those who have effectively altered the traditions of the Church. In certain experiences of the saints, there is an authentic originality, an authentic independent illumination, which brings into the development of the people of God something wholly congruous with the primal sources and yet new and independent. St. Ignatius remarked that if all of the sources of belief in the Trinity were eliminated, he would yet believe in the Trinity on the basis of his own mystical experience. The prototype of all such cases was, no doubt, St. Paul, who taught the same doctrine as the twelve Apostles, but claimed for it an independent and personal source.

The point, finally, is that it seems to me that the religious and mystical experiences of many founders constitute just such an authentic intervention of God, and consequently brought to the Church and to society an "inspiration" and a "spirit" that is authentically new and divine and yet totally congruous with Scripture and Tradition. This appears to be the reason for the implication of the council's insistence on renewal by a return, not only to Scripture, but to the original inspiration of the founder. Everything else, not excepting constitutions (even though written by the founder) and primary members, can be changed and adapted. The first task, therefore, for each religious is to renew in himself—in this period of grace and change—basic inspiration, for this is, for the individual religious, his total and absolute commitment to God.

For the rest, we must examine with absolute objectivity and courageous prudence the difficult matter of the structure and activities of the individual community. In the years ahead, Christian prudence is going to be severely tested. In a time of radical reassessment, when there is a ferment of ideas and a flood of proposals, it is difficult to distinguish between the wave of the future and a fad of the present; it is difficult to tell who is the creative innovator, the prophet of the future, and who is the crackpot.

Accordingly, when we face the topic of "Communication as Charity" we realize that we are involved in a very primitive sense with the following factors:

1) The spirit of community and the communication propositions;
2) The nature of the person;
3) The dimensions of the total apostolate;
4) The knowledges and skills necessary for authority figures and for each community member to make communication and charity flourish.

The Spirit of Community

Any society and religious organization can function productively and harmoniously only when community exists. To have a community of persons working jointly to achieve common goals, three conditions must exist: mutual understanding, mutual respect and acceptance, and mutual supportive mental and emotional activity.

No society or group can proceed further than the primitive, fundamental information which forms the basis of its judgments. There is need for continuing research. We must constantly increase and improve the information upon which each group—younger religious and older veterans—operate. We dare not indulge longer in the wasteful luxury and the time-consuming process of merely exchanging personal opinion based on personal feelings, rooted far too extensively in myth, legend, faulty memory and unreal generalizations produced by unchecked impressions. We need hard-nosed facts.

There is an absolutely necessary period of dialogue that must go on to improve the climate and dispositions for joint, cooperative action to achieve constructive progress. Dialogue needs facts—not rumors, misperceptions, and wild speculations rooted, on the one hand, in the driving needs of youth, and on the other hand in the equally real driving needs of more threatened persons, that is, older adults.

If we are to achieve a sense of community, a *sine qua non* is the awareness that each individual has an obligation and responsibility to exert that amount of discipline and skill which yields the ability to confront and to sort out the meanings and feelings of "the other." There appear to be no conflicts leading to the clarification of issues and the mental growth, development and maturity of both groups—youth and older adults.

Looking now to the community precisely as a group structure, we find that in the Pauline sense the community must be viewed as a cell of the Mystical Body. All aspects of the doctrine apply to the concept of community.

In a very real sense the community springs from the Trinity which is the first and most perfect society. One of the characteristics of the Trinity is the love and unity which permeates the Persons. The bond here is Christ; the Holy Spirit, the soul.

Without individuals' loving other individuals, there is no community—no society. A religious community emerges from persons sharing values: personal, Christian, and particular institute-values. In this sharing there is typically a strong basis for mutual trust, respect, and support. Traditionally, it may well be that there has been too much stress on community as a means to institutional efficiency. The spirit of Vatican II would now have us reorient that focus to a stress on the person—the member of the community.

When we realize that in some sense a community is a microcosm of the Church and has all the weaknesses of any human organization we will not be surprised to find in it the usual conflicts and abrasive frictions. For the good of the Church, the Mystical Body, and of the individual members, every effort and strategy must be employed to minimize these purely human drawbacks.

Love and dedication must order the lives of the individual members and the community as a whole. Because the turnover of religious personnel in a given house is so frequent, religious must live, as it were, without roots. This reality can militate against community cohesiveness, and can generate lifelong tension and restlessness unless the individual religious gives complete fidelity to Christ as a living, ever-present reality whence will flow a dynamic love and concern for his religious colleagues. Lacking this, the person will shrink into himself—withdraw—causing a hollow, non-productive existence.

Service as an expression of perfect charity is the essence of community. This must be the service of God, the Church, and fellow religious.

Better and better service should produce more and more love, internally and externally. This service is basically an enduring spirit that will show itself in deeds. Properly this virtue of service avoids two possible extremes: antagonism and isolationism. It is in an atmosphere of wholesome service that the person has the optimum context in which to grow.

A religious community, either as the total congregation or an individual house, is a human construct with traditions, customs, "by-laws," etc.: things it does and does not do. It can happen that gradually and almost inevitably it slows down under the weight of its own baggage.

Regrettably, all human enterprises suffer from slow hardening of institutional arteries. The impact of this degenerating is deadening for the members. There must be a constant counterforce from constant evaluation of objectives and purposes, the adapting of new methods and reshaping of objectives as a new age progresses and fresh needs are revealed. There must be a brave effort for updating, for the releasing of untapped energies, the stepping out of ruts and irrelevant routines into new endeavors.

Change, whether in the form of a break with the past or a new initiative, is upsetting. It is also a normal process in any living organism. The one clearly unhealthy thing that can happen to an institute or community is to set its face against change when all else points to a new day with its own demands. To meet change requires sound mental health and deep religious and apostolic motivation on the part of all members. In many ways, the mental health of a person depends upon his communications skills. By communication skills we mean those human methods and processes by which the rational psychosomatic unit relates to his world of persons, places, issues, and things. These particular skills encompass not only the continuing operations of the individual, but also embrace his capacities and abilities for receptivity as far as his environment of persons, places, issues, and things is concerned. Patently, then, we are immediately in the area of the nature and quality of the individual's sensitivities, his perceptions, and his ability at empathy as well as sympathy.

The term "mental health" is much harder to describe. The approach one takes in defining this term will depend pretty much upon one's central philosophic and theological position. The deep sense of adequacy and security which indicates the presence of mental health for the Christian, for the serious Catholic, for the religious, obviously will be quite differently characterized. Fully cognizant of the presence and meaning of the cross, steeped in an understanding of the purpose and meaning of life, the religious gives evidence of the presence of mental health when he can say, with objective validity, "With the help of God's grace, I am equal to the demands that reality puts upon me, and where I want to improve I can succeed," or in the same vein he may express himself by saying, "Before God, I accept my assets without smugness, and my liabilities without apology."

Behind both of these expressions we understand that the state of mental health exists, since here we are faced with an individual, laboring with only minimal need to escape from the reality with which he is faced. He manifests that he possesses at least an adequate amount of confidence and security to carry out the many roles which life puts upon him. Further we are impressed with the fact that this type of individual has seen the need for and has succeeded in achieving that amount of knowledge and skill which is necessary for carrying on as an adequately functioning person. This, then, describes the presence of mental health.

At this point certain propositions regarding the individual, his mental health and communications skills, and the community should be considered. These propositions are:

1. The human being functions adequately and securely in direct proportion to the quality of the emotional supports which sustain him in his environment of fellow human beings. Every human being has a deep need for this support. The very complementary nature of man, which is, in part, confirmed in the doctrine of the Mystical Body, indicates each individual's relationship in God's plan with every other human being, past, present and future, and particularly with those fellow religious who make up his religious family, his community.
2. The converse is also here entertained: A human being's mental health and sense of adequacy deteriorate to the extent that his necessary emotional supports are withdrawn.
3. A third is that the individual has mental health and a sense of adequacy to the extent that he can securely invest something of himself in other people and habitually manifest a well developed skill in securely and confidently permitting others to invest something of themselves in him. This is a demonstration of the great law of charity in action, and in no place should it be more visible than in one's own religious setting—one's community.

To make these propositions fully operative we need only to recall Christ's injunction to mankind: "A new commandment I give you,

that you love one another: that as I have loved you, you also love one
another. By this all men know that you are My disciples, if you have
love for one another."

The era of intuitive knowledge is over. People must be taught, and
they must be taught in the extremely sensitive and central area of communications skills. Under guidance and supervision, they must be aided
to have clear-cut values, loyalties and commitments that have been
thoroughly internalized. This requires the ability, with grace, to have
accurate self-knowledge, to have the skill to make corrective changes
in one's behavior whenever and wherever these changes are needed.
Further, people need the presence of constant good examples and ad-
mirable models that can be imitated. People learn how to relate securely and adequately with their fellow human beings when they are
nurtured and reared in an environment of other noble people who
show the way.

The community should, therefore, focus its major energy on the growth
and development of the individual person precisely as a unique, special
individual of inestimable worth.

The individual religious should spend himself generously for the good of the
community, its members, and its total goals.

The term "community" can be distracting. In some ways the term is
an abstraction. The tangible realities are the individual person in the
community and its apostolic works. Viewed as the latter the individual
religious can better come to grips with his part of the contract.

The community on its part, through superiors, major and local, as
well as all other personnel working in formation programs, pre-service
and in-service, will carry out its task responsibly when it places its efforts primarily on the total good of the subject rather than on community or institutional efficiency.

The Nature of Person

The evolution of a technological culture is yielding new insights
into the operational nature of man, his motivation and behavior. In
using these studies, however, we are faced with the task of sorting out
and judging the scholar's findings to judge them objectively in the
spirit of faith. We cannot ignore the fact that we live in an age which
has become supersaturated with the labels and clichés of psychiatry.

There is a current tendency to place most phases of human activity under some psychiatric label. The awesome dimensions of technical achievement, even in the behavioral sciences, intoxicates contemporary society, especially the young. If we allow ourselves to be dragged around under the influence of this intoxication, we run the risk of following a rootless naturalism. We are thus robbed of perspective and proportion regarding the human condition.

The fact is, our age is filled with positive values but these are often lost in a morass of ambiguities. We must love this age, yet defend ourselves against it. We must admire this age and use its best, yet be shrewd enough to sort out the best.

In the wholesome work being done on person and personhood, there is much we must incorporate into formation programs of religious communities as well as into all the houses and works of communities.

Since the 1940s both the sacred and social sciences have dug deeper and deeper into the nature and strivings of the human individual, creating momentum which has intensified delving into the realities of personhood in both the abstract and the real orders.

The human person is an embodied spirit. He has a body; therefore, he is subject to all the laws of matter. In space he is confined more or less to one small corner of the universe. In time he emerges (birth) and falls back (death) in due course at defined points in the history of the world. This individual is resistant, impenetrable and divided off in his individuality from all others. He is an assemblage of forces only momentarily composed.

More significantly, however, man is a spirit. In a mysterious way, because of this reality, he can transcend the laws of the body. Because of this spirit, there is no limiting man to space and time. His spirit comprehends space and surpasses time. His inner being or spirit urges an experienced awareness that he is made also for immortality. In addition, man is made for understanding and loving, and is in a state of constant tension to further his understanding and to deepen his love.

Man is much more spirit than body. It is this spirit that brings radically new values into the individual person and through him into the universe—the values of known loves, known choices, known commitments and known communions. At the root of this spirit lies the power of knowing and loving God. Spirit itself is an image of God Himself by which God appears through the person in this world in a unique manner. Each individual is so unique that God shows forth in him in a way in which He appears in no other human being.

Still further, a baptized and consecrated person participates in a finite way in the divine power of knowing and loving, not only the triune God but also creatures *as* He sees and loves them. Would it be too much to suggest that this special participation into the "insights" and "loves" of God is the radical heart of personhood? The individual person in a true sense exists to unfold a particular and unique aspect of the content of humanity within the human family; to carry it on, to perfect it, and to add his bit of growth and uniqueness to it.

When individuals reflect within themselves, they find certain real personal ties with the entire human community. They sense the active power of knowing and loving the whole human family. Even as the individual person feels these ties with the whole human community, he realizes paradoxically that these ties will not and cannot engulf and absorb his own individuality.

If the individual religious is properly formed and is maturing typically, he grows in the realization that these ties with the human community not only integrate but actually fulfill his individual personality. This is no doubt one of the greatest gifts that one's own religious community and the community at large through the apostolate can give him. The developing religious through the formation program should begin to see that his truest individuality is actually achieved through his freely responding to insights into his own unique role of valued part within the human family known, loved and redeemed by Christ.

The individual religious person must realize and accept the fact that he personally in his own unique nature and individuality is the term, the object, of the knowledge and love of God. Each human being is divinely called in space and time; he must respond to this call (vocation) in his own unique manner. Although man deals with many related responses, in his vocation he is alone—as he is alone in the presence of God. The individual person's deepest reality is achieved, is realized, in his responsive act to the will of God addressed lovingly to his own person.

In being called, the individual religious person must understand that he is called to confront the world, other men, himself, and the Father. Accordingly, properly trained the formed religious person's first, fundamental and enduring response will be to respond, to fulfill and to transcend his individual personality by entering relational, committed union with God, himself, the world, and men.

It is precisely this invitation to a unique, personal, individual witness by and for God which calls forth, structures and ultimately defines the profound worth of the individual religious person, and presents the law of his action.

The individual religious person's response to this personal divine invitation constitutes his struggle for self-realization and freedom. This struggle is the tension of self-conquest to achieve true self-realization within the family of God, to win which he must keep his own sincerity and integrity. Here the religious person needs understanding, patience, insight and help.

In the encyclical *Pacem in terris*, John XXIII spells out what this means for the individual, and at the same time describes the climate of the times in which today's religious is working out the fullness of his vocation.

The pontiff speaks to all of the civil and spiritual rights of man. Taking for granted the time-honored theological tenets regarding the origin of these rights, Pope John immediately finds their eternal, inalienable source in the nature of man himself. He stresses the need to reach an order where all men and all nations may possess what is due to them. In this encyclical the Vicar of Christ proclaims anew the dedication of Christ's Church to human freedoms. At this point could we with any profit ask ourselves how much of this human freedom our training and formation programs extend and foster in one preparing for the modern apostolate? Can the modern religious we are attempting to form communicate this encyclical message of Christ if he or she has never, or too seldom, personally experienced this freedom even in analogous forms? Does the old scholastic maxim have no bearing here: *Nemo dat quod non habet?* Do we not all have to give some hard-headed thought to the extent to which we have realistically attempted to provide experienced freedom in our own familial formation programs—in the areas of prayer, types of prayer, differences in daily-order schedules which still do not interrupt community schedules; interests and desires for particular works of the apostolate within the framework of the overall work of the order?

In training persons with a grasp of vocation such as is here being described, the concept of "normalcy" will be at best only minimally helpful. Perhaps a more helpful orientation and concept is the whole idea of adequacy. As we view all world cultures and even what might be termed specific subcultures, such as the priesthood and the religious life, the concept of adequacy seems more realistic and more rewarding for the individual; more productive for the apostolate itself. A person is adequate when there is a proportioned response between his performance, internal and external, and the responsibility placed upon him by life, natural and supernatural. This concept can be thought of as a total continuum ranging from complete inadequacy at the extreme left, up through simple, minimal adequacy, to the far extreme on the right, or maximal adequacy.

This concept of adequacy as a substitute for the more unrealistic concept of normality, prompts us to suspect that the nomenclature of psychiatry, personality studies, psychology, and the traditional ascetical types is outmoded and at times misleading.

To train the adequate person for the modern apostolate and its demands, it would seem reasonable to assume that we need a new orientation concerning the individual and his freedom, for it is only the free individual who can be a full person, a truly adequate person, a unique image of God. A person is free only when *he* takes the personal initiative for his will acts, and deliberately and responsibly lives with the consequences of his decisions. Any other state leads to mere conformity, which is a kind of death state.

When we think of the nature of the religious and the extrareligious environment or the public arena, we immediately visualize the individual religious sustaining the stress from the routine living of his religious life, meeting the various crises that usually turn up in the career of each individual. The dimensions of the stress of routine as well as of the incidental crises will be drawn in terms of the individual's perception of the particular reality and responsibility involved. It cannot be emphasized too much that the result of the individual's perception is "his truth." Here we have one of the factors which cause individual differences within a group, and at the same time one of the reality forces that account for each individual uniqueness.

There can be no safe generalizations here other than to indicate that in the formation of the individual for the modern apostolate, care should be had to help the individual in every way to clarify his truth and to internalize it into his motivational and behavioral life. His grasp of the meaning of the religious vocation must be such that he is personally and emotionally supported by its nature and function. Cardinal Suenens feels that we can best understand the religious vocation by asking of the Lord one question:

What are the thoughts and wishes of the Master to be played by religious in our times? What help does He require from them for the salvation of the world? . . . "Lord what wilt thou have me do?" Everything is in that question. How to make God better known, better loved and better served. As Pascal said, only God can tell us about God. Only God can speak about the salvation of souls whose worth He alone knows. What matters is the glory of God and the salvation of the world: everything else is relative to this absolute. Being open to the breath of the Spirit, to His views, not our own, this is the first thing required of those who, whether from within or without, are responsible for the destiny of the religious life. For the others the sure way is to respond with their whole heart to the demands made of them by their superiors. The generous carrying out of allotted tasks is an infallible channel for the grace which not only renders their work fruitful, but also advances the time of the hoped-for apostolic revival.

This then is the mode in which the developing religious is to form his own life, and prepare himself for the rigors of the apostolate. The religious life and the apostolate should be presented as serving the religious, otherwise distortion, nonproductiveness and final deterioration will be the result. It is of paramount importance that those in charge of the formation by reason of their own personal wholeness, training, and insights are able to demonstrate for the young religious that even as he develops his own life he is actually meeting not only his own needs but the needs of the apostolate itself. This is the delicate and complex task of manifesting that the vocational value and the apostolate value are actually complementary and not in opposition one to the other. The stable, mature, well-integrated person is the one who is always needed to represent Christ. Individual differences being what they are, the uniqueness of each human person being what it is, there will be no one human type that can be aimed for or desired.

There are some all-important factors to be taken into account regarding each religious: the condition of the individual's biochemical makeup which undergirds all mental and emotional life is a significant force.

While brightness, mental clarity, and the biochemistry of one's temperament do undoubtedly play major roles in the development of the individual, the whole group in formation must be given the common experiences that will allow each according to his native endowment to develop in terms of his own capabilities and potential. To start the young person in the desired direction of maturity and stability, he must have the opportunity to learn to be free. At first this may appear paradoxical for a religious who is to spend his life dependent upon authority. Paradoxical though it may be, it is in no sense a contradiction.

The freedom I want to stress is essentially an inner thing which exists in the living person, as Dr. Carl Rogers teaches.

It is the quality of courage which enables a person to step from the uncertainty of the unknown as he chooses himself. It is the burden of being responsible for the self one chooses to be. It is the recognition by the person that he is an emerging process, not a static end product.[2]

The young religious must fully identify with the fact that it is not only absolutely necessary for his own development, but that superiors desire him to be a person who deeply thinks his own thoughts, becomes his own uniqueness, responsibly choosing himself. He must realize that he will make mistakes in deciding choices among the many, many alternatives open to him, but that his freedom exists regardless and in this freedom lives his greatest potential.

It should be realized that some will raise their eyebrows in concern at the above statement, but a little reflection will bring home forcefully the truth of the reality herein described.

Unless the young religious at each step along the way of his formation can identify with the truth of the values being taught, he will not incorporate these values into his motivational life.

Freedom rightly understood is a fulfillment, by the person, of the ordered sequence of his life. Rogers would say that, "It is freedom in which the individual chooses to fulfill himself by playing a responsible and voluntary part in bringing about the destined events of the world he lives in."

If the knowledge of the values and objectives the individual possesses is seen as something which enhances the self (particularly in the deepest ascetical sense), then the individual's emotional reactions will be a support in living both the values of the vocation and of the apostolate—of giving to the individual greater and greater personal adequacy in both his religious life and his apostolic activity.

On the other hand, if the individual's knowledge about himself, his vocation and the apostolate is perceived as not enhancing the self, his emotional reactions, far from giving support, will inhibit the individual, causing him to give way under stress and to be proportionately inefficient, non-productive and unhappy. For example, in the multi-areas of sexuality, in routine relationships, in and out of the religious community and in work performance, it is necessary that the individual

2. Carl R. Rogers, "Learning to Be Free," *The NEA Journal*, March, 1963.

perceive his self as equal to the demands that reality puts on him, and capable of improvement whenever and wherever he has the determination to try.

The key factor is habitual, interior security in accurately perceiving the self, in accepting the self as it is when objectively confronted, and in living with the self as it is and in terms of its real and ideal potential. For the religious to develop constructively along these lines, the quality of rapport between the individual and his superiors, local and major, is a condition of prime importance. Aside from the juridical nature of the vow, the "spirit of obedience" depends very much upon the quality of this relationship. This relationship in turn is highly significant in the development of a sound self-concept. The latter either makes for a strong person or a weak person, an effective apostle or a non-productive one.

The type of training program which obtains in the formation of the individual is of great importance in these considerations. This formation program must involve a process which makes it possible for the young religious to confront himself realistically, and to understand his many roles and the knowledges and skills necessary for each role. For example, the most basic role to be understood is that of one's creaturehood. If this fundamental reality is not clearly appreciated, the individual cannot develop a sustaining, operative, highly personal relationship with God, the Creator, and Christ, the Gift. Similarly, there are the roles of "personhood," of maleness (femaleness), of priest or brother (or sister), of group member, of apostolic worker, etc. There is the added knowledge and skill to be gained which permits one to change from one role to another as circumstances demand. As these knowledges and skills are learned, the training setting must constantly take into account the uniqueness of each trainee. The expectations of faculties and superiors must effectively appreciate the implications of this uniqueness.

Interior acceptance of self yields interior security. Interior security produces the ability at the minimum simply to endure, and beyond that gives the ability to grow spiritually. Spiritual growth results in serenity and equanimity, producing the conditions in which the Holy Spirit can work in the person and through him for the accomplishment of apostolic gains. It is the presence of the Holy Spirit in the person which insulates the self against abrasiveness and panic from self and from the apostolic arena.

More specifically, the outcome for the individual who is developing a high degree of adequacy is a substantial amount of maturity. This maturity can be expressed by the individual through an habitual point of view which might somehow be stated as follows:

I accept my personal limitations and weaknesses without apology and com- pensating defenses. I accept my strengths, opportunities, talents and spiritual growth without smugness. I am equal to the demands that my life puts on me and where I truly want to improve, I can succeed.

To form the sound person, in each individual case the situation de- pends upon a variety of factors. Among these factors are such realities as the wide range of individual differences, the kinds and breadth of past experience each person has had, the type of childhood experiences, including home, parents, brothers, sisters, schooling, travel; the kind and force of the models one has had to imitate in his most formative years and in his religious life, and the opportunities one has had for achieving special insights, formal and informal, in and out of the re- ligious community.

One of the most important factors to be considered in this series of realities which form the truly strong apostolic person is whatever truly freeing experience the individual has had. By "freeing experience" I mean those experiences which take from the person his need to be de- fensive, and which have given him a genuine understanding of his constant dependence upon God, on his religious community, its spirit and its rule.

Whatever else is to be said about the factors that form the religious for the modern apostolate, it could not be stressed too much that the central reality is that the individual must understand in an operative way that his own faith and his own vocation give him a deeply per- sonal relation between himself and God. Thus does he become genu- inely related to the others loved by Christ—His apostles. It is not enough to have a kind of official knowledge that each one of us is truly called a son and is in fact a son of God; that each of us enters the life of the Trinity by sharing the sonship of the Son. In Him we have the Father for our Father, having a part in His relation as Son. This is ac- complished by the gift of the Spirit. Father and Son bestow their love on us by sending the Spirit, their gift; by the Spirit we are united to them. Each individual must internalize the central Christian truth that we are first possessors of the Spirit, then messengers and Christophers of the Spirit, brothers of the Son Incarnate, sons of the Father, not in name only, but in reality with the mutual knowledge and love that such personal relationships demand. And this new relation with the triune God sets up a network of personal relations among men themselves. As sons of God we are a people, not a mass of individuals.

Psychologists, psychiatrists, physicians of internal medicine, clergymen with sound professional training, and great teachers have found that the one real source of personal happiness is personal relations. If these are sound, nothing else matters; if they are defective, all the wealth in the world is no substitute. Our faith tells us that at the root of all our personal relations is a new personal relation with God. Mere theological knowledge in abundance is no substitute for the individual if he is to be a true person. He must have internalized an awareness of, a feeling for, and an habitual readiness to act on, the truth of our deeply personal relation with God. Only such a person is ready to work securely and productively in the modern apostolate.

No treatment on the topic of forming the religious person for the modern world can long avoid what has regrettably become known as the "crisis of authority." The person in formation, as well as even the relatively young religious out in the active field, is feeling the impact of the authority phenomenon.

Some will say that much of the preceding development in this paper adds to the so-called crisis. In the same vein not a few may claim the crisis is such that the whole doctrinal and teaching position of the Church is by implication under attack; that there is abroad a spirit which indicates a genuine unwillingness to accept the rulings of those who govern the Church and each smaller aspect of the Church. Such is by no means the case.

In thinking of developing a person toward his goal of personhood within the framework of the religious life in a given religious community, attention is being drawn in no sense to traditional authority but only to the mode of its presentation, extension and exercise. Too often the traditional teaching about the function of authority has been such that individuals in obeying could and did use authority as a substitute for deep personal living, and sought in the authority of the Church and of the individual religious community a means of escaping from responsibly conducting their own lives. It must be re-emphasized that authority addresses itself to will-life. Acts of the will are immanent acts. No one can make a will-act for another. No man may lean on authority, merely conforming to its dictates, and then assume that he is fulfilling a vital and rich personal life. To gain from authority one must

spontaneously possess and internalize it and then jubilantly will it into
the pattern of his life.

Today we have witnessed in the Church a reassertion of the rights
of conscience. In the new look at authority there is no rebellion. There
is, however, a highlighting of the fact that for authority to be intelli-
gently used there must be a greater stress on rightly forming con-
sciences. This can only be done through a higher intellectual grasp of
the teachings of the Church, the Gospels, and the individual institute's
original intent.

Two dimensions in the authority phenomenon are clear: the one of
legalism (which so readily degenerates into the shallowest nominalism
and formalism) which has disfigured so much of Christian living, especially that mode of Christian life followed in religious communities;
the other is a new orientation in religious life itself—a shift from a
primary focus on authority's role and the subject's inferior status, to a
concentration on the person with authority, and obedience's being
supportive to give the religious life its fullest meaning.

These two dimensions immediately indicate that human dignity receive an appropriate stimulus, and the religious life a more properly
enriched direction when the individual person can see himself as a co-
operator and a partner in authority in a manner not unlike the process
involved in the individual person's being an image of God.

Lawrence Cardinal Shehan of Baltimore brings the above discussion
down to the practical order in his statement of January 28, 1966:

There is a call for much more discussion between priests and bishops, between assistants and their pastors, between subjects and superiors generally
than was customary in the past. I don't think that exactly the same traditions of authority and obedience that prevailed in my day in the seminary
can be expected to prevail today. When I was a seminarian . . . we grum-
bled at times, but we never thought of challenging or even discussing decisions with our superiors. This situation has changed.[3]

This whole question is not so much one of authority as one of the approach and atmosphere of authoritarianism. The latter problem is indeed a very different matter from the former, and one much easier
to solve. In this matter the teacher needs intelligence and charity.

Too often, in the past, religious entered and were trained in a highly

3. From an interview with Lawrence Cardinal Shehan, Archbishop of
Baltimore, in the *Baltimore Catholic Review*, January 28, 1966.

stylized institutional atmosphere. Within the confines of this milieu they were expected to develop mentally, emotionally, and spiritually. The door has slammed on that past! Today's religious recruit (and the seasoned veterans too!) need living space where they have regular, extensive, significant and continuing person-to-person contacts with mature adults and authority figures who are not afraid to demonstrate that they value them highly. There is need for an atmosphere of love, truest charity.

Harry Stack Sullivan defines love for us:

When the satisfaction or the security of another person (persons) becomes as significant to one as one's own security, then the state of love exists.[4]

Erich Fromm indicates that love has the characteristics of care, responsibility and knowledge and that ". . . the essence of love is to labor for something to make something grow." [5] These two expressions help to clarify the fact that true love is quite possible within the setting of the religious community.

How does the content of this discussion correlate with the dicta of Vatican II?

The religious state is defined in the Church today as the "regular way of living in community in which the faithful agree to obey not only a common rule but also the evangelical counsels."

The Dimensions of the Apostolate

Today's apostolate is to be found wherever the people of God "move and are and have their being." This apostolate will take the form of those works or activities in which a given religious community engages: education, hospitals, social works, civil endeavors, orphans, the aged, youth groups, etc.

The people of God—wherever they are and in whatever condition they are—the old, the middle aged, the senior citizens; with all their varying needs and expectations—look to religious for three never-failing qualities: sincerity, integrity and credibility.

Each of these characteristics, to exist and flourish, demands that each

4. Harry Stack Sullivan, *Conception of Modern Psychiatry*, New York: W. W. Norton and Co., Inc., 1953.
5. Erich Fromm, *The Art of Love*, New York: Harper and Brothers, 1956.

religious community must ruthlessly evaluate itself and in so doing ask
three questions:

1) What is our "image," internally and externally;
2) What adjustments must we make to exhibit a positive and constructive
   "image";
3) What must we do in our internal organization to generate a reality
   which apostolically effects the production of sincerity, integrity and
   credibility?

These three questions might well become the agenda for a year's meeting of any community.

The people of God today are, in a new way, a searching people, a
questioning people, a hopeful people—and, ironically, a simple people.

To be won, to be engaged for true involvement, they tend to respond to religious who are: open, unaffected, simple, unafraid, secure
in themselves and convinced, enthusiastic, unflinchingly committed,
and undistracted in their sense of purpose and the pursuit of God's
kingdom.

When one observes the breakdown in charity in any group setting,
he invariably finds that blocked communication was the immediate
cause. What, then, causes these communication blocks? These blocks
are the result of personality malformation and malfunctioning.

Not perfectly but to a significant degree, personality malformation
and malfunctioning can be off-set by the acquisition of and constant
exercise in specific communication knowledges and skills. To acquire
these and to exercise them requires great self-discipline, true penance.
Here is meaningful self-sacrifice, for it prepares the natural foundation
for supernatural activity and growth.

The knowledge and skills required are:

1) The ability to keep an open, searching, growing mind;
2) The ability and will to listen to all information, no matter how challenging or threatening it may be;
3) The common sense never to laugh or scoff at a new idea, a new way
   of doing things, a new approach to ancient truth;
4) The habit of cross-examining daily one's daydreams, one's most cher-
   ished principles and convictions, one's pet axioms and sayings;
5) The consistent effort to discover and develop one's strongest talent,
   and to desist from the destructive need to apologize for talents not
   possessed;

6) The insight to seek and to use the good counsel and advice of competent colleagues;
7) The ability always, hourly, to be a forward, outward-seeking person;
8) The unfailing habit of mind to seek and cultivate the beautiful.

Conclusion

The far-reaching results of Vatican II in all phases of its work, including its re-evaluation of religious life, are yet to be learned. This we know: the Holy Spirit seeks through the council the accomplishment of Christ's goals for man.

Renewal and adaptation involve growing pains and trauma from change. Sacrifice and pain are involved but these are always companions of love. Whatever else pertains to the essence of religious life, love is at the center. Any community which grasps this point will serve well now and in the future for the great honor and glory of God.

PART
III
THE LOCAL SUPERIOR

The Local Superior as Guide to Renewal

MOTHER M. THOMAS AQUINAS CARROLL, R.S.M.
Mount Mercy College
Pittsburgh, Pennsylvania

There is a hierarchy in the documents of Vatican II which we must respect. For instance, the starting point for my comments is paragraphs 25 and 26 of Part II of the norms of *Perfectae caritatis*. These paragraphs must be studied in the light of the other norms, especially those relating to experimentation and to the special general chapters. They explain specifically Chapter 15 of *Perfectae caritatis*, which again must be seen in the context of that whole document, and of Chapter 6 of the Constitution on the Church. Finally, all this matter relating specifically to religious must be studied and interpreted against the background of the whole of the Constitution on the Church, the Constitution on Revelation, the Constitution on the Sacred Liturgy, the Constitution on the Church in the Modern World, and very many of the decrees.

If there is any one change of focus which the contemporary Church is eager to place before religious it is that we are very much *part* of the Church, a very important sector, but a sector nonetheless of the whole people of God graced with the ultimate goal of perfect holiness. The evangelical counsels are a special gift to us from God to be exercised for the welfare of the whole Church. They are to make us "a clearer revelation of Christ to believers and non-believers." Hence we are called upon to be "not strangers to our fellow man nor useless citizens of this earthly city." It is our brotherly unity that is "to show that Christ has come, and is to be the source of our apostolic effectiveness."

Another principle emphasized in the council documents is subsidiarity. Pastors are called upon to assign duties in the service of the Church to the layman, "allowing him freedom and room for action." In educational organization and international life we are reminded that as much as possible should be done on the *local* levels of competency.

The norms on religious life specify that "superiors on every level should be given specific powers so that useless and too frequent recourse to higher superiors is not multiplied." So also the norms of *Perfectae caritatis* start out with the revolutionary statement that "the most important role in the adaptation and renewal of religious life belongs"—not to the Sacred Congregation of Religious, not to canon law, not to bishops, but—"to the religious themselves."

A striking element in the council directives is the concern for the person.

It remains each man's duty to preserve a view of the whole human person, in view of which the values of intellect, will, conscience, and fraternity are pre-eminent. . . . The human spirit must be cultivated in such a way that there results a growth in its ability to wonder, to understand, to contemplate, to make personal judgments, and to develop a religious, moral, and social sense.

Pastors are asked to acknowledge respectfully "that just freedom which belongs to everyone in this earthly city." So far as we are concerned, it is ruled that "the cooperation of all superiors and members is necessary to renew religious life." And—most significantly—everyone is asked to realize that profession of the counsels does not detract from a genuine development of the human person.

If the Constitution on the Church and the Decree on Adaptation and Renewal of Religious Life had left religious any complacency, the norms for implementing the latter document were calculated to remove them—radically and universally. In a manner unique among the post-conciliar prescriptions, the post-conciliar commission on religious set a deadline for the beginning of changes (three years) in every religious congregation. This apparent urgency was difficult for most women religious to appreciate. There were no grave and persistent scandals among us; our "works" were meeting with some criticism, but on the whole they were still efficient, highly praised, and, in fact, in many aspects improving as our young sisters became better prepared. We were almost totally unaware of how legalistic and form-bound our way of life had become. Perhaps our reluctance to heed Pope Pius XII's directives on change of habit were more indicative than we realized of the closed, self-satisfied vision of our lives. An unshakable trinity supported us: our holy rule or constitutions, the Sacred Congregation of Religious, and canon law.

We had been taught and had completely built our lives upon the idea that the rule was something completely finished, sealed, with the approval of the Holy See and consequently with the approval of God Himself. All that we had to do was live that rule perfectly, and we would become saints, possibly even canonized ones. (What many of us overlooked was that the rule became more and more narrowly interpreted in those phases of it which could be measurably sensed, like silence, being "at prayers" on time, or avoiding idleness.) Though prayers might be long and monotonous we accepted them as God's will for us, and worked hard to put spirit into them. Common life was interpreted rigorously as the greatest possible uniformity, including not only common chapel, recreation room and refectory, but even, in some places, common study-hall and dormitory. Even recreation was an "exercise."

In very many instances our spiritual life became intense, and our pursuit of the "virtues" of our vows led us deeply into God's charity and taught us compassion. Yet even in these cases it was difficult to transmit our spiritual vision to our pupils or the laity because it was so rooted in monastic practices. In other instances the harsh regime did produce a certain hardening and dehumanizing which led to scorn for the weaker brethren and a fear of God ever remorselessly seeking us out in our deviations. The cloister was protected in canon law, as it was frequently interpreted, by threat of excommunication, and the companion-rule was strenuously enforced by zealous bishops.

It is unbelievable to us today how mechanistic were many of our attitudes towards the sacrament of penance, poverty, silence, even the Sacrifice of the Mass. Chastity meant keeping the external rules of modesty and avoiding particular friendships. It was the superior's duty to see that we were kept protected from the world; that we went to confession weekly; that proper books were read at lecture; that loud and open "breaches of charity" were atoned; and that the rule was kept faithfully. In retrospect, the role of the superior was relatively simple and easy. It was each individual sister's responsibility to find in the patterned life her own interior growth of humility, poverty of spirit, joy in the cross, faith and love and confidence in God.

And now the props are gone! Canon law for religious is to be reformed—after *we* have experimented! The Sacred Congregation of Religious will "willingly permit experiments contrary to canon law"— provided that they are undertaken prudently! And all the constitutions, *typika,* rules, all the supplementary codes, "directories," books of customs are to be revised!

What is involved is a revolution in attitudes which must be assimi-
lated if changes in structure are to be adequate or profitable. The sisters (including superiors) are to be the source of the changes, the experimentation. These are to originate *within* each congregation, not
in Rome, not in any chancery office. And further, they are to originate in the cooperative efforts of all the sisters. The principle of subsidiarity as well as practical considerations dictate that a great part of
the burden (and the joy) of preparing for such changes devolves upon
the local community.

This means that, if it has not already been achieved, now is the time
for the current local superior to create an environment adapted to
change—but a change which is according to the spirit of the Constitution on the Church. So very easily can change be a change in forms, or a
change of extremes where the central goal of individual and group
holiness is cast aside for all the "freedoms" induced by casting off one
old restriction after another. The purpose of the Vatican Council's proposals to revise religious constitutions is not to make them less demanding, but to make them demanding of the person in a freer, more
responsible way—a much deeper way of personal choice and initiative
and continually renewed decision *for* the Lord. For some, those who
have really animated their previous observance of the rule by utter
conformity of spirit, this newer approach will be a beautiful flowering
of graces already cultivated. For others, the changes will mean a painful, slow and agonizing assumption of self-responsibility which will
show that the previous apparent conformity had been merely the easy
routine of habit. Others will be crushed by the requirement of authenticity, and will suffer emotional collapse or will leave the congregation.

It was to religious women that Pope Paul said before the council:
"You are the Church of God, her most genuine, most authentic, most
complete and most vibrant expression." The council fathers have emphasized the absolute importance of *every* individual person in the
Church. Everyone is necessary. The importance of each one of us must
arouse in us a corresponding sense of responsibility. Every one of us has
been created uniquely by God to worship Him. Every one of us here
has been fortunate enough to be baptized in the Holy Trinity,
to thereby be made capable of communing with God and of entering
into close communion with others because of our communing with
God through the gift of Baptism.

And then in addition to that, everyone here has been called specifically by God to the counsels, and each of us has responded to that call with faith. This is what Pope Paul meant when he addressed the sisters as "blessed are you who have believed," because our vocation is senseless unless it is based upon a spirit of *faith*. We have answered this call, and in answering it we have accepted risk. We have asked for risks. We have said, "No matter what happens to me, no matter what happens to all around me, I intend to keep troth with God in the vows which I am making." Therefore, every one of us, because of the requirements which will be made of every individual in the Church, because of the fact that we are considered by his holiness the pope the most authentic expression of the Church, has an enormous responsibility to make herself mature in the fullest sense of this word: mature emotionally, mature intellectually, and, above all, mature spiritually.

Now, we do not, however, live as individuals. Part of the glory of our life is that we live in common; we live in community; we live in convents. Each convent should be the common life of mature people who love God, and who serve each other—whose love and zeal for service then pour out beyond the convent into our greater work. But our convent must be the nurturing place of maturity, of love, of service to each other and to God in order that we will have the energy to go out and do great things within our institutions, within our schools, within our hospitals and outside of them, in the works which the needs of the times make evident, and which will probably become more varied, more multiple, and more demanding than at present.

Therefore, each convent must generate a supportive environment. Each convent must be a place of freely given and continually willed obedience and poverty, trust in one another, and generosity and love. There is no place—no matter how we look upon the life of a convent— for fear or repression or resentment or retaliation. We owe to each other this spirit of free obedience, freely assumed and freely continued, mortification, trust in one another, desire to serve one another, generosity. And if we have convents of this kind we shall be so animated with zeal we won't be defensive or fearsome when we hear the "lay apostolate" being praised, being held out to our young people as a great opportunity. We shall rejoice that all these opportunities are being made available. But we shall know that no group, no individual will be able to match our energy, our zeal, our capacity for leadership if we are surrounded by people and go forth from convents which do radiate this spirit.

According to *Perfectae caritatis* "a religious community is a true family." It seems to me essential that we read this sentence as poetry rather than sociology, or in other words that we clearly define for ourselves what we mean by "true family." A religious community cannot be a family in the sense of setting up relations of a mother or father with children. All the professed members of a religious community are adults, and even the novices and postulants have exercised or should have exercised a serious adult responsibility in entering the community. The obedience which a religious professes is not the obedience of a child, nor can authority be exercised in the authoritarian manner which has in the past characterized the behavior of a parent to a child. The recent talk of Pope Paul to women religious is instructive in this matter. While he insists upon the need for obedience and rejects the use of majority vote as constituting law in religious congregations, he also calls for new approaches in the expression of authority. These approaches must be built upon the recognition of sisters as mature persons, where the outstanding relationship is that among peers.

Opposed to such a spirit are the rigid forms which in some communities have built themselves around seniority. A dichotomy even to the youngest sister in our congregations, seniority is usually the first structure to be attacked verbally but the first also to be found useful. As a principle of order, it has a distinctive place, but not as a substitute for mutual service. Respect for elders, special consideration for the worn and the sick and those of whose strength the years have taken toll, should flow immediately from the spirit of charity, not from any formalistic procedures related to a legal date of entrance.

The phrase "a true family" must be understood as applying primarily to the spirit of mutual affection and concern, and of satisfying relationships developed among persons of specialized competencies, but sharing a similar dedication and heritage. In this sense, we may well need such a warm word as "family" has become.

This places upon the local superior enormous burdens. She will be the key to opening the convent to an environment which will set every sister free. She herself must possess a sense of the great value of every single sister—especially the weak, the non-efficient, the lukewarm, because they are valuable in themselves and in God's possession of them. She must convey this appreciation to them, and show that she is aware of the individuality of each. She should thus lead them to expect that they will not necessarily be treated alike, but that each one is met and responded to as a unique adult. It is of the essence that she *trust* her sisters and fully accept their sincerity as religious. As a woman of integrity, she must respect confidences. Observing much, commenting little about the interpersonal relationships of the house, she will be expected to be a bond of unity among the many unique personalities, to provide a foundation for their respect of one another. Upon this mutual respect should be built a natural and open dialogue. Therein should be found that politeness and consideration to be expected in any adult interpersonal relationship, but excessive formality, "standing on ceremony," should be avoided.

Charity of communication does not imply identity of outlook or opinion. In fact it is a means for reaching balance between the "new outlooks" and former points of view. The superior or sister does not need to convey to the other, "I think as you do," but she must communicate:

I trust your sincerity; I accept you as a person searching for the same life of dedication which I seek; I want to learn from you as well as share with you and perhaps offer some guidance; I want to be able to disagree with you, even fundamentally, yet still revere you.

Perhaps more than anywhere else it is imperative on the local level that the superior listen to her sisters, keep them well informed about matters that concern them all, and involve them in planning for the particular needs of the house. She should respect the dynamism of situations and of individual contacts, and not feel that the holiness of her office is impugned if she is not informed of everything first and most fully.

There has grown up among us a strange phenomenon—the unwillingness to speak about spiritual reality. The local superior must promote discussion groups, study sessions, and conferences to overcome this weakness. Thus, the sisters may learn to speak freely, frankly, exactly what their perceptions of spiritual reality are, to encourage one another, to help to deepen one another's appreciation of possibilities for spiritual growth.

These discussions, if the sisters are inexperienced in them, will undoubtedly arouse problems. Some training in group dynamics or sensitivity workshops is essential for at least the superior or leader of the group. The precocious verbalism of the young, their superior education, will deepen the embarrassed reticence of the older sisters unless there is marked stress laid upon the experience of these latter, the great advantage they have of teaching the young out of what life it-

self and God have taught them. The gap between generations, so
marked in our whole society, the prejudices and the narrowness of
view, may rub raw some individual sensitivities in free-wheeling discourse, but they are also made capable of being understood and gradually eliminated. It will take long practice before the average group of
sisters begins to like discussion. However, there seems to be no other
way in which a community can prepare itself for the role the Vatican
Council expects it to play in determining its own life policies. Sharing
the goods of our own personalities usually proves a far harder task than
sharing material goods. And yet it is precisely in this sharing that we
enrich and free our own selves. A mutual growth of interior independence and the interdependence of persons marks the successful community spirit. Hence, the superior who supports each sister in becoming
herself builds an environment of trust, mutual respect, and communication and is in a position to beg the descent of the Holy Spirit upon
her group that they may "renew the face of the earth."

For growth in fraternal love the sisters must depend upon prayer:
the liturgy which "inspires the faithful to become of one heart in
love"; divine office and mental prayer, especially. So far as she can control or influence the celebration of the Eucharist, the superior must be
willing to exercise leadership in augmenting the new liturgy. She should
work to motivate the sisters to give of themselves in singing, readings,
and the other aspects of shared participation. Her mentality toward common prayer sets the tone for the house. Especially on feast days or days
of leisure from professional work, she must help to build the horarium
around a genuine and creative prayer life. Her obligation is not so much
to see that the sisters are all "at prayer," as to plan or, better still, to enter into the planning of others so that a vibrant, meaningful community worship may be realized. If the growth-in-Christ life is to be found
in individuals and in the group, much deep, silent reflection will be
necessary. Therefore even as we recognize and give some scope to the
young sister for group meditation, we must also cultivate the spirit of
silence, the love of mental prayer.

The intensity of spirit which I am trying to emphasize is so important
because we are about to put greater demands and more strain upon the
essentials of community living than ever before. Common life can no
longer be used to protect sisters from the world. It must on the contrary so "charge" the sister that she takes from it the spark with which
to enkindle the world. The doctrine out of which her spirituality
grows must be the same doctrine which she imparts to others. She is

called upon to live before and within the world so as "to manifest the possession of heavenly goods here below; to witness to the power of the Trinity." So imbued with Christ is she to be, that, through her,

Christ should be shown contemplating on the mountain, announcing God's kingdom to the multitude, healing the sick and the maimed, turning sinners to wholesome fruit, blessing children, doing good to all, and always obeying the will of the Father who sent Him.

"To believers and unbelievers alike," the religious is to give "an increasingly clearer revelation of Christ" (Constitution on the Church, §46).

In order to do this, religious in the local convent must study, must help each other in discourse to know Scripture, to gain insights into the liturgy, and to understand the opportunities and problems of contemporary life. More than this, they must become involved with persons and groups outside the convent and outside their immediate professional assignment, if this latter is not conducive to normal adult contacts. Community life, in other words, must prepare the sister and reinforce the sister to play her new role among the people of God, to use the religious community as her springboard into the wider community of "the world."

The Constitution on the Church triumphantly announces, "All men are called to belong to the new people of God; all of us are creatures of God, made by Him to express His creating love, the object of His sacrificial redeeming love." Through baptism we are integrated into the very life of the Trinity, participating in the living mutual knowledge and love that animate the Father and the Son through the Spirit. It is this dimension of the life achieved through Baptism, perceived through faith, which is the most basic reality of our existence. It is this spiritual relationship, this hope of the total realization of ourselves in God, which defines us as persons, as the people of God. All of us thus transformed have a common duty to be perfect. It was to *everyone* that Christ spoke when He said, "Be perfect, as My heavenly Father is perfect." The Constitution on the Church expresses it: "All the faithful, whatever their condition or state, are called by the Lord each in his own way, to that perfect holiness whereby the Father Himself is perfect." The very difficulty of keeping alive in our day this meaningful reality must draw us together with unbreakable bonds, and induce in us the total acceptance of each other, not as categories, but as persons who can mutually rejoice in a common heritage and a common destiny. For too long the laity and religious in the Church have been "they" and "we." It is urgent, if the full abundant life of the Lord Jesus is to be shown forth in our day, that we all become "we." There must be the lived rediscovery that that which divides us is less deep, and less important, than that which unites us. What unites us is our membership in Christ's own Body, which draws us into the very life of the Father, through the Spirit, and places the substance of our being in *God*. If, though, we are all people of God, if we are all people on the pilgrimage to our eternal home, then it is certain that we should rub shoulders with each other, try to understand each other as fully as possible, and deepen ever more our mutual respect and trust in each other. It seems fundamental that we should be co-inspirers of one another.

The cooperation of laity and religious in the active works of the apostolate, the works of mercy such as education, hospital work, social work, become unlimited once we are willing to accept each other as co-partners to be trusted. Boards of control, boards of trustees, could and should be greatly strengthened in institutions owned and operated by religious by the addition of dedicated lay men and lay women who can bring specialized knowledge and techniques to bear upon the operations of our institutions. The day has passed when religious can ask laymen to contribute financially and to assist in the raising of funds, while denying them any part in the policy formation of the institution. In like manner, within the framework of our parochial schools, the religious must accept as full partners the parents of their students in the parent-teacher relationship. They should welcome the parish school board and use it as an instrument not only for effective action for the good of our schools, but also for beginning an exhilarating personal relationship among members of the laity, the clergy and the religious. So too, religious, when they are competent and knowledgeable, should be made welcome upon parish and diocesan boards to bring their particular experience and knowledge to the benefit of the entire parish. The cooperation of religious and laity in works of the poverty program, tutoring, and distribution of food and clothing, can be effective demonstrations of the Christian solidarity which exists among us.

The changes that I see being wrought and needing to be wrought are then the complete acceptance by religious and laity of each other as persons united in the common pursuit of perfection. They are Christians who should be looking for occasions on which to cooperate with each other in clarifying the meaning for our world of God's message: the sisters contributing mainly by being specialists in prayer and concentration upon the end of our existence; the laity by continually bringing to the fertilization of the religious spirit the impact of their involvement in all the clamoring problems of society. Both should unite forces to study, to pray and to serve.

Now let us look again at our norms. They urge that every means possible be used to promote the common life and fraternal cooperation. If the convent is, in the midst of all the sister's contacts with the lay world, to remain her best solace and most welcome home, its common life must be satisfying and nourishing. The norms call also for flexibility of the order of the day from convent to convent, but also for flexibility for individual sisters. If the role of the sister is to be as I have visualized it, one sees readily that the local superior will have to understand the varied demands of the sisters' commitments. In other words, she will be faced, in a much sharper way than is true now, with the task of building deeper community at the same time that there will be less uniformity than ever. This makes it clear that our efforts must be more directed to helping each sister build in herself a deep, personal commitment to Christ, so that, with her sister, she may indeed find herein "one heart and one soul" (Acts 4:32).

Our religious congregations exist to form and nurture women of prayer, of love, and of service. And *we* represent, under the Lord, the human agents mainly responsible for this formation and nurture. As such, our task today is more difficult, yet more wonderful than it was even in the recent past—before Vatican II.

Our generation has been granted significant insights which, as they are implemented, will largely and beautifully alter religious life. One such insight, to be emphasized here, is that external conformity does not produce the religious person. We have all undoubtedly experienced a feeling of inadequacy as we dealt with women who have never deviated from prompt fulfillment of every exercise, and yet are hard, judgmental, self-righteous, and proud. The literature of the past quarter century has dealt in depth with this phenomenon. On the other hand, it is not true to say that the really religious person does not conform. But we are escaping from that exaggerated mechanical concept of grace which associated its workings largely with the visible, observable, physical ordering of our actions.

Ours is so great an age in the history of religious life, precisely because *we are all asked to become founders*. In a real sense, of course, we are always founders, because by our observance or our disdain of each rule or point of discipline, we remold what is to be handed on to our successors. But in addition to this unconscious reconditioning of our structures we are today urged and commanded by the highest organs of the authoritative Church to rethink our structures, to refound our communities. Of course we have guide lines: sacred Scripture, the *spirit* of our founders, and the needs of our times.

What a wondrous opportunity! To place ourselves individually and as corporate groups at the disposal of the Holy Spirit, as we with our late-twentieth-century psyches read God's word and study our congregational origins! To seek the deepest meanings of relevance in meeting the needs of our own persons, of the contemporary Church, and of the poor, needy, and rudderless everywhere! To find the essentials of life in Christ and rebuild a fellowship upon them! The norms for *Perfectae caritatis* may sound formal and lifeless, but they arouse the poetry of great adventure.

The Religious Superior's Ministry

MOTHER ANGELITA MYERSCOUGH, AD.PP.S.
Ruma, Illinois

Not too long ago, every religious superior seemed to know what her job meant: taking charge of the community, issuing orders, giving permissions, having things well organized and running smoothly so that work and materialities as well as "subjects" were properly taken care of. Time was when you might find not a few superiors who could easily make their own the assured conviction of the Roman centurion when he tried to persuade Our Lord not to bother coming to the house to heal his servant-boy. "Just give an order," the official said, "and my boy will get better." With alarming self-assurance he went on to explain: "I myself know how authority works" (Mt 8:5-9). In the context of turmoil in which the Church of this post-conciliar period is laboring toward renewal, few dare be as sure as the centurion. Nor, in accepting the assignment to treat this topic, do I in any sense approach the question convinced that "I myself know how authority works." What I hope we can do is simply to think the topic through in a scriptural framework, and draw out a few practical conclusions.

We ask ourselves what a religious superior's ministry is, what he or she is meant to do. (In the present setting we may as well decide to talk about the superior as "she" or, rather, since so many of us are practitioners at the job right now, shall we say "we" or "I"?) We dare to ask so basic an identity-question because we are daughters of a Church which has been asking herself questions of like radicality. Pope Paul VI set the pattern when he told the bishops to ask just such a question— what is the Church herself? what is her mission?

Like the Church we want to ask our question in the light of faith. The talks and discussions in this Sister Formation Conference have made it clear that superiors have diversity of function. We are busy people with multiple roles—organizers, administrators, executives, principals,

143

fund-raisers, public relations experts, counselors. What we want to consider now is the superior's radical function precisely as religious superior; to assess, if we can, what it is the Spirit calls us to do, when in the course of our personal salvation history we are asked to serve a term as religious superior. Obviously we cannot and must not neglect the human, the psychological and sociological aspects of the work. Just now, however, we concentrate on the dimension that revelation gives for our task, for our ministry is primarily a *religious* exercise of authority in a community of faith.

When I speak here of a religious superior, I mean one charged with responsibility for directing a community of men or women religious. Primarily I have in mind local superiors, though I include all.[1] I do not distinguish the superior's ministry for the younger sisters, for I believe that our responsibility to them is essentially the same as it is for the rest of the sisters. I use the word "ministry" because it suggests service in a religious context. I employ it here in the New Testament meaning of *diakonia*, with the sense of a special kind of practical service for the Body of Christ, of which St. Paul enumerates many varieties in the churches at Rome, Corinth and Ephesus (Rom 12:6-9; 1 Cor 12, 4-11; Eph 4:11-12).

I. NATURE OF A RELIGIOUS SUPERIOR'S MINISTRY

A. *Vatican II Emphasis on Authority as Service.*

In paragraph fourteen of *Perfectae caritatis* we read this line that has already become a commonplace: "Let him use his authority in a spirit of service for the brethren." [2] Few themes are as basic and steady in conciliar teaching as is this theme of service. Already in their opening message to the world, the bishops proclaimed their intent to serve their brothers, after the pattern of Christ the Lord who "came not to

1. The word "superior" is inadequate, but it is used here because it is familiar; other titles that might be used are moderator, coordinator, chairman, president, minister, servant. Included here as "superior" are also the religious who serve as head of experimental groups which are trying to work out new structures, functioning without a superior in the formal sense that present canon law gives that term.

2. All citations from conciliar documents and the opening message of the bishops are from Walter M. Abbott, gen. ed., *The Documents of Vatican II* (New York: Herder and Herder, 1966).

be served but to serve." "The Church," they announced, "was not born to dominate but to serve." [3]

Yet it is a truism (of which Father Greeley has gently reminded us in a recent column)[4] that all human authority exists to serve the good of the members of the organization. Why then so stress the conciliar emphasis on authority as service? The first reason, I think, is the unpleasant fact that all too often in the past, sometimes in theory and sometimes in practice, authority in the Church was construed all too humanly as power, as domination and control, rather than as service, despite the fact that the successor of Peter had been signing himself since the sixth century as "servant of the servants of God." The council fathers wanted to correct whatever needed reform in this key area of the life of the Church. They seemed to recognize that if she was truly to be the "light of the nations" (Is 42:6, 49:6) in the modern world, the Church would once again have to manifest clearly (as the Decree on Ecumenism phrases it) "the features of Christ the servant"(§ 12).

Secondly, in using the servant terminology and theme, the council was drawing on an important scriptural insight. Today all recognize the centrality of the suffering-Servant-of-Yahweh theme in the New Testament. Indeed, this was *the* image in which Jesus chose to present Himself and His mission to Israel. More than any other Old Testament theme, the writings, especially of second Isaiah concerning the Servant of Yahweh, provided the primitive Christian community with the thematic for their earliest preaching of the mystery of Christ's saving death and resurrection. In the sub-apostolic age, the *Didaché* still used the servant theology, and Clement used it in the liturgical prayer of his first epistle. Beyond that, the servant theme did not continue as a strong characteristic of Christian thought or piety. It remains, it seems, for the Church of our time to recapture and explore anew the mysterious richness of this theme. The council points us in this direction, prompting all of us who bear authority to penetrate the meaning of the servant image (as well as, of course, the parallel image of the shepherd).

B. *Biblical Background of Servant Concept*

1. *General Old Testament usage.* The Old Testament is saturated with servant terminology. The psalms, for example, are the prayers of

3. *Ibid.,* p. 5.
4. Andrew Greeley, in *St. Louis Review*, 26 (Nov. 11, 1966), 16.

the faithful servant of Yahweh. The phrase "servant of the Lord" (*'obed Yahweh*)[5] was a term of nobility for a believing Hebrew, for it meant a faithful Israelite, called by Yahweh for a particular mission in behalf of God's people.

All the significant events in Israel's unfolding story of salvation were led by great servants of Yahweh—Abraham, Moses, Joshua, kings, judges, prophets. Theirs was the God-given mission to lead Israel in faithfulness to the covenant, to restore them to unity, to interpret the will of the Lord and the meaning of events. As those of us who are serving as religious superiors "take the Scriptures in hand each day . . . reading . . . and meditating" (*Perf. car.* § 6), we will find the Lord speaking to us through the example, the words, the deeds of these ancient servants of Yahweh. In their dealings with the Lord, in their dealings with God's people, in their grappling with personal difficulties, we can find guidance and courage. We can come to see that our mission as servants within our local community of God's chosen ones is in direct continuity with the work of Jacob and David and Jeremiah.

2. *Servant-of-Yahweh theme in Second Isaiah.* The classic expression of Old Testament servant theology is concentrated in the hauntingly beautiful poems of Second Isaiah, the great unnamed prophet of the exlie. Taking inspiration from the lives and deeds of all the great servants of the Lord before his time, the prophet limned the features of a mysterious servant in four beautiful poems.[6]

Tantalizing exegetical questions are raised by these passages. We must bypass them and simply note the portrayal of the servant. He is one of the *anawim* of Israel. Called by Yahweh for a special mission and endowed with His Spirit, he gives himself over faithfully to do the Lord's bidding. He is servant to his brother Israelites, whom he is called to liberate from captivity. Toward them he is patient, kind, humble; he is tender, sensitive to the needy. Yet more, he is destined to serve the nations beyond Israel, even to the ends of the earth. Fidelity to his mis-

5. In ordinary usage, the word "servant" or "slave" (*'ebed* in Heb., *doulos* in Gk.) carried the pejorative sense of submission unworthily of one man to another. In the biblical expressions meaning "servant of the Lord," however, it was a term of high praise. In Jn 15:15, when Jesus says that He calls His disciples not slaves but friends, the usage is this human pejorative sense. The image of "servant of the Lord" is one of many that are used in Scripture to express man's relationship with God. No image can ever fully express this reality.

6. The four poems are found in: Is 42:1-9; 49:1-13; 50:4-11; 52:13—53:12.

sion involves the servant in suffering, a voluntary sacrificial offering of his life for the redeeming of others. Through his sufferings, the servant is exalted by Yahweh and comes to glory.

3. *New Testament development.* We are all familiar enough with the Gospels to recognize how largely Jesus Our Lord utilized this Isaian servant image in presenting Himself and interpreting His mission to Israel, and how fundamental this theme was to the apostolic preaching and understanding of the paschal mystery.[7] From both the epistles and the Acts it is obvious that St. Paul understood Christ's work in terms of the servant thematic. Indeed Paul composed (or borrowed) his own servant song when he hymned the praise of Jesus who emptied Himself, taking the form of a servant, and so was exalted by God.[8] Paul's original development, however, was his realization that the community of Christians were to be identified now with Christ the Servant. Through them, the risen Lord would continue His service of preaching the good news, healing, bringing freedom, and suffering for the sins of the many. Paul delights in referring to himself as servant of his brethren, servant of the Gospel, servant of Christ, servant of the new covenant. He sees his sufferings as a fellowship and a filling-up of those of the suffering Servant, Christ Our Lord.[9] These Pauline insights obviously have inspired the teaching of Vatican II on the Church as servant, and the servant-vocation of all who have authority in the Church.

C. *Superior's Ministry Identical with Servant's: to Form Community of God's People*

1. *Scriptural basis.* In this light, we ask ourselves what is our function, our essential ministry as religious superiors. In the mission of the Servant of Yahweh, I believe we can identify our ministry. The mysterious servant of the exilic Isaian poems is called by God to serve his people

7. *E.g.*, the terminology of "beloved" and "chosen one" at Christ's baptism and transfiguration (Mk 1:11; Lk 3:22; Mk 9:7) reflects the Isaian servant titles; Christ's preaching and healing ministry is interpreted in Matthew as the servant's mission (Mt 8:16 ff.; Is 53:4; Mt 12:17 ff.–Is 42:1 ff.); the passion prophecies, much of the last supper event and teaching, and Lk 24 on the resurrection reflect the suffering Servant songs in Isaiah.

8. Phil 2:5 ff.

9. Paul identified his own vocation with that of the suffering Servant (Gal 1:15; Is 49:1-6); he interpreted his own labors as continuing Christ's servant mission (*e.g.*, Rom 10–Is 53:1; 52:7; 2 Cor 5:17-21); and his apostolic sufferings he saw as a sharing in those of Christ (Col 1:24; 2 Cor 4:7 ff.)

chiefly by leading them back from exile, forming them once again as
the Lord's assembled people (the *qahal Yahweh*). In the second poem,
the servant speaks thus:

And now Yahweh has spoken,
he who formed me in the womb to be his servant,
to bring back Jacob to him, to gather Israel to him (Is 49, 5a).

Through the servant's faithful commitment to the Lord, the whole people will be restored to covenant fidelity, for he himself, in a mysterious
way, *is* the covenant: "I have appointed you as covenant of the people" (Is 42:6). Yet the purpose of restoration lies beyond Israel.
Through this people God intends His salvation to reach to all mankind.

It is not enough for you to be my servant,
to restore the tribes of Jacob and bring back the survivors of Israel;
I will make you the light of the nations
so that my salvation may reach to the ends of the earth (Is 49:6).

The servant's mission, ultimately, is directed toward bringing together
all men as God's people.

Toward that goal, all revelation pointed. Prophets and poets sketched
in inspired imagery their vision of the unity of God's people: vine-
yard, sheepfold, flock, kingdom, temple, holy city Jerusalem, covenant
assembly, bridal union of Yahweh and Israel. For the achievement of this
goal, Jesus, loving Servant of the Father, labored. For this unity He died.
At the great supper of paschal covenant fulfillment He prayed: "Let
them all be one. Just as you, Father, are in union with me and I am
with you, let them be in union with us" (Jn 17:21-22). Having established the nucleus of a new people of God in His own Blood of the
new covenant, Christ sent the Spirit as bond of unity to make His
Church one Body, one communion in His love. The Church, the council
says, was made a "sign of the intimate union with God and of the unity
of all mankind destined to be a people made one with the unity of Father, Son and Holy Spirit." [10]

2. *Religious community.* Two thousand years of Christian presence
in the world have been a long, tortuous working toward that unity.
During these centuries, the Spirit has given to some Christians the
charismatic gift of entering into special evangelical brotherhoods (or

10. *Lumen gentium*, §4.

sisterhoods) within the Church, forming communities of "Christ's members living fraternally together" [11] (*Perf. car.*, §15). Their life-style expresses and pursues that unity in Christ which is the ultimate goal of God's salvific plan for the world. By their existence as gathered Christian fellowships, bound together inwardly by faith, hope and love, religious communities are meant to be a constant, dynamic witness to the community-reality of the Church and its unitive mission for mankind (*Lumen gentium*, §46). Religious communities, the Council reiterates, exist to be "ready for a ministry of service in building up Christ's body" (*Perf. car.*, §1). [12]

Now, within each community, each local community, all the religious share this ministry of building Christian community. The key person, however, by the laws of nature and of grace, is the one appointed with responsibility to serve the community with authority. Her service, our service, in the long tradition of the Servant-of-Yahweh theology, is essentially unitive. Our prime ministry, then, is to build up the whole Body of Christ through promoting genuine growth of the particular faith-community we are appointed to serve.

As superiors, our position is at the visible level. The essential unity to which we are called to direct our ministry is at the inner level of faith. What this means, then, is that as religious superiors we work in the visible, the tangible, the external level in such a way that we help create within our community a climate that favors inner growth in unity, which is the direct gift of the Holy Spirit. Ours is a ministry of so exercising authority that it tends to form this particular group of Christians into what they are meant to be, that is, a genuine interpersonally related fellowship of the baptized, who follow the Lord in the way of the Gospel counsels, working toward the upbuilding of the Body of Christ. To each of us, the servant vocation is addressed anew: "I, Yahweh, have called you to serve. . . . I have appointed you as covenant of the people" (Is 42:6).

11. For historical treatment of this concept, cf. Thomas Barrosse, C.S.C., "Religious Community and the Primitive Church," in *Review for Religious*, 25 (Nov., 1966), 971-85.

12. For additional references to this same idea, cf. *Perfectae caritatis*, §§5, 2, 14; *Lumen gentium*, §§43, 44, 45. Pope Paul VI emphasized the same idea in his address to nuns, May 16, 1966.

150

THE LOCAL SUPERIOR
II. HOW A RELIGIOUS SUPERIOR FULFILLS
HER MINISTRY

Our ministry as religious superiors, always working toward forming genuine Christian community, must be a service of love, for *community is the perfection of love*. Our task, we are told in *Perfectae caritatis* (§14), is to "reveal the love with which God loves" our sisters. How are we going to do that? Drawing our insights from the servant theme, we can see that this means we must be leaders in love. We must, first of all, lead our sisters in obedient, trustful love of Father, Son and Spirit. We must be leaders in fraternal love with our community of sisters. Finally, we must be leaders in redemptive love that is open to all mankind, fully embracing the cross that stands at the heart of the paschal mystery.[13] Let us look at these characteristics of our servant ministry with special attention to the statements in article fourteen of *Perfectae caritatis* that briefly sketch for us our task as superiors.

A. *Obedient Exercise of Authority—Leader in Love for God*

"For his part, as one who will render an account for the souls entrusted to him," we read there, "each superior should himself be docile to God's will in the exercise of his office." What does this imply for our ministry? It means that we try to echo in our lives the words of the Lord's great Servant, Christ Jesus, who said: "I do nothing on my own. No, I say only those things that the Father taught me. And the One who sent me is with me. He has not left me alone since I always do what pleases Him" (Jn 8:29; cf. Is 53:10; Is 50:4, 7-9). Here two basic demands are made of us: first, a realization that our ministry is a God-given trust; second, a faithful readiness to search out and to pursue whatever it is that the Lord seems to want for our faith-community.

1. *Trust in the Lord.* At this time when the whole Church seems somewhat disoriented and confused, in the midst of an alienated and despairing world where psychologically God does seem dead, when religious life is in a state of turmoil such as it has not been in for centuries, the need for religious superiors to live in strong and steady trust in the Lord

13. Cf. Thomas Dubay, S.M., "Renewal in the Exercise of Authority," *Review for Religious*, 24 (Nov., 1965), John L. McKenzie, "Authority and Power in the New Testament," *Catholic Biblical Quarterly*, 26 (1964), 413-22; and *Authority in the Church* (New York: Sheed and Ward, 1966), *passim.*

is the first imperative. No matter how the winds of prophecy or public opinion, of the Holy Spirit blow, we must remain firm in trust. What Isaiah wrote about the servant holds true for us: the Lord will send His Spirit upon us, the Lord will grasp us by the hand, and be with us, for He has called us to this work of being superior Himself. Of us as of the ancient servant it can be written:

Though he walks in darkness, without a gleam of light,
let him trust in the name of the Lord,
and rely on His God! (Is 50:10)

No matter how busy we are, we must somehow find the space for reflection and prayer that nourishes trust. The most important kind of openness for us is openness to the Spirit. There must be times when we seek solutions on our knees. I wonder whether there is any more urgent aspect of our ministry than to lead our sisters in the work of renewal, in a spirit of openness and much prayer, with steady optimistic confidence that the Spirit is indeed breathing in these winds of turmoil. Trust in the Lord is the first consequence, practically, of leadership in obedient love.

2. *Docility to the Lord's will.* The second aspect of a superior's exercise of authority is leading her sisters toward a loving unity based on humble, faithful commitment to Father, Son and Spirit. The superior must be first in obedient love. Now what I mean here by obedience is the definition the council gave it in *Perfectae caritatis,* and as Pope Paul VI stated it some time ago. The pope said:

Obedience, even before being a purely formal and juridical homage to ecclesiastical laws and submission to ecclesiastical authority, is first of all a penetration and acceptance of the mystery of Christ, who won our salvation by means of obedience. It is a continuation and imitation of this fundamental act of His: His acceptance of the will of the Father.[14]

It is of obedience in this sense that the council speaks when it directs us superiors to "be docile to God's will in the exercise" of our office.

Obedience reverses the great primeval temptation to be like gods, determining good and evil for ourselves. Much of the strong reaction today against authority in the Church, and in religious life in particular,

14. In an address to pilgrims at the Vatican, Oct. 5, 1966, cited in U.I.S.G. Bulletin on Special General Chapters, Via Pomponio Leto, 2, Roma.

may well derive from a too frequent yielding in the past to the very human temptation to identify or substitute the superior's will with the divine will, as if the superior were the sole determiner of good and of evil. This is a subtle way of yielding to what Jacques Leclercq has called the greatest temptation facing all who govern: that is, the impression that they can do whatever they like.[15]

No, superiors cannot simply do as they please. They *do not make God's will—they find it*. The servant of Yahweh was conscious of this search and of how the Lord had equipped him for it:

Each morning he wakes me to hear
like disciples do.
The Lord Yahweh has opened my ear (Is 50:4–5).

Vatican II asks of us religious superiors this same docile attitude of discipleship: it is our job to seek God's will together with our sisters. "Therefore the superior should listen willingly to his subjects" (*Perf. car.*, §14).

Successful renewal and proper adaptation cannot be achieved unless every member cooperates. . . . In decisions which involve the future of an institute as a whole, superiors should in appropriate manner consult the members and give them a hearing (*Ibid.*, §4).[16]

Does this mean, to quote comments not infrequently heard, that: "there's no more obedience in religious life; today, it's the subjects who decide everything; today, it looks as if everybody is supposed to do as she pleases; the young people want to be listened to—they don't want to be told what to do; they don't want to obey!" So runs the confused Jeremiad, and with some truth! Only a few weeks ago, Pope Paul answered this type of questioning with a reaffirmation that, of course, there must remain obedience, together with "wise and loving authority"—but for both, he pleaded for new forms that our own times demand, forms that will be "more profound, more virtuous, more worthy of ecclesial community, more in harmony with the spirit of Je-

15. "The Use of Authority," in John M. Todd, ed., *Problems of Authority* (Baltimore: Helicon, 1962), 254.
16. Cf. Norms for the Implementation of the Decree of the Second Vatican Council *Perfectae caritatis*, #4 and #19.

sus Christ." [17] The council has pointed us toward the goal of renewal in authority and obedience by emphasizing the fundamental mystery of Christ's acceptance of His Father's will as central in obedience, and authority.

To discover the Lord's will, we superiors must do many things, and we must do them together with our sisters. For principles of faith to guide us, we must return constantly to the word of God in Scripture, to listen as disciples do to what He tells us there. We must listen to His word of self-giving deed in each day's Eucharist. We must listen to His word echoed in the teaching and the laws of the Church, and in the specific interpretations of the Gospel in our own community spirit, its history, its constitution (with proper limitations, with revision under way). We search for His will also in directives of our superiors and in chapter decrees.

But this is not all: we must pay attention to the actual, human-dimensioned situation in which we live. We must open our ear to the needs, the talents, the insights of our fellow sisters. We must be attuned to the signs of the times, to the "physical and psychological conditions of today's religious," to "the needs of the apostolate, the requirements of a given culture, the social and economic circumstances" of our time and place (*Perf. car.*, §3). We must listen, for the Lord speaks therein.

As superiors striving for the obedient exercise of authority we must listen to all our sisters. We must promote dialogue. Young sisters speak without inhibition; we must not silence them too quickly, nor label their questions as disobedience or rebellion. Rather we must listen to what the Spirit may speak through them (and be alert to winnow out the chaff!) We must encourage middle-aged and older sisters to speak out, too. By our actions we must encourage all to listen to one another in love, to learn to differ with another's opinion without condemning the person, or to interpret as personal dislike a disagreement with our suggestion. I like to think of community as meaning the group of those who disagree in love. As superiors, we cannot any longer expect to be shielded from complaints; we must be alert not to take personal affront at suggestions for doing things differently from the way in which we have been proceeding. Obedient love for the Father means honest searching for the truth of things. It demands of us the humble maturity

17. "Discorso del Santo Padre all'Assemblea Straordinaria dell'USMI, 12 gennaie 1967," p. 3, on leaflets specially printed by Libreria Editrice Ancora, Roma.

of the Lord's servant who seeks the best advice available, even when that means turning to a young sister who happens to be the best informed or the most creative thinker.

Clearly the reason for consulting the sisters, for encouraging them to speak out, is not so that each can do as she pleases. This would mean the very opposite of renewal in charity, for this would canonize selfishness. To be free as a Christian never means simply to do as I please because I so please, for my own selfish interests—even if I try to label it "God's will"! To be free as a Christian means to be able always to do the things that please our Father, as did the free Son of God, who became obedient in love unto death.

When the moment of decision arrives, the superior makes it as servant-leader of the faith-community. Hopefully, that decision will correspond as closely as human insight can discern with the objective reality of what the Lord wants of this sister, or this community, in these given circumstances. No superior has a private charism of infallibility, nor is she impeccable or omniscient. That is why we must search out the Lord's good pleasure humbly and honestly. Perhaps we should advert to the fact that at times a superior is going to be humbly convinced that the decision the Lord really wants is not in agreement with the consensus of the sisters. These times may be expectedly rare, but when they occur, there is nothing to do but to make the decision that we are convinced is best, having listened and prayed and honestly searched for the truth. There will be times, too, when we may have to be firm when someone disagrees or rejects decisions made. Like the faithful servant of Yahweh, we will try not to bruise the bent reed nor quench the smoldering wick, but neither will the superior "flicker nor bend till justice be established" (Is 42:3-4).

Another aspect of this problem needs a moment's consideration. I speak of the present transition to a situation where there will be less detailed regulations and where more things will be left to the personal decision of each sister. Clearly, the extent to which we consult and the degree of our listening must be correlated to the importance of the matter. Small matters of group living that can be decided quickly and efficiently by the superior should be decided by her that way. Matters which sisters can more readily decide personally should be left to them to decide. By our own attitude of humble fidelity to the Lord's will, we can help our sisters make their personal decisions with the faith-inspired commitment that each is called to by the Spirit. We can help our sisters see that the Lord wants a modicum of good order in group living, through having some ordinary established policies that save endless decision-making on trivialities. Clearly, too, the Lord wants simple courtesy and good common sense in our interpersonal relations. Less detailed regulations will not cancel out these basic needs of the group.

Our ministry, then, as superiors forming community among our sisters, is to lead toward a unity that is built on faith-recognition that we have one Lord, who is truly Lord for us, whose good pleasure we seek with docility. Our leadership in the common struggle to discover the Lord's good pleasure can help each sister recognize the Christian prudence of accepting the final decision made by the superior as at least an approximation of the Lord's will in the concrete situation. Hopefully, too, this leadership on our part can help sustain our sisters with courage and joy in accepting the difficulties, when a decision is made quite contrary to their original suggestion. We can expect also that the communal search for the Lord's will may help eliminate false servility and infantilism, as well as aggressiveness and hostilities toward authority.

To live by the Lord's will as our communal norm gives an abiding impetus toward our ultimate communion in trinitarian love. If as superiors we humbly carry out our ministry of authority in the daily humdrum realities, then we are truly laboring for the progressive gathering-in of God's people. For all men and things will be unified in Christ only when the prayer He taught us comes to fulfillment: "Thy will be done on earth as it is in heaven." It is our ministry as superiors to lead toward that realization with firm, trusting love.

B. *Fraternal Exercise of Authority—Leader in Love for Sisters*

It was His own brothers of the house of Israel that the Servant of Yahweh was called to serve. Christ Jesus, though Lord and Master washed His disciples' feet, as one who serves. The apostolic Church was a communion (a *koinonia*) of brothers. A religious superior, too, is called to serve as brother among brothers, as sister among sisters, in a community of Christian love.

1. *Essential equality as persons, as children of God.* Fraternal exercise of authority means leadership in fraternal love. In essence, that means an exercise of authority between those who are basically equal, though on other grounds there may be a hierarchy. Superiors and sisters all stand together in loving obedience before the same higher authority of the transcendent Father.[18] Two cogent phrases in *Perfectae caritatis*

18. For some development of this concept, cf. Alcis Muller, *Obedience in the Church* (Westminster, Md.: Newman, 1966), 141 ff.

direct us toward such an exercise of authority: "Governing his subjects *as God's own sons,* and *with regard for their human personality,* a superior will make it easier for them to obey gladly" (§14). As servants of the Lord leading our sisters toward loving unity in Christ, we superiors should stand "in their midst as one who serves." We ought not to stand as one who is over or above them. Rather we should function fraternally within the community, at the heart of it. Through the mystery of our own Christian personhood, standing fraternally in the midst of our sisters, listening and directing, we who are superiors will most effectively form a genuine faith-community that bears witness to the Lord's living presence in this brotherhood, this sisterhood.

To govern with fraternal authority means that we respect each sister as person and as daughter of God. In the past we have insisted strongly on respect for authority. It will remain necessary, wherever human beings live and work together, that there be some who exercise authority for the ordering of common efforts toward common goals, and this authority must be respected. The conciliar documents take this for granted. Conversely, however, they also emphasize the need that those who are ministers of authority respect those whom they govern. The need for us superiors to maintain respect for our sisters, we must remind ourselves, continues even when they manifest apparent infidelity, crassly unChristian attitudes of hostility and aggressiveness toward us who bear authority. Traditionally, ascetic writers have stressed the need for subjects to try to see Christ in superiors, even in unholy and unreasonable superiors! That is still sound advice. But it is equally sound to suggest that we superiors try to see Christ, the sin-laden Redeemer, in our sisters in whom His image is obscured, perhaps terribly defaced. As superiors we must be first to follow Christ's difficult command of fraternal charity:

Love your enemies, treat those who hate you well . . . pray for those who abuse you . . . help them and lend to them . . . and you will be sons of the Most High, for He is kind even to the ungrateful and the wicked (Luke 6:28, 35).

To govern "with regard for the human personality" demands that we respect the uniqueness of each of our sisters, with her own gifts of mind, heart, emotions, background, heredity and education, her own God-given spiritual gifts and destiny. We must, with fraternal love, try to be trustingly open to each sister's uniqueness, willing to accept each

as she is. This demands of each of us a steady effort, by power of the
Spirit, to rise above our pettiness, our tendencies to mistrust, suspicion,
or jealousy in dealing with our sisters who are obviously better educated, more creative, more efficient, perhaps holier, than we are. The
insecurity of the present transition period probably triggers us to use
these defense mechanisms more than usual. We might also remember,
too, that over-insistence on uniformity, or needless uniformity, is a violation of respect for the uniqueness of our sisters. What will probably be
most helpful in this matter of accepting each sister as she is, will be our
humble and joyful acceptance of our own uniqueness. Each of us must
be willing to be the kind of superior that only she can be, granted her
gifts and her limitations. We must not forget the ceaseless variety and
diversity among the faithful servants of God's people down four thousand years of unfolding salvation history!

Respect for our sisters as persons demands that we respect their
minds, too. That is a reason for giving explanations of decisions, as far
as we prudently can, so that our sisters be able to carry them out in-
telligently. The emphasis that the Decree on Religious Life and the implementing norms gives to involving all members in renewal, shows
how important it is that we superiors do everything we can so that all
our sisters will understand the true situation of the whole community.
The principles of subsidiarity and collegiality that are an integral part
of conciliar teaching about authority in the Church are based on the assumption of genuine respect for each person. All that we said a few minutes ago about listening and dialogue in the communal search for the
Lord's good pleasure, presupposes genuine respect for our sisters as
intelligent, well-meaning Christian women.[19]

To govern our sisters as God's children, and to respect them as persons, demands that we be deeply interested in their steady growth toward full Christian maturity. This holds true not only for the young sisters, but for all, because all must keep growing in life, ever more abundant life. Because we have so many jobs to do and problems to solve, it
is easy for us superiors to exercise authority exclusively in administrative terms. Fraternal authority demands of us an effort to create a climate of growth. For that to happen, there must be room for mistakes,
space for trial and error and for risks. It takes genuine self-denying as-

19. Cf. many examples of God's servants in Scripture explaining situations and events to others: *e.g.*, Lk 24, Christ explaining His passion to the
two disciples on way to Emmaus; Acts 11, Peter explaining to Jerusalem
Christians why he baptized Cornelius.

ceticism on our part and real fraternal love to risk our own reputation
for the sake of our sisters. None of us likes to be considered inefficient,
careless, irreligious, or a poor manager. We so often try too hard to be
good superiors by making sure that every sister does just what we think
she ought to do. We are so tempted to "handle" the sisters, or to "manage" them. Especially if we are teachers or principals or hospital administrators, we may be inclined to treat our sisters as we do our pupils
or other subordinates in the office. Respect for our sisters calls for an
atmosphere in which they can, with reasonable and humble frankness,
state complaints and make suggestions, and expect to be heard. If we
have a real climate of growth in our community, our sisters can be less
cautious about watching for the moment we are in the right humor
for them to present proposals or questions that require our approval.
A climate of growth fosters mutual trust, too, when sisters know that
things told confidentially to the superior are going to be held sacred.

It is not easy to govern with fraternal authority. Yet this is the challenge of the servant ministry the Lord has given us. If, in the power
of the Holy Spirit who has been promised, we calmly do our loving best
to respond to the challenge to govern thus, then we will be faithful servants who are spiritually opening blind eyes, making the lame walk, and
the deaf hear. We will be setting free those imprisoned in the dark dun-
geons of their own selfishness. Only love that is a gift of the Spirit sets
men truly free. The Church wants our sisters to experience that love in
our dealings with them. It can be done. Here is one sister's comment
about her own local superior:

In my limited experience I would say that Sister N. is the best superior
I've lived with. Sister is really inferior in some respects when compared
with others. . . . I'm not sure if the word I want to use here is "humility"
but there is something about sister that brings her down off that pedestal of
being superior to being one of us. Sister is a member of our little community; she is not *the* member about whom all else and everyone else re-
volves. I don't fight to be an adult here. I am an adult and recognized as
such, responsible for many of my own decisions and actions, but not wholly
independent either.

Love liberates and opens the way for genuine Christian freedom. Christian community is the perfection of such love. It is our ministry as
superiors to lead toward that perfection through our fraternal exercise
of authority.

C. *Redemptive Exercise of Authority—Leader in Love for all Mankind*

We come now to the final point in examining our servant ministry of forming community: redemptive exercise of authority. Here we have in mind two aspects: first, openness to the world; second, readiness to bear the redemptive cross.

1. *Openness to the world—fostering apostolic involvement.* As religious superiors we are meant to be leaders in a redemptive love that embraces all mankind. Religious community is supposed to be community for the world. It should be a "sure seed of unity" (*Lumen gentium,* §9) planted by the Spirit, whose blossoms are not wasted on desert air. The mission of the servant of the Lord concerns the salvation of the nations, even to the ends of the earth (Is 49:6, 12). Christ fulfilled His servant ministry establishing in His blood a new covenant of people from all tribes and tongues and nations. Similarly, through our immediate fraternal ministry that deepens the bond of community among our sisters, we superiors are to be servants of the Lord whose vision goes to the far edges of mankind. It is our task to lead our sisters in community toward apostolic cooperation in the great continuing work of redemption, to lead them in concern for men in their complexities of social problems. Racial injustice, poverty, fair-labor standards, peace— we cannot remain unconcerned in any of these matters.

Perfectae caritatis directs us thus:

> Let him [the superior] give the kind of leadership which will encourage religious to bring an active and responsible obedience to the office they shoulder and the activities they undertake. Therefore . . . they should encourage them to make a personal contribution to the welfare of the community and the Church (§14).

Clearly the council bids us superiors do all we can to foster the fruitful involvement of our sisters in the paschal work of redemption, which is the Church's service to the world. The "active and responsible obedience" that this calls for will be an obedience in which there are less specific directives, few prefabricated answers to problems, and greater possibility of failure. Such obedience calls for adaptations that lead to honest practice of subsidiarity and delegation. To encourage our sisters to "make a personal contribution to the welfare of the community and the Church" will necessitate more flexibility in our routines and house rules. Paradoxically, it means allowing for the diversity that leads toward true sisterly unity. Redemptive authority means weighing the balance between present apostolic commitments and meeting new needs, facing questions and confronting situations where it is very difficult to discern what the Father wants us to do.

2. *Readiness to bear the redemptive cross.* These are difficult challenges. Redemptive authority means accepting the cross, bearing the burden of our ministry as superior. Today's urgency of adaptation and renewal brings us a very special fellowship in the sufferings of Christ. What one local superior wrote recently is typical:

I sometimes wish that everything that is to be done would be settled. I suppose the younger sisters don't mind the confusion and unsettled conditions. We oldsters have been living so calmly for so many years, that it is difficult to adjust ourselves.

Yet if our religious communities are to be effective signs of the kingdom for our contemporaries, then we superiors must lead in the difficult work of removing all that is obsolete, outmoded and meaningless in our religious-life patterns and practices. To do this responsibly causes painful tension in our keeping a balance between immature and ill-considered changes, and inflexible resistance to the far-reaching changes that are needed. Patiently we must bear the tension of differing viewpoints—between young and old, between those who oppose and those who favor change. Even if we try humbly to draw all our sisters into true community search for the Lord's good pleasure and into a true fraternity of love, we will probably sense a failure in attaining what we strive for. This may be our darkest sorrow. Awareness of our limited vision and insights, consciousness of our fallibility and sinfulness, of our failure to stand really in the midst as one who serves—these, too, form part of the everyday cross that Our Lord asks us to shoulder with redemptive love for the world. These are healthy crosses, if we confront them with joy and trust. They unite us with the suffering world, and remind us to share its sorrows, too, in fellowship with the suffering Servant who bore our pains and carried our sorrows all the way to paschal exaltation and glory! (Is 53:4; 52:13)

CONCLUSION

Let us return to our initial question: what is our ministry as religious superiors? Our ministry as servants of the Lord is to work toward the building-up of the Body of Christ through obedient, fraternal, re-demptive exercise of authority within the faith-community of sisters whom we serve. As servants, handmaids of the Lord in company with the greatest woman in history, we must be leaders in love: love for our Lord, love for our fellow sisters, love for all mankind.

Ours is a challenging ministry today. We must not be afraid. We must not fail to serve in love. As we celebrate the Eucharist with our sisters, we share together the cause of joy and peace, the very source of com-munity, for the fruit of the Eucharist is the unity of the Church. Through renewal together of our covenant loyalty to our Lord, we grow together in love that is strong enough to pour itself out in daily redemptive work for the world, docile to the Lord we serve, struggling together to know and to do His bidding. To lead our sisters, from our place in their midst, toward becoming true community within the great community of the Church, and so tend toward the final unity of all mankind—this is our ministry. Christ is with us in our service, giving us His Spirit, to serve with so much love that He can one day say to us: "Well done, good and faithful servant, enter into the joy of your Lord" (Matt 25:21).

COMMENT

by Sister M. Dorothy, B.V.M.
Chicago, Illinois

I AUTHORITY

Mother Angelita states that the role of authority in religious communities is one of service, whose end is the building up of the community of faith, and love. It seems important to me to stress further that authority is a function of love, and love presupposes some interpersonal relationship. This form of authority introduced by Jesus Himself was revolutionary: the leader would be the *diakonos*, the servant; the leader would be the servant, and, in this case, one rendering service in love. If we really believe the Christian message we will agree that the first duty of authority as well as of those under authority is to foster love, and each fosters love best by performing the works of love. Jesus went about doing good. Even more, Jesus, warm, openhearted, sensitive, anticipated needs.

As Father McKenzie says (and we can apply this to the religious superior):

What authority *can* do is show the Christian what the Christian life is—and move the Christian to desire the fulness of this life. [What authority in religion *can* do is show the religious what the Christian life is—and move the religious to desire the fulness of this life.] Authority will not do this by control but by the full proclamation of the gospel. . . . Authority proclaims the gospel by exhibiting in itself the Christian life to which all members of the Church are called. If authority does this it shows leadership.

Proclamation by action is true leadership, and it is the only kind recommended in the New Testament.

In speaking of St. Peter's concern, his loving concern for the flock, Father McKenzie says that Peter's love for them, that is, the Church,

162

will be the medium through which they experience the love of Jesus the shepherd. We are somewhat remote from ideas of domination when we read that Peter proves his love by feeding the flock, i.e., by loving service.

Consider St. Paul for a moment. His personal dedication to Jesus Christ is not conceived as something detached from his dedication to his Christians. In them and only in them could he find a real Christ to love and serve; for they are the body of Christ.

Authority for Paul was a function of love, a personal love directed to individuals whom he could name [it was not an organizational function].

Authority is *diakonia* only if it is service to real existing persons.

This then is my first point: in our present system, which apparently will undergo more radical changes in our lifetime, it does make a difference what the superior is, and says, and does and thinks. Let her then be an active inspiration to the other sisters, especially by following Christ in his exemplary role of *diakonos*, servant, one rendering service in love.

But my second point, and the one I consider the chief point, is this: perhaps the best service we can render to our fellow sisters is not to try to form them. The sisters, or better still, all Christians, share authority through the Spirit. To presume that we have a better idea of what they should be then they have, is, I believe, an error. We must, it seems to me, have the courage to let them be.

I don't mean to imply passivity: it's not a case of leave her alone—I'll keep my hands off; let her vegetate. Fromm says that love is the active concern for the life and growth of that which we love.

Father Kennedy says that authority implies a living relationship. "A child grows because the father is able to grow in the relationship. . . . The child grows because someone loves him enough to provide the healthy conditions in which he can grow." The relationship in which we are interested, that between superior and sister, should also be a dynamic one, that is, one characterized by growth for all parties involved.

Etymologically, authority means to make able to grow. For us it means to provide an atmosphere wherein each sister has opportunities for choice, and, therefore, opportunities for becoming the mature woman she has always hoped to be. (It is good for me to be reminded occasionally that we are supposed to be mature women among mature women.)

Katherine Byrne, in *New City* (September, 1965), makes a statement which might well be applied to authoritarianism in religious life. She says: "a child rendered artificially silent is annihilated, not disciplined. Discipline is freedom to act in the right way. It is acquired slowly and painfully through many opportunities for choice."

I wonder if the same criticisms could be leveled at us which have been directed toward canon law. In *America* recently an article by Father Peter Shannon on "Changing Law in a Changing Church" states that canon law has been criticized on these two accounts:

1) It is universal, detailed and specific;
2) It favors institutions rather than persons.

Haven't we been too specific? A sister says she is going to Dubuque. We are both experienced drivers, and I say to her, "Take the route through Beloit," and really, she much prefers the route through Freeport. What difference! Let her make the choice.

I apologize to Paul Tillich when I say this, but the courage to let be should perhaps be the chief characteristic of superiors these days. The risk involved is real. We shall find the sisters growing into individuals we never dreamed possible. But they will be themselves. Perhaps then we shall become more aware that our sisters are persons, unique individuals who should not be treated in a mass, and that they, as persons, are much more important than the institutions and structures which surround us.

An awareness of this individuality and concern for our fellow sisters as persons would perhaps prevent our falling into that deadly authoritarianism which depersonalizes the group members and reduces them to a mass. This kind of concern for the individual, this kind of awareness of the person, this kind of loving service, this kind of courage to let be, can only stem from the genuine selfless love of a true Christian leader.

COMMENT

by Sister M. Francine, O.S.F.
Joliet, Illinois

II THE JUNIORATE DIRECTOR

As a juniorate director, I have had illusions and have been disillusioned; I have dreamed dreams and have been made to face reality; I
have had faith in the juniorate program and in the junior sisters, and
I still have faith. As I read through the questionnaires, the realization
came to me, black on white, that all juniorate directors have also
dreamed; and much the same reality I faced was theirs to face. They,
too, have kept faith.

By way of comment on Mother Angelita's paper, I should like to
make use of the responses of juniorate directors in the following areas:

1. The juniorate director's goal for the junior sister while she is in
the house of studies;

2. The juniorate director's relationship to the same sister while she is
in temporary profession on the missions under the direction of a local
superior;

3. The relationship hopefully existing between the juniorate director
and the local superior;

4. The continuing formation or growth of the sister after her departure from the house of studies;

5. My conclusion will center on the dreams of the council fathers in
this regard as they set them forth in the documents of Vatican II.

A juniorate director of even one year's experience will underscore
the following response from one of her colleagues:

Working with junior sisters is a very special apostolate and provides many
opportunities for the director to come to a deeper understanding of how

165

to live the paschal mystery in her daily life. This calls for greater holiness
and is indeed a trembling experience and a challenge.

What are the goals of the sister entrusted with helping sisters to bridge
the gap between novitiate formation and full apostolic mission? She
wishes to form mature, Christian, religious women, imbued with the
spirit of her institute and able to grow in fulfillment. She plans the formation of a whole person through an integrated program of spiritual,
intellectual, apostolic and professional formation, so that each sister can
truly be a "daughter of the Church," eager and enthusiastic to fulfill her
role according to God's plan, thus bringing about the reincarnation of
Christ in her particular milieu.

    She tries to create a climate of growth in community through experi-
ences that involve awareness of the conflicts and needs of other persons
in the religious life, the Church, and the world community. She is there
to love, guide, support, share success and failure, and help the sisters to
live in the mature tension of human dignity and sinfulness. She exercises them in making prudent decisions, in growing in awareness of
apostolic possibilities, in being responsibile for their work, prayers and
studies, and permits them to learn by making mistakes. She does not
force them into a mold but is fearless in pointing out their faults. She
encourages a deep spiritual life, a sense of responsibility, and a generous attitude toward work and sacrifice. Finally, she attempts to produce an integrated person, coupling idealism with realism, confident
of her identity as a Christian religious woman, equipped with theological virtues, an intelligent understanding of her role as a sister, humbly
convinced of her continued need for formation, secure in her trust in
God, and eager to contribute to the growth of God's kingdom in obedience to the Church and her community.

    And the reality. The junior sister belongs to the human race. There-
fore, she does not progress at the same rate as every other sister in the
juniorate or scholasticate. When the juniorate director sends her out to
assume her assigned obedience and responsibility, she is quite aware of
the fact that the junior sister is not perfectly formed. Although she pro-
gressed during her five years of pre-service training, she is facing new
circumstances and new realities; she is sailing uncharted seas, and is
moving into a new environment with different and unexpected challenges. The sister who will now be her superior and guide is experienced
in school, mission life, convent life with other than peer groups, and
may not understand that the newcomer in this confrontation will need

a little time before she operates as securely or as maturely as she did in her pre-service surroundings. Patience, understanding, and love will certainly be called into play at this moment.

What is the relationship of the juniorate director to the sister who has left the scholasticate and is now engaged in full-time apostolic works? On this point, practically every juniorate director is in agreement that the local superior is now the key person in the life of the sister in temporary profession, and any function the juniorate director still maintains is only advisory. It would be difficult for a juniorate director to reach into the local mission and fully understand the situations existing there. She must not interfere with activities or policies of the mission nor lessen the influence of the local superior. She ought not to try to solve local problems nor take away from the competency of the local superior. She would definitely impede the maturity of the young sister if she continued direction in any absolute or structured form. However, there still is a relationship that ought to be guarded and preserved, especially when it is the custom in the community for the sister in temporary profession to return to the juniorate during the summer. Such a relationship is secured by letters, visits when possible, continued interest and availability, a yearly day of recollection, a guided reading program, etc. Wise local superiors will not expect a sister to review all the history of a problem with her, but will permit her to return to the juniorate director if a problem continues in new surroundings to be acute and yet solvable. The wise local superior will also be understanding of the trust and friendship that have been awakened in the young sister during juniorate days for the sister who has prepared her for her mission life, and will permit this to continue in a mature way. By so doing she will gain the esteem of the young sister, and will find herself to be very soon the trusted guide in matters of moment.

Perhaps this is an area where reality has been more difficult to accent, because juniorates were new ventures in every community, and the local superior often felt threatened by the junior sister. The present situation is better, and the future is much more rosy. Local superiors are better prepared now to see the value of the juniorate, to accept the young sister for who and what she is; and despite the millions of demands made on their time and attention, they are more cognizant of their role as the continuers of any formation that has been the policy of their community for young sisters.

You will not argue with me, I know, on the relationship that should exist between the local superior and the juniorate director. This is most essential for the health and sanctity of any community. A mutual trust and understanding, a spirit of cooperation and support, an open and frank and constructive critical approach to each other—all this should characterize this relationship. As a juniorate director I would want the local superior to understand that she has not received into her house a finished product, but that I have done my best with this sister up to this point, and that she still needs help to assume her new responsibilities, to live with different age levels gracefully and helpfully, to realize her potential in the service given her, to integrate her spiritual and apostolic life. I would want the local superior to uphold the formation program and to do all she can on her part to understand what the Church wants in the formation of sisters today. I would wish that she would recognize the junior sister as a unique individual, knowing that there is no typical junior sister. If she does this, then she will not give her special treatment, refer to her as the baby of the house, or tune her out when she presents her problem of adjustment to a life she finds different from her previous religious experiences. I would also like the local superior to create community in her mission house. The young sister today is taught to live community from the beginning of her postulancy, and her advent into a house more like a hotel is almost a disastrous experience. The common complaint is: "But there is no love there." My expectations of the local superior are contingent with her expectations of me. Therefore, we must be collaborators; we must discuss ways and means of working together more effectively. We must communicate our doubts, our beliefs, our satisfactions and our disappointments. We must understand and respect each other's rights, problems and efforts. Anything that will, with the help of God, produce for our community the sister who will be a living personification of Mary in her work in the Mystical Body is our common field of endeavor.

With this ideal collaboration between the local superior and the juniorate director, what are some of the ways in which formation can be continued after the junior sister leaves the scholasticate? The questionnaires yielded the responses that I think are quite natural and apparently show a common consensus of opinion that a complete cessation of formation should not occur after the juniorate. Many communities have weekly instructions given by the local superiors. In other communities the discussion in the local houses for all the sisters supplants this, and the junior sister is taken into these discussions on an equal basis with the other sisters. A coordinator of the formation program has been established in some communities and this sister visits the junior sisters several times a year. The juniorate director herself visits the missions or conducts a day of recollection in specified places to which the junior sisters can easily travel. In many communities the junior sister, as long as she is in temporary profession, returns to the motherhouse for the summer program, which is both spiritual and intellectual. In other communities a Christmas renewal program for the junior sisters is held in the motherhouse. The summer before final profession in most communities is devoted either entirely or partially to spiritual renewal. Many juniorate directors write a monthly open letter to all junior sisters in something of a conference fashion, and personal letters as frequently as they are wanted or needed. Continued classes in the constitutions, guided reading programs, self-appraisal programs, specific persons assigned to be of help to the junior sisters, are other ways in which the formation is continued. No matter what has been established by a community in this regard, it is imperative that when the junior sister leaves the motherhouse or house of studies, her continued formation should not be neglected.

This brings me to the final point, the dreams of the council fathers in regard to formation as manifested in the Second Vatican Council documents.

Perfectae caritatis, after stating that adaptation and renewal depend greatly on the education of religious, stresses positive necessity of juniorates:

Consequently neither non-clerical religious nor religious women should be assigned to apostolic works immediately after the novitiate. Rather, their religious and apostolic formation, joined with instruction in arts and science directed toward obtaining appropriate degrees, must be continued as needs require in houses established for those purposes.

Later, describing the continuing formation it says:

Superiors therefore should give serious attention especially to the spiritual training to be given members as well as encourage their further formation.
   Religious should strive during the whole course of their lives to perfect the culture they have received in matters spiritual, and in arts and sciences. Likewise superiors must, as far as this is possible, obtain for them the opportunity, equipment and time to do so.

In the Decree on Mission Activity we read:

Habits of mind should be earnestly exercised already in his time of training;

they should be cultivated, and should be uplifted and nourished by the spiritual life. Imbued with a living faith and a hope that never fails, the missionary should be a man of prayer.

Elsewhere, the same decree enjoins that beside the moral and spiritual training required, the missionary

must have the spirit of initiative in beginning, as well as that of constancy in carrying through, what he has begun; he must be persevering in difficulties, patient and strong of heart in bearing with solitude, fatigue, and fruitless labor. He will encounter men with an open mind and a wide heart; he will gladly take up the duties which are entrusted to him. . . .

This, as well as this next injunction, is applicable likewise to all of us:

The heralds of the Gospel, lest they neglect the grace which is in them, should be renewed day by day in the spirit of their mind. Their ordinaries and superiors should gather the missionaries together from time to time, that they may be strengthened in the hope of their calling and may be renewed in the apostolic ministry, even in houses expressly set up for this purpose.

Any dream manifested in the Decree on the Lay Apostolate can be realistically true of religious also. The document says:

He should not cease to develop earnestly the qualities and talents bestowed on him in accord with the conditions of [his] life, and to make use of the gifts which he has received from the Holy Spirit.

In a special way, however, adolescents and young persons should be initiated into the apostolate and imbued with its spirit. This formation must be perfected throughout their whole life in keeping with the demands of new duties which are assumed.

The fact of the necessity of continuing formation is more forcefully repeated in the following passage:

Since the apostolate cannot consist in theoretical instruction alone, from the beginning of their formation the laity should gradually and prudently learn how to view, judge and do all things in the light of faith to develop and improve themselves through working along with others and thus enter into active works and service to the Church. This formation, always in need of improvement because of the increasing maturity of the human person and the proliferation of problems, requires an ever deeper knowledge and adapted activity. In the fulfillment of all the requirements for formation, the unity and integrity of the human person must be kept in mind at all times so that his harmony and balance may be safeguarded and increased.

Two passages from the Consitution on the Church serve as a closing to my contribution to this panel since they stress the formation unto the end. We read:

Let each of the faithful called to the profession of the evangelical counsels, therefore, carefully see to it that he persevere and ever grow in that vocation God has given him. Let him do this for the increased holiness of the Church, for the greater glory of the one and undivided Trinity, which in and through Christ is the fount and the wellspring of all holiness.

All the members ought to be molded in the likeness of Him [the Holy Spirit], until Christ be formed in them. For this reason we, who have been made to conform with Him, who have died with Him and risen with Him, are taken up into the mysteries of His life, until we [and the addition is mine], "those who form and who are formed" [since reciprocity of action is evident here], reign together with Him.

The Understanding Superior

SISTER ROSE ADELAIDE, S.C.
Cincinnati, Ohio

Although the Sister Formation Movement was generated nearly two decades ago and is progressing on national as well as international levels, much help and guidance are yet needed for local superiors in understanding their role in formation—especially in their work with young sisters. It would be next to impossible to train all of the local superiors, currently in office, who have not benefited from the type of pre-service programs now being developed. However, it is possible for many of them to draw readily on several of the broad principles of the formation program to assist in solving some immediate problems.

In keeping with these principles each local superior must understand:

> *First*—that what served past society will not serve it today. This is because of the rapid change of the past decade—changes involving family living, social values, educational aims, economic opportunities, class structure, etc.

> *Second*—since the local superior is the one most directly responsible for the "in-service" training of these young sisters, she should recognize that a balance exists between the spiritual, intellectual, social, apostolic and professional facets of formation. This thinking is necessary, if each sister is to fulfill worthily the canonical mandate of doing the specific work given her by the Church.

Sister Bertrande Meyers in *Sisters for the Twenty-First Century* states that, in our present setup, local superiors are principals of schools and executives of many and varied offices. Manifold responsibilities and directives from school or hospital authorities keep them from having

172

large blocks of time for the close supervision and attention to counseling of the young sisters which less harassed administrators had in the past. Thus it is good that sisters are coming to the local superior as well-prepared religious, and as completely grounded as possible in the spiritual and social life of the community.

On the other hand, Father Eugene Kennedy, M.M., in his speech in August, 1965, to major superiors, pointed out the fact that much valuable time is spent by local superiors in handling the problems of maladjusted or psychologically shattered religious. Blame was placed on recruiting in quantity rather than quality. We agree with Father that time which could be spent helping the well-adjusted, normal and healthy women to become greater, better trained and advised, is frequently spent in patching up difficulties or in planning ways to avoid trouble from the misfits who have been permitted to join community ranks. Many of our convents have become rehabilitation centers. Is the superior, then, expected to do a balancing act as untrained psychiatrist and spiritual guide to those whom God must surely love, but does not expect to undertake a life they are unable to lead?

Much of the screening is done now by testing before entrance, and by dismissal during the postulant, novitiate, or juniorate years. However, the first years with a local superior in a school or hospital setup often bring to light unwholesome characteristics and adjustment difficulties which do not appear in larger groups. Required periodic reports to their superiors make it possible and of obligation in the best interest of the Church and community for the local superiors to make known serious difficulties or maladjustments.

One trait most important for those undertaking the role of superior today is understanding. A superior must be aware of the variety of connotations underlying the word "understanding." It is a characteristic frequently looked for in superiors but not as frequently found.

To define it is rather difficult. Those possessing it must have a broad grasp of human psychology, or a practical grasp of human traits made possible by serious personal study and experience. They must likewise be able to put themselves in the position and mental frame of the other person, to try to see how a matter appears to them before a decision is made. An understanding superior is never unduly disturbed by a wrong, and at the same time takes steps to right what is wrong. She treats insignificant difficulties or infractions as insignificant.

Younger people resent (often silently) the superior who offers "pat" solutions to every situation, one who tries to fit all into the same mold.

They admire the understanding which shows itself in a sincere love, displayed by taking time for each as an individual, offering a warm welcome even to the delinquent, and creating a family spirit of trust and affection. Real understanding should curtail early feelings of frustration, help toward permanent solution of problems, and give a spirit of mutual trust and cordiality befitting the elite members of Christ's Church. But characteristics comprised in what we call "understanding" are the most elusive in human life.

Another important task for superiors is to preserve a sense of values. Foremost must be the ability to recognize the importance of person over things, or relationships over customs, and of the family over any organization. It is strange how easily we become preoccupied with the need to organize efficiently. Is this urge for well-ordered things the reason why religious houses usually look as if nobody lives in them?

Superiors are charged with the responsibility of assisting to build communities, not community centers; of letting others experience love, not power. "The heart of the young," Freya Stark tells us, "goes out to people who have a feeling for the living space of other human souls." There is a way to God through small things, but there is no reaching Him through petty things. Christianity surely will mean little to souls in the hands of one whose main concerns are skirt lengths and schedules.

One of the titles which future generations may affix to our times is "The Age of Automation." It should be realized that certain dangers are attached to dependence today, upon mass production and mechanical control. Superiors must be on the alert lest this same blind, automatic obedience be transferred to constitutions, rules, and customs of the order. Here could be a spirit of the world carried into the religious life under the mask of virtue.

In a recent *Sister Formation Bulletin* we were reminded of the need for being aware of the uneasiness and agitation in this world of change. Young people are imbued with this spirit. Four dangers underlying these world conditions were listed. All four dangers began with the letter "d." They are:

First the danger of *dilettantism*—or the fascination with being everything, as is in the tendency to be "go-ers," "name-droppers," and such. It includes having a superficial involvement and surface enthusiasm which often discourage those in earnest.

Second is the danger of *dissipation*—or a weakness spreading from individual to community. With this, the extra or outside work becomes so interesting or time-consuming that energy is spent before primary matters are given proper attention. Thus, assigned work is neglected for what appears to be more apostolic or ecumenical.

The third danger is *dissatisfaction*—or thinking our community pace is too slow, and our work at renewal is retarded.

The fourth is the danger of *disillusionment*—or thinking our community has let the Church down by refusing to exploit the potential of so many of its gifted members.

We may take a cue from the eagerness of youth to be up and doing by abandoning some of the trivia in our lives, and the uncoordinated round-about delays in accomplishing the assigned work. We must remember also that experience is a valuable resource and needs to be tapped regularly.

The superior's role is above all a spiritual one. It is likewise human, since it is her task to influence the spirituality of human persons. But her obligation is to govern people, and not only to administer things; in this she must manifest interest in the care of the interior life and not merely in external order and regularity.

The local superior must make certain to acquaint each sister with the fact that a religious community is not a commercial, industrial, or professional organization based on self-interest, but is a state of perfection founded on the desire of each person to seek personal sanctity, and to cooperate with Christ in the sanctification and salvation of souls.

St. Paul's epistles frequently center on three reminders: *instruct, exhort,* and *admonish.* What better framework could local superiors use in carrying out their responsibility in formation?

We know of no instruction which is more effective than example. Father Joseph Gallen, S.J., lists fifty qualifications for superiors. In summing them up he states that a superior must be a very superior kind of person, an example of every virtue, especially humility, and the possessor of the highest qualities even on a human level (including a sense of humor).

Over and above the instruction given by example, an important responsibility of the local superior is to give periodic formal instruction to those not perpetually professed. Any topics of practical concern or current interest to community living could be utilized in a group discussion or collective meditation, as well as in formal instruction.

Superiors best follow the counsel to exhort by considering each sister as an individual. If exhort may be interpreted to mean "encourage," then many opportunities will present themselves for the practice of this precept.

The negative duty of the superior, but one with a positive purpose, is admonition or correction. There are manifest signs that superiors are failing to correct, and the principal reason without doubt is that subjects universally resent correction. The substantial cause is pride. But, a superior who habitually fails to correct ceases to be the primary directive force in helping a religious attain her vocational ideal. To take correction is not easy, to give an efficacious correction, in many cases, is even more difficult.

Most sisters in early formative years are eager to do what is the right thing and they accept suggestion wholeheartedly. They should be told personally of matters in which they are not measuring up. It seems unfair that often they are not made aware of their faults until they apply for vows, and a report of failure is read to them by the mother or provincial general.

Correction will without doubt help to lessen the frustrated and empty lives we see so often in the middle-aged or aging religious whose lives appear to contradict their vocation; those who are idle, who have returned, even physically, to their family and relatives, who are immature, who are absorbed in a social life, or are obsessed by sports and television, whose teaching and apostolic work is mediocre; and those who live apparently with little or no consciousness of their religious state.

Many defects that have seriously impaired the lives of religious later, can be corrected or minimized in early years without demanding heroism in effort or constancy: for example, indolence, a hasty temper, irritating mannerisms, pretentious speech-mannerisms, talking too much or too little, coarse language, a "tough-guy" exterior, talking too much about oneself, and an exaggerated idea of one's abilities. A superior should surely pray for God's help in this duty of correction as well as in all others. All efforts will fail unless God touches the will by His interior grace.

The ultimate aim of the superior must be to advance the glory of God as well as to promote sanctity in the house and institute. The immediate objective, however, should be care and anxiety for the sanctification of the individual subject.

Apostolic Aspects of the Local Superior's Role

VERY REV. MSGR. D. JOSEPH CORBETT
Rector, Cathedral Latin School
Washington, D. C.

The precise apostolic aspect of this Conference's theme—The Role of the Local Superior in the Continuing Formation of Sisters—sounds and is both current and complicated. It also stimulates; makes us look within; forces us to confront and to struggle. It is part of the present-day-life crisis that surrounds us, where we experience both the opportunity and the danger, the promise as well as the threat, the hope of growth as well as the specter of deterioration.

My reflections are the perspectives of a priest; I have not the slightest intention of being dogmatic in any sense. I have only some suggestions, some questions, and a few recommendations.

Your experience certainly has taught you that achievements always bring more problems than failures. While you rejoice in the success of the Sister Formation Conference, you must be prepared at the same time to face the problems that inevitably come with success. Crucial to the development of the religious life in our time is the unique and pivotal presence of the local superior. It is the local superior who provides the leadership and initiative in the formation of a true community of worship and service. Under her inspiration and by her formation, the spirit of the community and the founder's dedication are kept alive and vital.

The responsibility of the superior is to all the sisters; her work must guarantee that this community be bound together without any divisive elements, despite generation gaps, education gaps, formation gaps. The local superior stands in the middle of a series of vital relationships involving the whole religious family; her leadership is manifest in many ways, but especially in her recognition that every segment of the religious house supplies a wealth of its own—the enthusiasm of youth, the experience of years, stability in religious life, wisdom born of struggle, maturity developed in diversity of assignment.

A tremendous asset to the local superior's apostolic leadership would be the development within the community of what might be called a "philosophy of formation." Such a philosophy would involve a dynamic synthesis of the intellectual, professional, spiritual and apostolic goals of the community. The harmonious blending of such a formation would of necessity be: *developmental,* according to the maturity and growth patterns of the sisters as persons, women, and religious; *consistent,* applied at all levels of religious life with varying intensity, yet always consonant with the purpose and goals of the community; *mutually fostered and refined* with the local superior assuming a guidance role of vital importance. Such a philosophy would involve a deep and satisfying insight into the nature of the religious vocation, positive formation in the spirit and work of the community, and a clear understanding of the relationship between the apostolic life and the community existence of the sisters. It would demand continued communication in apostolic perspectives within the total community, especially in the matter of new trends or emphases in the apostolate, the presentation of the gospel spirit in new accents to meet the new needs of the Church, with a built-in capacity for change and flexible adaptations, emphasis on the supernatural nature of the religious life, and clear presentation of answers to the two questions, "Who am I?" and "What am I about?"

Living in days of extremes, the important word for all our endeavors would seem to be "balance"! There is some validity in the concern of many that our intellectual and professional preparation be balanced by a more solid spiritual and apostolic growth as well. We must seek more than human excellence, more than a humanistic perfection in our program of personal development. Holiness of life and consecration of spirit are linked irrevocably to our vocation of service and witness. Professionalism makes heavy demands on time and interests; there is a real danger that the intellectual formation, accompanied by isolation from the real work of the religious community, might actually dim the desire for personal service. It is the religious sister who must emerge from preparation. We are concerned, and we must be, about new approaches, new areas of the apostolate, widening responsibilities and broader visions—all signs of a true and generous response by the alert religious aware of the needs of the Church today. But while we are concerned about the real needs of humanity, let us not become unmindful of our attachment to divinity. The need for God and His grace is always a relevant conviction; the teaching of the Gospel is central to every age. The purposes of the apostolate, no matter how ennobling, can never diminish the value of personal prayer, community life, community worship. Without these ingredients in our life, our apostolic endeavors will become mere movement, without direction and without inspiration.

As the Constitution on the Church in the Modern World warns us, ". . . the future of humanity lies in the hands of those who are strong enough to provide the coming generations with reasons for living and hoping" (§31). Our spiritual life gives us these reasons; without a sound spiritual existence, even we may begin to wonder about the reasons for living and hoping.

The apostolic formation of sisters should involve healthy experimentation within the essential framework of the community's work in the Church. There is no doubt that educational communities will become increasingly involved in adult education programs, Newman apostolate, urban centers, parental education, retreat work for adolescents, inter-community projects, inner city apostolates, etc. The educational mission of the Church is so varied in scope that there is ample opportunity for diversity of function within the same community. The local superiors will be alert to seek and provide opportunity for involvement of interested and capable sisters, provided there is no danger of dissipation or danger to health, and provided the essential task to which the sister is assigned is carefully and professionally cared for.

Success and happiness in our apostolic endeavors depends in considerable measure upon our mature view of celibate love. The virgin consecrated to God has a message for the community of Christians, but one that risks being misunderstood or ignored by the community of believers. The motivation of the celibate is altogether unique, in that the total gift of self to the present task is an entirely special type of consecration, a truly fulfilling kind of love, which provides the stable joy of fidelity in Christ who is our fulfillment. Much of our work is like throwing pebbles down a deep well; we do not hear the splash of our efforts. "The world in which we live and the way in which we converse with this world is a gift of others who went before us" (van Kaam, *Personality Fulfillment in the Spiritual Life*). We benefit from the rich sowing of the holy people who have preceded us in the service of the Lord. "To give and not to count the cost; to labor and not to seek for reward" is the motto of the celibate. Our love is a truly sacrificial love blending poverty and chastity into a generous gift of self that does not supply immediate and visible gratification; this fulfillment, unlike that of a woman who is mother, guardian, and teacher to her own children, does not come to those engaged in teaching and nursing and social service. Part of the sisters' apostolic formation must include an insight into the rich satisfactions of the religious life, even though these satisfactions are less tangible and less sensible than those of other women. Our marching and moving generation finds this virginal love of others a difficult generosity—and so it is—yet so much of our effectiveness and our appreciation of our tremendous contribution to growth in others depends upon grasping solidly this concept of celibate devotion.

Part of the apostolic formation of the religious community will be the presentation of the educational dimensions of the social apostolate, and the social aspects of the educational apostolate. Of late, there seems to be present in our writing a gigantic myth that all the action of the Holy Spirit is rooted in the inner city, and that this same Holy Spirit seems to have abandoned the classrooms of the country, as well as the hospitals and social institutions for the young and the aged. The enormous social ills of our day cannot be solved merely by the presence of religious in the inner city. The preeminent task of Christian education, made more demanding than ever by recent national studies on the educational programs of the Church, may not seem as glamorous as walking in a picket line, visiting the poor, caring for expectant mothers, or marching for justice in housing and employment. But when the picket lines have been walked and their causes won, when the poor have been visited and served and their ills alleviated, when the social ills of our day have been exposed and diminished, the remaining and most important task will be the quality performance of the "impact" teacher who offers the seed of God's truth in accents of love and devotion.

Part of apostolic formation, however, will certainly be exposure to various areas of social interest and social service. Visiting the sick, caring for the mentally ill or the retarded, aiding in various inner city educational and social projects—all will reveal the vast preparation necessary for a quality performance in such areas of the apostolate, and the opportunity to serve in these programs will take away some of the unrealistic glamor that may surround such programs, especially in the minds of those who have never experienced them. There cannot be and should not be any conflict between the social and the educational mission of the Church today. While the traditional role of the teaching and nursing sister has been subject to some vocal, adverse criticism of late (and this criticism has often come from religious women!), some of the statements have been undoubtedly irresponsible. (Some contemporary writing on the religious life and the apostolates of teaching and nursing has been both bitter and empty.) The local superior in her leadership role within the community should discuss these points of view, and strive to inculcate a questioning and discerning spirit so that truth is not confused with mere hypotheses.

The clear and strong relationship between the teaching and the social apostolates in the Church today is manifestly clear in that many of our current social ills are the result of educational failures in the past, while many social crises will find their stable and long-range solutions only in increased quality education.

A strong factor in apostolic enthusiasm will be the healthy openness which authority supplies to the life of the community. Linked with the mature relationship of true sharing is the instilling of confidence into the lives of the sisters. When friends, classmates, and relatives are so personally involved in the giving of self to husband and children and community, the sister needs a comparable sense of self-donation. Without such a recognition, she may begin to feel that her mission is indeed weak and impoverished. The apostolic outlets of the religious life must include some opportunity for humanness that is deeply personal. It is quite imperative to inject here the further thought that the superior must keep the confidence of the sisters—both personal and familial.

What Dr. Tom Dooley said of the doctor is equally true of the local superior: "doctors can cure sometimes; can relieve often; but can always be compassionate." A most important element of this compassion is the formation of a community in which the apostolic approach to others is humanly full and satisfying. There should not be even the appearance of any sterile concept of service. Such compassion will manifest itself in many ways—but especially in the provision for a fine spiritual library in the convent, the opportunity for honest and fruitful discussions within the community of the "problems that unite a family," freedom and leisure for attendance at lectures, seminars, institutes of value for the spiritual and apostolic strength of the sisters, and an abundant supply of listening love.

The impetus to apostolic effort must flow from a true and valid concept of the religious vocation, not as an event in the past to which

I responded with love and generosity, but as a consciously present Person to whom I am responding at this moment in my life. More than analyzing and proclaiming our seeming irrelevancies, we might better spend our time revealing to our communities the glory that is ours, loving what we are, and loving what we can become. Too many of us seem obsessed with our image and much less concerned with our reality. True, the modern image may be a burden that we would rather not have to carry with us, but the integrity of our lives will provide the new image that will be no barrier to communication, and will, in fact, invite the accepting approval of the young who discern the reality of things and persons with a special facility.

The superior should be well informed concerning the apostolic formation of the novitiate and the juniorate. If her role is that of continuing formation, it seems obvious that she herself must be convinced that what the young sisters of the community are receiving is worthy of being continued. In fact, for the sake of continuity in the religious life of the sisters, it seems imperative that the local superior positively endorse the work of the juniorate and see this preparation as practically linked to the life of the sister on active mission assignment.

The local superior will certainly be more inclined toward such enthusiastic approval if the early work of formation involves no isolation from the real work of the community, and if the local superior is in some way involved in the formation of the young religious. A definitely difficult factor in the apostolic formation of a total community is the public relations task of the superior in preparing the present community of religious to accept and to absorb graciously the new life that comes from the juniorate programs. At the same time, since the function of local superiors relates very importantly to the apostolic formation of all the sisters—including her own formation—such previous knowledge and understanding will be of immeasurable value. In this way, there will be no overemphasis on attention to the youth of the community as if they contained all the wealth of the religious family. Nor will they be ignored and neglected as if they had nothing to contribute. The members of the religious community cannot be allowed to think that religious formation is the sole burden of the superior; the formation must be seen as a community endeavor. In this way the formation will be more solid and consistent, and the mutual sharing in a common endeavor will weld together a richer family life and offer a much-needed support to the superior in her increasing service to the sisters. In this way, too, there is highlighted the truth that much of our present crisis in religious life centers not so much on the crisis of authority, or the crisis of obedience, as on the crisis of community. The formation of a community must become the cardinal concern of all, lest the local superior find herself in the unenviable position of presiding over a divided house.

This group endeavor will provide a more sympathetic and compassionate relationship with the local superior. She will be respected as a sister of known stability who is conversant with the signs of the times, experienced and self-possessed, of sound inner religious strength with ability to bear up under the stress and strain. The manifest joy and serenity of her own life will be in itself a requisite base upon which to build apostolic desire and zealous performance in the service of God. The local superior must be secure and communicative. The right person can be taught these things, and perhaps "teachability" should be considered in the appointment.

Since the local superior's first and most important duty is to the sisters of the house, the growing policy of limiting the superior to this one consuming task and not burdening her with any administrative assignment in the community seems to have much value. Perhaps the greatest gift the superior gives to her sisters today is her time; her availability is perhaps the greatest part of her poverty. If the superior were removed from all administrative functions (although she must engage in the normal apostolic work of the community) this assignment in itself would highlight the community's concern for the good of all the sisters and greatly enhance the local superior's position in the community. Also, the local superior's active engagement in the apostolic functions of the community bring her even closer to her sisters, indicate her appreciation of their problems in the practical order. The superior's cooperative work, under the leadership of the principal or administrator, will also be an example of the type of community cooperation so much desired by all. The superior, then, is a contributing member of the apostolic effort, and not just the guide, leader and educator.

If the local superior's role of service to the sisters and the apostolic work of the community is to be of a high caliber of excellence, and still a deeply personal service to the sisters, it seems to me that a cumulative informational record of each sister should be available to the superior. This record, comparable to the professional summary of a teacher, or the up-to-date record of a staff member in a governmental agency, would indicate the strengths and weaknesses of the sister, her talents, past assignments and involvements in the apostolate of the community. Such a cumulative record is indispensable for the guidance of the sisters as well as for their appointment to the various missions.

Self-criticism that is positive and constructively charitable is vital for the growth of religious life in our country. The superior with the closed mind is like the woman with the walled-up heart—both are traitors to their own humanity. The local superior, in love with her community, must impart the vigor and the spark of the founder's dreams; she must revere antiquity—but not be bound by it. St. Cyprian's words have special meaning for her: "Custom without truth is only the antiquity of error; and the Lord did not say I am the custom; but I am the truth." The local superior must be a woman of the tradition; and a woman of the tradition today is a woman of the Council. The local superior must also be relevant, alive, fulfilled, contemporary, and involved in the real action of life! She will be all of this if her heart is readied for the guidance of the Holy Spirit, and her apostolic leadership exhibits flexibility and an abundance of prudent judgment, if her whole life speaks to her sisters of her genuine concern for them.

The role of spiritual and apostolic guidance is the indispensable task without which all psychology and all human competence is so much straw. The local superior is expected to bring to life in her sisters a vibrant faith, apostolic enthusiasm, culminating in and flowing from a community of worship and love. It is through the acquisition of these various elements of community that the superior will draw members of her household to her as leader and thus strengthen the unity within the family.

This is a task that calls for more than human excellence and efficient organization. This task which is so central to the religious life of the Church calls for local superiors to be living parables of the kingdom; the local superior must be a superior person, a superior Christian, a superior religious!

Prudent Guidance of the Young Sister

MOTHER M. THOMAS AQUINAS CARROLL, R.S.M.
Mount Mercy College
Pittsburgh, Pennsylvania

Nuns represent one of the strongest formative forces in the Church today: religious women in the United States have their greatest days before—not behind—them only if superiors and the hundreds of others they represent do not betray us. Criticisms today do not come from the Know-nothings or the American Protective Association; they come from within. Shall they serve to make us healthily vigilant and alert to change or shall they rob us of our confidence? You will largely decide that issue. Hence the topic is of profound importance and long overdue. More and more major superiors reach the conclusion: the local superior is the *key* person in the practical effectiveness of every Sister-Formation program. It is to her guidance that the Lord confides the young sister when He calls to her: "Come, my beloved, let us go forth into the field, let us abide in the villages" (Cant. 7:11).

The topic "The Role of the Local Superior in Sister Formation" may be applied broadly. Every sister, please God, will be forming herself until she dies. In that process she may well welcome the aid of a good local superior. Here we limit ourselves, however, to the role of the local superior with relation to those sisters who have recently completed their juniorate studies.

Today we take it for granted that every congregation has established a basic formation period of at least five years. May I at this point be allowed a *caveat!* The Sister-Formation program as we have inaugurated it in most of our congregations is in its completed form not more than three or four years old. We have, as we might have expected, discovered weaknesses within it. My plea is that we correct the weaknesses, but not destroy that which is good, that which is not yet even completely tried, in favor of a program which in its essence may

185

be very much weaker. We must have specialized formation aimed at laying a firm basis of spiritual strength and providing adequate professional preparation, usually the basic academic degree, before assignment to responsible involvement in fields of service.

Throughout the period of formation the young sister is instructed in liturgical and meditative prayer, in Holy Scripture, sacred doctrine, and the practical living of the spiritual life according to particular rule. At the same time she has, typically, received a liberal arts education and a more or less sophisticated initiation into the world of contemporary culture. In most formation centers she has learned to appreciate beauty, and to love to produce it in its various forms of liturgy and paraliturgy, of song and dance and visual arts. As part of her generation's heritage, and as a result of her own philosophical and literary studies she is deeply person-oriented. She is very much aware of her own "need to be fulfilled"; she will often feel that only *she* can respond to the needs of another soul. The poor, the culturally deprived, anyone who appears to be suffering from "the system," has a natural claim upon her concern. She wants desperately to be honest, genuine, and open. But though she is honest in seeing the deficiencies of others she can frequently rationalize her own. She possesses a strong desire to build community in order to find her own self-fulfillment through interpersonal contacts, and to express Christian love.

During this long period the directors of formation have sought to know and to understand this sister as an individual. They have aimed to help her experience deeply spiritual realities in faith and hope and love, and to base her total experience of life upon these. At the same time, in her studies the young sister has, hopefully, acquired a habit of testing ideas and opinions, of exercising constructive and critical judgments. She has literally grown up in the give-and-take of discussion, and adapts easily to teamwork in planning and executing projects. The influences upon this sister have been, as far as has been possible, rational, fair, and Christlike in giving her kindness and leading her to faith-values. The sister has verbalized, often brilliantly, her own aspiration to become a woman of great love, of prayer, of service. Like most of the rest of us, she is more disturbed at finding these ideals poorly realized in others than in herself. Her greatest weakness, of which she is dimly aware, is that she has not met many tests of her own fine dreams and commitments. Poised, articulate, joyfully anticipating her first apostolate, and almost paralyzed by fear, she presents herself to her first superior outside the house of studies.

And the superior, as she reads the notice of the sisters to be in her house, does she gasp as she sees the name of a temporary-vow sister: all the other responsibilities of the house, and now this? If such should be her response she is already defeated. She may be thinking primarily of the fact that she must give a very influential opinion as to whether or not this sister should make final vows, and be caught in a web of fear at the awfulness of the decision required, wherein "yes" or "no" will be said to a sister for life. She may, on the other hand, be concerned about the edification which the sisters in her house will give to the young sister. She may conceive her position, as canon law has enunciated it, as the keeper of the rule, and wonder in these days of change how she can know what is the rule which is to be kept. She may think of the stories she has heard of the brashness of the young sisters, of their lack of maturity, of their pride in superior education and abilities. She may feel that she is no match for this youngest member of her household. Any one or all of these thoughts form, of course, the worst welcome she can give to the young sister approaching her so hopefully and yet so fearfully.

Let the local superior, rather, from the depths of her own faith and trust in God's providence, greet her young sister with joy, receive her as one sent from God. Let her see her not as a child, but as a woman who is in at least her 22nd or 23rd year and has, through realistic preparation in her years of study, gained a concept of herself as an adult. Let her respect her as a person, unique in her gifts and unique in her deficiencies. Let her thank God that He continues to draw from the so-attractive world young people of generous self-sacrifice. Above all, let her look upon her as her sister, bound by vows which differ from hers only in their time-span, already committed to the extent that her weakness will allow, and eager to become the fully mature religious able to say firmly, "I vow . . . until death." If the superior's gaze is big enough, open enough, to thus extend herself in gracious welcome, half the battle is won. The young sister already has one of her greatest needs fulfilled; to be wanted, to be accepted, to feel that her superior expects her to function as a womanly woman. And the superior has opened to herself a wonderful opportunity which will challenge every bit of ingenuity she has, her spirit of prayer and her confidence in God, but will at the same time be completely life-giving.

She will find that her newest recruit is anxious to be part of the family, to work with these sisters she has not known before, to form deep and pure and lasting friendships with them. But they must accept her as she is, pray for her and work *with* her to help her become all that she desires to be. To this end the local superior must make heroic efforts to understand her and to help the other sisters understand her. I say this, not in the sense that the world is to be made over so as to be intelligible on the wave-length of the new sister, or that all obstacles are to be cleared from the path of the young, but because this generation must be approached in its way, and, if it is approached properly, will enrich our lives immensely.

The young sister has been drawn to religious life in the first place by love of God, the desire to give love, and the need to give herself in service. She is committed to Christ, but in expressions different from those which animated earlier generations. Whereas most of us here have based our spiritual growth upon the imitation of the historical Christ, it is Christ in His Mystical Body who attracts our youthful member. Her thrust goes naturally outwards, to find Christ in serious soul-revealing dialogue with others, to find Him in the child, the wretched, and the sick. Group meditation not only appeals to her, it really helps her. It is only with difficulty and with help that she can give herself to prolonged personal prayer, and appreciate the value of silence and recollection upon which this is based. She differs from the sisters who are older than herself in finding more nourishing food in Sacred Scripture than in visits to the Blessed Sacrament, reserved or exposed. She is not less capable of deep spirituality, but if she is to make headway in it, she must find in her sisters, and especially in her superior, a willingness to accept the genuineness of her dedication and to allow her to express it in her own way. The superior must be keen enough to accept the differences of expression and yet guide the young sister in the principles of religious life which remain basic to both the older and the newer expression.

The young sister is not helped when the superior recoils in horror at the statement that the rosary does not mean anything to her; rather the superior should frankly raise questions: "What is it that you find so difficult about the rosary? What is it that I find in the rosary which it is important for you to find in some other devotion? What other devotion have you found or can you find which will do for you what the rosary has done for me and my generation? In what ways can I help you to build into your life this newer form of devotion? Is there anything which your devotion has to teach the rest of the community?" With such an approach the superior is not only helping the young sister; she is growing herself, and she is opening the door for growth within all her sisters. (This is not an attack upon the rosary, but it is a recognition of the fact that the rosary is a cultural expression of a particular devotion to the human life and mystery of Our Lord and His Blessed Mother. It came into being as a popular devotion, in the present form in which we have it, only in the sixteenth century. For about a millennium and a half Christians were able to serve God meaningfully without it. If it is now to yield to other devotions, let us bless the Lord, let us find these other devotions, let us make them meaningful to this contemporary generation as the rosary was to preceding ones.)

It is in the Holy Sacrifice of the Mass that all generations must become as one, entering profoundly into the meaning and the reality of Christ's transformation, presence, and worshipful sacrifice to His Father. Yet again one of the great areas of increased difficulty for the young sister going into her first local mission is the expression of this participation in the liturgy. In the novitiate, the juniorate, the college, the young sister has undoubtedly been taught the centrality of the liturgy for her spiritual life and for her affective life. Beauty, care, reverence have marked every detail. She has delighted in being as active a participant in the liturgy as in the classroom. Through identifying closely with the actions of the priest in the new rubrics, singing joyously her "great Amens," reading the epistle, bringing the offertory gifts, sharing her deepest and most intimate aspirations in the bidding prayers, calling out the names of her loved ones in the mementos, greeting her neighbor in the "Pax," and singing, singing, singing, she has experienced life in the liturgy, she has shared, with all her senses, in Christ's sacrifice; she has communed with God, with all her associates present, and with all peoples everywhere. The Mass has become the core of her daily life—her "experience of God." She is easily swayed to any external manifestation of her acknowledgment that Christ "is" in her sisters. Her mood has become expansive and joyous.

To transfer from such a *celebration* of Holy Mass to a parish church of Barclay Street art, often cold and dark and empty, with the priest far removed, back turned to the congregation, secretively whispering the prayers that should be soul-shattering and breath-taking, is a deprivation of monumental significance to the young sister. Mass becomes dry and, in a sense, unyielding. A portion of her dies right there.

She desires feverishly to convince the older members of the community of her conviction about Christ—present in the others. She yearns for Mass to be alive and to be allowed to put herself into it. In the local convent this satisfaction drawn from daily immersion in the liturgy may fade, and something happens. Mass is no longer *the thing*.

Her drive for spiritual depth must suddenly seek another path. If her suffering in it is met by smug ridicule ("Well, at least we have this much our way.") or by pretense that all is as it should be, she will be scandalized and rebellious. If on the other hand it is honestly pointed out to her that here there is deficiency, that she hereby has an opportunity to share in the suffering many others endure from the human weaknesses in the visible Church, she will ponder more maturely what it means to believe, to participate "interiorly," to seek the beauty which is within. Now, the young sister will not readily be willing to accept this state of affairs, or to go along with the element of self-immolation which is being asked of her and which she does not understand or consider relevant. She will allow her energy to be sapped. The local superior must be ready for this. Since potent motivating force has been withdrawn from the sister she must give her the opportunity to talk about the Mass, to move to a new level of understanding. Her most important task is to help the sister keep the Mass as the core of her life, to make use of monotony, carelessness, lack of concern (human failure of all kinds), to find new meaning. In general, she must help her transcend the external.

At this point all the young sister's spiritual forces ought to be open to new ways of finding God. The local superior must be prepared to feed her the "milk and honey" of our ascetical heritage. Be assured that the motivation of the concentrated formation periods will fade, and new ways, new reasons will be essential to pursuance of depth. Perhaps it will be here that she should be reintroduced to treatises on virginity, to works on faith and the meaning of consecration. More than ever the office should be studied, psalmody, its meaning and its primacy as pure prayer. She should be led to works which will encourage potent apostolic attitudes.

When the young sister receives her first full-time assignment other than study, she feels as though she is just beginning to live. All the hopes and dreams of giving herself to the apostolate which she has built up through her training and through her contacts with local houses, visiting hospitals and poor homes, and observing classes, are at last to be realized. With the exuberance of youth she pictures herself—admirably so—as affecting apostolically the people she will meet. Her assigned charge may be the classroom or the hospital department and she accepts this. But, she will want *apostolic* contacts with parents, with youth groups, with poverty programs. She will want to be involved in the parish, ecumenical meetings, and freedom rallies. The superior might meet this enthusiasm with a tired "I've seen all this before"; or worse still, she could condemn the young sister as superficial, wanting to run around, or seeking to escape "cloister." Or, judging her to be brash, and giving her "enough rope to hang herself," she could allow her indiscriminately to take on tasks and commitments, to overdo, and attract the carping criticism of the sisters and others. And the young sister would become disillusioned and embittered, set back many years in her course of doing great things for God.

But how much better if the superior would recognize in the young sister a zeal related to the theology of the Constitution on the Church, commend her for it, and then prudently, in partnership, work out with her the demands and opportunities of her main assignment, then any other significant work needing to be done which was within the young sister's competence. Here the superior should help the sister to see the possible effects of her inexperience, her *untested* capacity, and, if applicable, the temporary nature of her assignment which might make it impossible for her to carry out the full responsibilities of the task. In such a discussion the young sister could grow in her own self-awareness, in realistic appraisal of situations, and in gratitude to her superior for taking her seriously, and treating her aspirations with respect. She would feel encouraged, too, as she grows in experience and self-knowledge, to approach her superior again with the proposition that she become more involved in additional responsibilities. Hence the vitality and generosity which the Church needs so desperately will not be crushed, but only ripened!

As we said earlier, the young sister has been drawn to religious life in the first place by love of God, desire to give love, and the need to give herself in service. She has brought many weaknesses, particularly noteworthy insofar as they differ, at least on the surface, from the characteristics of former generations. Perhaps most shocking to the older sisters are her repugnance to anything negative, to the cross, to suffering, her repugnance particularly to any mortifications which look contrived or artificial. Her directors of formation have already been working with her in these areas. They have presented to her the classic doctrines, they have taught her Our Lord's description of the need for suffering and the cross. Yet as she emerges from the juniorate she would probably still recognize only that mortification as advantageous which arises from situations wherein she may suffer with those who suffer. "Uniting herself to the sufferings of Christ" will have meaning for her only if by it we understand Christ as the Christ living now in our neighbor who is needy.

She rejects the concept of voluntary mortification as a means to ensure acceptance of life's difficult moments or to make her "strong" in temptation. The word "strong" communicates to her a snobbish ideal, a state in which she might think of herself as superior to the weaknesses of human nature, actually a state which would reduce her to a worse level—that of separating herself from her fellowman. Such a sister looks forward to leaving the juniorate mainly to be in the active apostolate, able to relieve suffering humanity.

However she soon recognizes that her life is virtually without suffering. While she becomes keenly aware that she is not "one" with a large part of the suffering world, yet she senses that she could probably not live out successfully a life of destitution and loneliness. Here mortification begins to take on meaning in her life. Because she wants to be one with the deprived she is drawn to seek this oneness deliberately, and to seek it in actual privation. "Fasts for freedom" are meaningful. Cold feet and empty stomachs during a demonstration speak to her. Walking instead of riding or taking a streetcar instead of a cab becomes her way of participating in reality.

The local superior may quench something very beautiful if she insists upon the ways of the past, spurns or laughs at these unfamiliar ideas! The young sister might then well remain on the plane where the privation of the needy speaks, and the privation of religious life becomes frustration, unnecessary and without potential for good. If, instead, the local superior recognizes that the hard ground is yielding when a sister arrives at this stage, that it is time to plant the seeds of a deeper ascetical life, she will help the sister transform her love of privation into a love of the cross.

Those of you who have been working with or keeping abreast of the Canon Law Society of America are aware of the vast shift in underlying philosophy that has taken place in the approach to law. Attempts to revise the code are being built around the criteria of Christ's double commandment of love and the primacy of the person. If you understand this you will find acceptable also this next attitude which we find characteristic of our incoming sister. The rule has very little meaning to her. She is apt to look upon a correction for "violation of the rule" as ridiculous. To her a law is good if she has found it to be so. Each part of the rule, hence, will be tested against her freedom to love.

Does the rule arise from her needs and those of her sisters here and now, or must she suffocate as she studies it? The law of charity often seems to be in opposition to the law, especially when the law or the superior refuses to be flexible.

In the course of novitiate and juniorate much of this conflict subsides. Again and again the sister faces a crisis with the law, and is led, through penetration of its spirit, to transcend her objection to the particular regulation. Nevertheless, the process of acceptance will probably remain the same with each new regulation (depending of course on the type of restriction and the degree of importance the sister attaches to it). Hence the tremendous patience needed with our young sisters! Their obedience, to be authentic to them, must spring from a total embrace of the matter commanded. This is, ultimately, a very healthy state of being. (How many neuroses appear in middle-aged persons who have half-accepted obediences, sacrifices, humiliations, and unconsciously left the other half to rankle into bitterness and rebellion!)

Neither can the young sister be readily moved by the consideration, "the good of the religious community." This again is something she must grow into with experience and patient discourse. It is not the community but the sister next door, or the sister "in trouble" (whether personal trouble or trouble with the superior) who claims her sympathy and who usually constitutes the reason for her lack of conformity. "Community" only appears to her as a good, if she sees it as a sincere relationship with the sisters as individuals. The people she lives with are "persons"; the rule, congregation, even "religious community" are abstract. That the congregation should have overriding rights to regulate is oppressive to her; the needs of a sister are personal, can be known and satisfied.

This devotion to the good of the other person in the concrete is, in itself, wholesome and Christlike. The superior ought not to ridicule or snub it, but use it to help the sister develop a really selfless appreciation of others' needs. That there is much of the selfish satisfaction (e.g., of her need to be needed) in the earliest stages of the sister's expression of love of neighbor, will be clear to the superior though quite unrecognized by the young sister. Here sincere dialogue, patient and serene answering of the sister's "whys" will promote the young sister's self-knowledge, purify her love, and lead her gradually to confidence in her rule and love of her congregation.

It has been abundantly clear from these illustrations that I sense a prime role of the superior to be that of a "sounding board" through which the young religious comes to know, improve, and direct herself. More will be accomplished in five minutes of real listening and responsive, challenging comment as to an equal than in hours of haranguing or talking down to the sister as a subject. Such dialogue is possible only if the superior has created an environment of trust, kept confidence, and made approach to herself easy. The indispensable key to such an environment is the superior's own life of faith and prayer. From this stronghold she will draw the principles which direct her to be flexible or to be firm as total circumstances warrant. The local superior will also be of immense help to the formation of the young sister if she fulfills faithfully her role as a link between the adjusting young sister and the others in the house. It must be apparent that she really is superior of the house, of the whole house. If her attention or her directives are aimed only at the young she risks imbalance. If she regularly makes distinctions between what she asks of them and of the more senior members of the house in the way of fidelity to the constitution and customs, she will not be taken seriously by either group.

The young sister easily ferrets out instances of what she considers gross irresponsibilities of older members, whether these relate to community living or to professional inefficiency. What she is not competent to judge is precisely what is crucial: the *value* of what she is judging. The local superior is in an excellent position to help the young sister realize that mediocrity, weaknesses exist in all of us, that perhaps the most poignant suffering can come from our inability to accomplish what we feel we should. She can help her to see that the perfection of Christian charity is not built upon perfect people, but upon a compassionate, humbling realization that "we are all likewise sinners." In helping the understanding and acceptance to flow both ways, toward the young and toward the older, she helps the community perform one of its main functions as an agent of continuity, imparting to the young an appreciation of past attitudes and achievements as a genuine response to the needs of the past and a respect for present forms as a genuine response to present needs. The young sister will be helped toward a mature depth of spirituality by the older sisters; and the older sisters will be stimulated by the freshness of outlook of the younger. Through her eyes they will cope better with other young people they meet. In the shift of emphasis being forced upon our congregations in attempting to understand the young, we should learn, above all, to be grateful that we are thus rethinking, re-evaluating what are the really *basic* values of our lives. If we can all move from emphasis on externals and formalism to the freer expression of deep faith, hope, and charity, who can deny that in the challenge of the young lies the breath of the Holy Spirit moving over today's troubled waters?

The Local Superior as Spiritual Guide

MOTHER CHARLOTTE MARIE, F.C.S.P.
Spokane, Washington

"Come Creator . . . to create, re-create and re-construct; bring us down to death and back to life again" (Louis Evely, *That Man Is You*, p. 99). May your consuming Spirit destroy all that is irrelevant to modern living in our religious communities.

Thomas Merton writes, "The most hopeful sign of religious renewal is the authentic sincerity and openness with which some believers are beginning to recognize their often rigid faith" (*Apologies to an Unbeliever*). I think we all may be counted among these believers and thank God for it.

To be aware of the Spirit is to recall how Christ lived for the same goals as we, namely, the glory of God and the salvation of mankind; and how He adapted His approaches to people and events, His instruction and Himself to the variety of people and situations. His new requirements for religious living caused no little disturbance among the smug leaders of His day. In moments of crisis especially, the principles of Christ's teaching became obvious. In our times, also, ". . . crises are the essential human elements in the life of *Christ in the world*. In fact, it is precisely in and through crisis, and in our engraced answer to it, that Christ fulfills his promise to be with us always" (Paul Barrett, O.P., "Source and Center of Tradition and Renewal," *Worship*, Vol. 39, #7).

We have been warned in the scriptures of the priest and the levite who did not submit to the crisis of an expression of love of neighbor. They, no doubt, had set ideas of what God wanted of them, and did not allow for unforeseen incidents of manifesting their love of God and neighbor. Nor can we be like the rich young man who would not risk the security of his planned way of life in the following of Christ, Christ's way. As in the life of St. Paul, in these times when religious life has been criticized and we have been directed to become renewed, and to adapt to the times more quickly, the Spirit has smashed our defenses so that we *will* give in to His revolutionary presence. This giving in is accompanied by the pangs of insecurity and some degree of anxiety, and by consequent participation in the ferment of all peoples in the modern world. With Pope Paul VI, we welcome this ferment because it is a healthy sign of growth and progress. The rapidity of growth on all levels of society is unusual, due to the limitless discoveries of man necessarily followed by frequent changes in his outlook and in his concrete living. Change requires constant renewal, detachment and adaptation, all the more for us if we are to become and remain vibrant and effective for Christ in the world—if we are to genuinely witness to Christ and to His Church. In "Words to Remember," Cardinal Newman reminds us:

> But here below to live is to change;
> And to be perfect is to have changed often.

Every change implies hurt which must be accepted to complete the effectiveness of the new insights and consequent decisions.

Happily, it is the Council of Vatican II which has provided us with the new insights: "with the new vision of government in religious life . . . that . . . gives us a better understanding of God's plan for men and women called to live under the guidance of a religious superior" (Ladislas Örsy, S.J., "Government in Religious Life," Supplement to *The Way*, May 1966). This plan places the superior as Christ placed Himself with His apostles and disciples—as one having authority, but only because He received it from His Father, exercising it as a servant of His followers, looking upon them as friends.

Some of the new emphases that affect our governing are:

1. The realization that the Holy Spirit speaks not only through the superior but also inspires every member of a religious community.

2. An awareness that the highest form of authority in the Church is collegial, and surprisingly, this aspect strengthens the authority of Christ's visible representative. In the religious life, the collegiality aspect is effected by the close union of superior and sisters, with the sisters taking active part in deliberations. The authority of the superior is, by this means, confirmed rather than lessened.

3. A greater stress on the fact that all authority outside of the episcopate is subject to failure. It is believed that the charism in the very

nature of episcopal authority is not so possessed by the superior of religious institutes, but the charismatic qualities originate from the charism received by the founder or foundress when he or she with docility followed the inspirations of the Holy Spirit in providing a new institute for continuing the work of the Church.

4. The understanding given by Christ and restored by the Church that all authority is an opportunity for greater service.

5. The development of the theology of the divine indwelling and of the Mystical Body of Christ, by which God's grace to a religious community is given through all its members and that, likewise, if communications break down, all the members are affected.

In a recent Bell Telephone Hour Presentation of the Berkshire Music Festival, Mr. Warren Wallace asked Erich Leinsdorf, conductor of the Boston Symphony, if he experienced a feeling of power and gratification to so ably lead other talented artists. Leinsdorf thoughtfully replied that, no, he didn't feel a sense of power as he stood before this group of gifted people. Rather, he said it was a humbling experience. Then he added, "think of it this way; at this time I just happen to be the first among equals."

Our attitude should be very similar to that of Erich Leinsdorf. Though we may not be unmindful of the responsibility our authority involves, we must be, as a leader among equals, *in*, not above, the group we govern. Thus we are among other consecrated adult women witnessing to the perfection of adult virginal love. We share with our sisters the task of establishing the kingdom of God upon earth. I am sure that Christ, Pope John XXIII, or Pope Paul VI would not object if superiors looked upon their sisters as associates, even corporate members of the religious community.

In fulfilling Christ's command, "Love one another," we will be wise to apply Pope Paul VI's qualities of dialogue. In his first encyclical, "The Paths of the Church," he defines dialogue as ". . . the internal *drive* of charity which tends to become the external *gift* of charity." This charity is characterized by reverence, solicitude and love as first manifested by God the Father, as expressed by Christ: "When God sent His Son into the world, it was not to reject the world, but so that the world might find salvation through Him" (John 3:17). By means of dialogue, we superiors are to accomplish our apostolic mission with our sisters, listening not only to their voices, but also to their hearts, to their needs on all levels of their personality, to their sensitivities, accepting them as they are, trusting and respecting them for what they are—as we are—members of Christ's body. Such Christlike love becomes increasingly a self-forgetting, self-donating concern for each member with whom we live and work in any way. We then can truly shepherd our sisters, lead them to the progressive development of maturity and the sense of responsibility. Perhaps it would be helpful to consider ourselves as coordinators—aware of each group as a group and the individuals within the group as individuals.

Adults need coordinators because they need to know how their judgments fit in with the common good. They need to know that someone besides themselves is interested in their part, and they need to feel the assurance that their part is contributing to the whole. Coordinating is no easy task. However, we are not asked to do it alone but in union with all our sister associates. Not versed in all specialties, we are the master listeners even though, in the end, the actual decision rests in our hands.

And decisions must be made—decisions to eradicate every rule, custom, and practice that destroys the equality of love and the adult-to-adult relationship among us and our sisters. It is no longer a privilege for the members of a religious community to be *in* on the revision of the constitutions taking place in most congregations today. It is a must! Otherwise the revision will be a failure followed only by extinction. Let us prepare by study, dialogue and experiment as much as possible in order to discover the theological implications of our rule; what in our rule and customs it is that lessens charity among us; to discern all that tends to cause resentment and/or rebellion in our sisters; to delete whatever makes religious less than fully human and fully woman, thus preventing young women from becoming attracted to the religious life.

Would it be too drastic to have the law of charity as our only rule? As women, we, no doubt, would need a few more details! Seriously, we should, for example, study our rules of silence, our observance of recollection, our laws of cloister and those concerning communication with "outsiders," to see if they are conducive to failings in charity and consideration of the neighbor.

Some of the difficulties we encounter regarding outmodedness stem from the rules and customs handed on from contemplative religious that existed when women's place in society was at a much lower status than it is today.

We cannot shut our eyes to the inconsistencies that may still remain in our religious living. We know they destroy the exercise of authority

by reducing it at times to mere police activity, causing almost insur-
mountable obstacles to the freedom of spirit consistent with intense
commitment and the state of consecration. Vatican II has reiterated the
basic truth that the purpose of religious life is to follow Christ more
freely and imitate Him more nearly by the practice of the evangelical
counsels.

I believe it would not be amiss to cite a few examples of possible inconsistencies. (a) We, following the principle of subsidiarity, leave a
sister on her own to organize a department in the hospital, or the de-
partmental team in a grade school, or to be a principal of a high school,
yet require her to report telephone calls that come to her when she is
in the convent. The sister is the same person in both situations. (b) We
give a sister freedom to order supplies for the dietary department, or
to equip a surgery or a business office with expensive equipment, then
deny her the exercise of good judgment in deciding her personal
needs. (c) We unhesitatingly take it for granted that a sister will be
mature and prudent in her professional activities eight to ten hours a
day, but we limit her freedom in her personal correspondence. (d)
Many of our customs reduce the sister to the stature of a permission-
asking child, but this same sister is credited with common sense and a
love of poverty when handling hundreds and hundreds of dollars in
her work as a treasurer. Younger members cannot understand these
evident contradictions. They just don't make sense! "Why the double
standard?" they argue. If a sister actually is efficient and economical
in her apostolic field, and becomes inefficient and extravagant in her
convent life, is it because she is expected to act differently in the two
situations? Do we set up two different norms for our sisters? We must
be honest and admit that the exercise of authority needs reform. The
apparent lack of virtue on the part of the sisters in the presence of inconsistency is a logical reaction. To be a freedom-giver rather than
the upholder of every custom whether it is relevant or not takes someone with a great capacity to love.

Another responsibility of superiors which I would like to mention,
and which is being experienced throughout the world, is to help re-
establish within community life the sister who has returned from
higher studies. We simply must not close our eyes to the difficulty involved, but do all we can to prevent unnecessary suffering on the part
of the sisters in the convent, and the sister who returns. Sympathy and
understanding must be developed on both sides. On the one hand,

those who have remained at home must show interest in the sister and for all she has learned, as she should in their apostolate, which perhaps was somewhat handicapped during her absence. All should try to realize how the sister who has been away has had to re-evaluate her life in adapting herself to a new environment which required self-imposed discipline and a flexible schedule in order to fit in her classes and other activities. Her association with her peers reached the degree of an intimacy in which they respected her judgment and sought her advice, and this resulted in a development of deeper personal views and values on her part. We can readily see that the sister who has been away will find it the more difficult to readjust to the convent situation than the other sisters to her. She has discovered the importance placed on essentials against the somewhat out-of-proportion emphasis placed upon nonessentials in religious living. She finds the sisters at home have changed, having also met people and lived situations that were maturing. Sister must be guided to accept the sisters and the circumstances in the convent as she finds them, and again, to be ready to generously share the inconveniences of common living. If both the sisters at home and the sister who has just returned listen to each other and remain open to one another, the possibilities for renewal and adaptation are tremendous. Since we do send sisters away for graduate study, we must be willing not only to bear with the consequences; we must want them! We must be ready to accept these sisters with their new ideas. We must encourage them to contribute their all to the Church through the religious community in which they have chosen to persevere, while some of their companions at study have requested dispensations from religious life, or have chosen to live the counsels in other circumstances.

Father Bernard Häring, C.Ss.R., has said that it is much better if the sisters who have had the privilege of higher education remain in their congregation to aid in the renewal process, but often they do not have the humility or the patience to wait for the natural procedure of progress (CMSW Meeting, Denver, Colorado, 1965).

On the other hand, we know that the delay toward renewal can sometimes be the fault of the religious congregation. It has lost its real sense of purpose, its original dedication to the goal established by the founder. Members recognizing this may either remain, trying to influence a "reform" movement, or leave if not suited by nature and grace to involve themselves in such a movement, particularly if they

receive no encouragement whatever for the help they desire to contribute. We also know that unless the life of consecration has been
thoroughly integrated into the sisters' personality, the religious interest stands little chance to survive, in view of the rather thorough integration that has taken place during the recent educational process.
However, let us be convinced that renewal and adaptation are possible only with love on the part of each sister for the other along with
respect for each other's opinions.

The relationship which we develop with our sisters is the basis of
success or failure in our religious apostolate and other living. The sisters are our most valuable resources and deserve our understanding,
hope, patience and sense of humor. We can't afford to sit back and
watch immaturity, or inconsistency, or a want of genuine love and
concern, cut away at the religious community spirit.

Truly we are blessed to number many religious who are mature;
but what a *greater* gift of service we will have to offer the Church if
we can structure our lives in the spirit of trust and friendship, of guided
initiative and mutual support. Charity will then be our light and the
hard things in the obedience-authority picture will be overcome by
service and respect made mutual.

To speed up the implementation of the decrees of Vatican II, com-
missions were appointed to establish norms for new adjustments to new
goals and areas of the apostolate. Just recently, these norms have been
published on an experimental basis, due to the changing characteristics of discipline and to the present-day revision process of the Code
of Canon Law. Though the experiments must have the approval of the
Holy See or of the general chapter, there is much religious can do on
their own, such as:

1. Fulfilling all the possibilities of improvement in our existing apostolates, which through the years may have been imperceptibly made
to yield to custom that may *not* be meeting the needs as they totally
exist.

2. Studying additional needs of people in the areas; to discover if
these will fulfill the function and aims of our respective institutes, and,
whether or not these needs are being taken care of by other agencies
of service.

3. Making studies of religious life in order to make it a sufficient symbol and sign to help mankind to the utmost degree.

By way of parenthesis, it may be well to add the following possible
clarification of *spirit* concerning religious community:

The importance of the past lies not in the details of what was done or what was said for its own sake, but rather in what facets of the personality of Christ these things embodied and revealed. The importance of historical *action* is *not* in the historical mode but in the character and motives of the person who confronted the world in and through this act. [Paul Barrett, O.P. *Art. cit., Worship*, Vol. 39, #7].

We must encourage our sisters in experimentation prudently allowed, hear them out, guide them to be practical in the following of the Spirit, and to note the advantages and disadvantages for the good of the Church. The experiment should be followed with a report of successes and failures, plus the advantages and disadvantages of the experimentation. Such reports are of value to preliminary meetings in preparation for provincial and general chapters. One example of experimentation may be for a local group of sisters to improve their daily schedule by making it more relevant to the needs of the students, or to professional groups with whom they work, or to be at the patient's bedside when he or she most needs a sister. Our mission is always *people*, not things.

For better or for worse, religious today must cast their lot with the needs of the Church as a whole, abandoning whatever "go-it-alone" policy they have. Vatican II points out the Church as a pilgrim church going forward together with humanity and experiencing the same earthly lot. As a portion of the pilgrim church, we become aware of contemporary human conditions, and the temporal, psychological, and spiritual necessities of man. If contemporary life is to be taken seriously, and it must, the pat phraseology that the religious ideal is to be *in* the the world, but not *of* it, contains only a half truth.

It is a fact bearing on the very person of man that he can come to an authentic and full humanity only through culture, that is, through the cultivation of *natural* good and values. Wherever human life is involved, therefore, nature and culture are quite intimately connected.

We must, then, recognize cultural forms, participate in them and adapt to them, seeking to "render social life more human . . . , expressing in its works the great spiritual experiences and desires" of man (Pastoral Constitution on the Church in the Modern World, Chapter II).

To be of religious Christian influence, it is understood that the religious is to always maintain her state of consecration to the full, no matter what type of adaptation she must make in her apostolate. Thus the difference between the secular and the religious, for example, will be manifest. This is because, as you already know, the religious is animated and strengthened by the conviction that the very success of her apostolate depends on the quality of her living relationship with Christ.

Although the Church is not a democratic society, still, in order to be up-to-date, it has accepted democratic means in so far as they are consistent with the Church's supernatural origin and its service on behalf of the human family. Now, is there any reason why we could not introduce whatever democratic procedures would be conducive to improvement in our religious structures? In ordinary living, it is very natural for a group to choose its leader. I look forward to the time when religious on the local level will vote for their own superior. It would be worth experimenting on such a procedure with its consequent living. I do know of a province, whose provincial superior's term of six years will soon be over, in which each sister was asked to forward her recommendation of a provincial superior to the superior general.

I believe that it is quite apparent that Christ favored the psychology behind the idea of natural selection. At the time of the promise of authority to Peter as recorded in the gospel account, the Lord quizzes the apostles about what men say of Him. Various apostles answer that some think He is Elias, others, John the Baptist or one of the prophets. Then the Lord springs the sixty-four dollar question. He asks them, "Who do you say I am?" Perhaps the apostles looked startled, confused and concerned. They may have nudged Peter, urging him to formulate a reply. At any rate, it was Peter who answered, and his answer was evidently accepted by the rest of the apostles. Peter accepted leadership and Christ accepted Peter as the first leader of His Church.

Also, there was actual voting in the form of casting lots in the Scriptures. One example you will recall, is that after Judas had defected and Christ had ascended to heaven, the apostles decided they should be twelve in number once again. To replace Judas, they cast lots and the lot fell upon Matthias.

Whatever we do for the renewal and reform of our religious institutes, we surely cannot replace or go ahead of the Holy Spirit, but we can *help* Him accomplish the complete springtime to be finally fused into summer within the Church. We must desire what God desires for us, with no preconceived notions on our part of what He wants, while following the light given us by the Spirit of Vatican II. The details of what we should do are left to us. We have the "go ahead" sign. Let us not be as those who yearn for freedom, but after they have it and realize its accompanying responsibilities begin to wish for the good old days. The authority we have been given, and which we have accepted, will best achieve its purpose when it is exercised for the service of the common good, while keeping in mind the proper development of the individual in the world of today. If authority extends beyond the point where it is needed, it is no longer justified. Also, flexibility of methods in applying principles is most fitting to the dignity of the human being.

When the sisters have been able to retain their freedom of spirit in their obedience, the more fully will they and we witness to Christ and the Church. Together, we will

spread the good news of Christ by the integrity of our faith, our love of God and neighbor, our devotion to the cross and our hope of future glory. Thus will our witness be seen by all and our Father in heaven will be glorified. [Decree on the Appropriate Renewal of Religious Life, §25.]

With courage, joy and love, I know each one of us must go on with a song in our hearts—a song with words similar to the following:

> I walked one morning with my King,
> And all my winters turned to spring,
> Yet every moment held its sting.
>
> It's a long road to freedom
> A winding steep and high,
> But when you walk in love
> With the wind on your wings
> And cover the earth with the songs you sing,
> The miles fly by.*

* Record: Medical Mission Sisters, "Joy Is Like the Rain," Song #6 Avant-Garde Records #101. Used by permission of Vanguard Music Corp., 250 West 57th Street, New York, N.Y.

The Role of the Local Superior as Spiritual Leader

Rev. Shaun McCarty, M.S.Ss.T.
Father Judge Seminary
Monroe, Virginia

The tempest occasioned by Vatican II is rocking many a boat, but the waves it is making, I believe, are bringing in a high tide of renewal. When the debris has been cleared and old structures rebuilt, I think we are going to find the shoreline not just modified, but also beautified and further fortified. In the meantime, however, it is important that boats don't capsize, valuable property not be lost, and anxious Christians not become flotsam and jetsam on the angry seas.

If there is anyone at the eye of the storm today, it is the local superior. Not that the exercise of authority has ever been easy; becoming the object of criticism and reaction has been a perennial occupational hazard of holding office. Never do one's faults loom so large as when she assumes the burden of governing, and part of the "spoils of office" includes becoming an automatic target for every subject with an authority problem. If the superior happens also to be popular, then she has two strikes against her to begin with, for all those confronted and affronted by her gifts. Her challenge then becomes how to succeed as superior in spite of power and popularity.

And all this in ordinary times! When the very concept of religious life is called into question, when communities are faced with the prospect of fewer coming, more leaving, and demands growing, is the superior denied the luxury of a crisis of her own? More than likely an alumna of the old school of formation, she faces the task of continuing the formation of those fresh from the new school. Hers is the task of helping the young keep their ideals intact while they make them com-

206

patible with reality. Hers is the further task of helping the older religious to respond to rather than react against those young people and their new ideas. Perhaps the most difficult task she has is to save people from surrender; not only from the surrender of leaving religion, but from capitulation in apathetic non-involvement.

Before considering the role of local superior as spiritual leader, should we ask questions about the religious life itself? What is the purpose of religious life? Does it truly have relevance for the Church in the modern world? It is my contention that religious life is not only here to stay, but that more than ever before both the Church and the world have need of the unique prose and poetry by which it proclaims God's love to men. The prose of the practical service which it renders according to the needs of the times seems clearly legible. But perhaps even more indispensable is the poetry of sign it offers in proclaiming the Gospel in every age, a special need in our own depersonalized one. Who can adequately gauge the effect this intense individual and communal witness of real Christian persons living in genuine community has upon alienated individuals, a fragmented society, a divided Christendom, and a confused Church? Of course, this presumes that the genuine witness is in evidence where the action is!

Particular religious institutes have emerged in the Church under the inspiration of the Holy Spirit in response to contemporary needs. People have followed founders in performing specialized works for which the Church gives them a mandate. Individual religious houses of a given congregation have the responsibility of implementing that mandate at a local level. In other words, the prose and poetry that religious write with their lives proclaim the Gospel at a given point of contact—in this place, with these people, under this superior. The quality of witness offered determines the effectiveness of their apostolate. The witness, in turn, depends upon the development of persons and community created in a given house.

The local superior is the person entrusted with responsibility for creating the climate for the growth of these persons and this community. At various times she performs different functions: provider, schedule-maker, rule-enforcer, traffic-director, work-coordinator, policy-implementer, complaint department manager, ambassador-at-large. But should any of these roles enjoy priority over that of spiritual leader? Has she any more important task than to help people be holy together, so that they can be witnesses for Christ and His Church?

Isn't the pivotal question of today's discussion, "How can the local superior best exercise this spiritual leadership?" Authority is not in question. The exercise of authority is.

It has been said that no person or situation is so completely useless as not to at least be used as a bad example. We know bad examples of spiritual leadership. On the one extreme, there is autocratic rule by which the superior imposes her own will on others and demands unquestioning conformity. Is this a witness to Christ or to Caesar? Can one command sanctity? Will persons develop when their consciousness is dulled or their freedom stifled? Will community come from dictating togetherness? There is a more subtle form of control by which a superior may stunt the growth of person and community. It is a maternalism. Instead of using harsh measures, she maintains a skillful hold on the affections of her subjects, and keeps them in a state of immature dependence upon her. Is this the way to provide for the wholeness and holiness necessary for an adult Christian witness? On the other extreme, there is a *laissez-faire*, overly permissive abdication of true spiritual leadership. Can one really lead a group with which she is overly identified? Are the young fully formed at their first assignment? Is it fair to expect them to make their own adjustments alone? Will persons automatically grow and community thrive in the absence of authentic leadership?

It is easier to state the extremes to be avoided than to designate the balance to be attained. Where does one find a manual of Christian leadership? In the code of canon law? In the holy rule? In a text on administration? Without a doubt, each has insights to provide. But where better to search for the unique ideal of Christian leadership than through the New Testament? Is not Christ depicted as a suffering servant who shepherded a flock? From the beginning, in the mystery of the incarnation, did He not empty Himself and take on the lowly condition of a man? At the end, in the mystery of the redemption, like the good shepherd, He laid down His life for His sheep. And in all the years between, he led by selfless service. Christ writes with His life the handbook for Christian leaders. And both theory and practice are evident among those who lead others by following Him. His first appointed pontiff was to echo His teaching in charging his fellow priests to care for the local Christian communities: "Shepherd the flock of God among you, watching over it, not perforce, but willingly, as God would have it; not in avarice, but generously; not lording it over your charges, but being examples for the flock" (1 Peter 5:2, 3). Sig-

nificantly, the passage is used in the liturgy for the feast of a pope, a
saintly superior. Perhaps local superiors would do better to emulate
a pope's charism of service than in assuming his prerogative of infallibility.

How does a superior best exercise spiritual leadership? Ideally, one
can best teach her subjects what they should be by being it herself. As
a fellow pilgrim-in-exodus toward the Christ-ideal, her leadership
might be enhanced by an increased awareness of herself as a servant
and her subjects as persons and their goal together—true community.

What does it mean to be a servant? A servant is one who provides
service and puts self second. An ancient Chinese philosopher, Lao Tsu,
described the leader as ". . . best when people barely know that he
exists. . . . Of a good leader, who talks little, when his work is done,
his aim fulfilled, they will say, 'We did this ourselves.'" That was six
hundred years before Christ expressed the ideal in kindred terms:
"And whosoever will be chief among you, let him be your servant."
To serve is to practice that poverty of spirit by which one is available
to all who need her when they need her. Does it call for a radical openness to the Holy Spirit?

Subjects are persons. Being a person implies being a conscious, free,
unique individual made in God's image to share in community with
others His divine life, and to render Him conscious praise. Because
conscious, a person is made for a meaningful existence, not one of mechanical reaction, vegetation, or mere instinctual drive. Because free,
a person has the capability of choice and the responsibility of decision;
she is not meant to be dominated by force or fear that would deprive
her of her freedom, rob her of initiative, subjugate her to passivity, or
stifle her creativity. Because unique, a person is not part of another,
but enjoys an existence of her own; she is not a cog in a machine or
an instrument to be used or a slave without rights. And yet this person
seeks the full growth of her uniqueness in community with others with
whom she can establish significant relationships, whose dignity she
must respect and whose uniqueness she, in turn, ought to accept. When
persons mutually recognize and unconditionally accept one another,
they truly love, they really create community, they actually free each
other for growth. Because he is made in God's image and capable of
sharing His life and responsible for His praise, a person is set apart
from, and lifted above the rest of creation. A person is made for worship and witness.

The superior's leadership is exercised over persons. Shouldn't it, then, reflect a respect for personal dignity? Isn't her first responsibility to remove the obstacles to, and provide the means for, living as persons in community? She is neither the straw boss of an assembly line, nor the executive officer of a military operation, nor the landlady of a boarding house, nor the house mother of a sorority. Rather, she is the leader of a Christian community of persons. And if this is precisely what constitutes the unique witness that religious life is supposed to give, there seems to be little doubt as to the direction in which her energies should be aimed. Would a fair gauge of her success as superior be the extent to which her sisters are living as persons in community? Perhaps if this were the focus of her efforts, many other concerns of the apostolate on the outside would take care of themselves.

How build community better than by a renewal and adaptation of the means available for spiritual growth? Perhaps we can express the formula in an equation: community proceeds from communion, communication, and cooperation.

By communion I mean the togetherness that begins in worship, that person-to-person relationship with God. Is it a fit expression of communal worship or more like a session in a language lab with many individuals working from invisible booths? Is the Sacrament of Penance the occasion for a real meeting with Christ and deepened awareness of communal as well as individual guilt, or has it become a sporadic occurrence when a long, black line moves in and out of an absolution machine with deliberate speed and majestic instancy? Are periods of prayer genuine opportunities for union with God, or have they become so many semicolons to punctuate the work day when conditioned organisms spin prayer wheels in a mechanical repetition of insipid phrases? Is there provision for religious silence to aid contemplation, or has silence become the mere absence of noise in places and at times unrelated to the needs of a given group? Are there availability of and guidance in spiritual reading to meet individual needs, or is this merely a penitential practice calculated to inhibit digestion at meals or engender hostility around the sewing circle? Is there a premium on time for reading, or is it regarded as a luxury, or disdained as an escape from work? Can a modern religious remain relevant without a well-balanced reading diet? Is spiritual direction considered a normal, healthy growth-oriented means for all, or is it regarded with suspicion as a problem-centered resort for some seeking sympathy? Does the superior feel secure in sharing her role as guide with others perhaps better equipped to help, or does she feel threatened by overtures made for additional guidance? Does she really trust her sisters? And if she does not, can she really lead them to holiness?

Communion should become communication. Persons in community should have the opportunity for genuine exchange. If there is one area in which the superior should be intolerant, it is in a prolonged breach of charity between or among the members of her religious household. Can anything more effectively negate the essential witness of religious life or more truly scandalize than the absence of real community? Privacy is a need, but should not people be kept from a short-circuit in communication resulting from isolation? Friendships are a must, but should exclusive relationships close-circuit communication? How much of the stress of the present crises in religious life could be relieved if those under pressure could feel the warmth of acceptance in community? Is it that people feel irrelevant or unwanted? Do they have problems with chastity or with alienation? Are they chafing under authority or personal oppression? Are they railing against structure or impersonal treatment? Is the basic concern one of poverty or personal impoverishment? What bothers them more—world hunger or their own starvation for affection? Are many people suffering vocation crises because they don't have one, or because the one God has given them is withering in the absence of the light and heat of love? What do you consider more important—a good school, hospital, or social work center, or a happy religious community? What is more important—efficient service or effective witness? (Not that the two are at all incompatible!) What occupies more of your attention—your job or your sisters? Are meals the nourishing and relaxing interludes they could be, or have they become faculty or board meetings, or extensions of periods of prayer or penance? Is recreation a time for really recreating, or recouping one's capability of bearing the burdens of the day, or is it a disintegrating experience of enforced togetherness? Is the horarium regarded as a means to serve the needs of a given house and provide for times when people can communicate, or is it a master to which all else must bend? Communications means that people know what's going on. Isn't it ironic that often the most widely broadcast items are the scandals or confidences, perhaps given superiors, while the most closely guarded secrets are items of community concern like the determination of policy?

Communication should become cooperation. If people are better informed and even have a share in shaping events in which they are to participate, aren't they more likely to cooperate? If the superior is to remain open to the Holy Spirit, should she not listen more to the Spirit as He moves and speaks among the members of the community?

I don't pretend to know the answers. I don't even know all the questions. Even the inferences I have drawn are highly tentative. They need discussion. But as you do discuss them, realize you have critical jobs at a highly critical time. I suggest that we must first discern clearly the place of religious life as a relevant force in the world today, and then see where our own religious institute fits into the picture. Next, there should be an understanding of the local superior's role primarily as one of spiritual leadership in providing for the growth of Christian persons in community. Then we will be in a better position to re-evaluate the use of means available for the exercise of that leadership, so that abuses may be corrected, more potential realized, and experiments tried. It is the least we can do, and perhaps the most!

This age of renewal is wonderful and it is terrible. It is a time when those at the helm must keep members of the crew working, and prevent them from either jumping overboard, or becoming part of the cargo. As in the case of St. Paul and his jailors on shipboard, it is wiser to forget differences and dump equipment rather than persons, and so together all may become better sailors for having endured the ordeal, and go on to bigger and better missionary journeys.

The Local Superior as Counselor

Rev. Carlo A. Weber, S.J.
Loyola University
Los Angeles, California

In my paper on "Person and Community" I tried to look at religious life from the point of view of the psychologist, with a glance at the contemporary emphasis upon personalism, and the revolt from structure. The natural practical conclusion relative to the superior as a counselor is that she cannot rely on structures either; and that it is of little value in this particular context whether we find this transition in which we are placed desirable or undesirable. The fact is that it is unrealistic for the superior to quote rules, to quote precedents, to quote traditions. The superior must deal with the subjects as persons. We have been told so many times that we must relate to one another as persons, that I am afraid there is danger that we make jargon out of this person-relationship and talk about it rather than engage in it. Action requires on the part of the superior warmth, openness, diplomacy, and intelligence. The superior in her relationship with the individual subject is not a mother in the sense of a woman with a cluster of children about her, nor is she a boss, or simply a traffic manager, nor is she the infallible voice of the Church in all matters. She is by and large a woman dealing with women, which is a specific modality of her role as a person encountering another person, and therefore, whether the superior wants it or not, she is often invited to be a counselor.

We get a little involved, I think, in what normally are considered the professional requirements for being a counselor. Counseling, as I intend to mean it in this particular essay, is not a specifically professional relationship. We who are specifically involved in therapy, whether it be group or individual, counseling, or another dimension of the therapeutic process, realize full well that a good bit of counseling is done every bit as well by bartenders, elevator operators, taxicab drivers,

213

and a whole host of other people who meet people—and really *meet* them. To hide ourselves behind the cloak of professionalism is often a very dangerous procedure. What I mean by counseling, therefore, is the meeting between two persons in which the skill and the presence of the one awakens the presence to the self, to the other, and to God, in the other person, who before this encounter was not quite in the world.

Now, this requires a certain amount of openness and a certain amount of skill. The skill is learned; the openness for the most part is a function of the personality structure. I think our communal experience as religious counselors is that this experience is above all extremely gratifying; in all our experiences, there is perhaps no religious activity, and I use the phrase advisedly, that is more involving, more rewarding, than the counseling relationship. On the other hand, it is an experience that can at times be enormously frustrating, for example, when someone looks at you very blandly and says, "Now what do I do?" and you don't *know* what to do. Our training, unfortunately, in this respect has emphasized rational responsibility, even in some instances legal responsibility, and this is qualified with a certain disdain for what may be emotional because we are at times threatened by the specifically emotional.

I want to say only one thing—for those who are uncomfortable with uncertainty, counseling is a bad place to be, because this is an area filled with uncertainty, filled with fog. Here is an art that is both new and old. I suspect the history of psychological counseling as such is scarcely more than thirty years old, and yet at the same time it is as old as the Sermon on the Mount. It is a hybrid skill, participating in the sciences of philosophy and physics; on the pastoral side it is a child of theology as well. Here in the United States especially, guidance is also a child of education, because it was in the educational milieu that counseling was born in this country. This is not true of Europe. The educational type of counseling that was prevalent up until the time of Carl Rogers, of course, was identified with Dr. Williamson, and was a very directive type of counseling, in which the assumption was that the individual who came had a problem; he came to an expert who gave him an answer to a particular problem. The whole concept of counseling was virtually turned upside down by Rogers, who in 1942 proposed for the first time the idea that counseling was not of this type. He based his entire theory on the personalistic premises that the individual has the resources within himself to resolve his problem; that he has the God-given freedom to do it; that the problem is basically an emotional one and not a rational one admitting of some rational solution; that the problem must be engaged on the present level; history is of no concern. Therefore, for him there was no diagnosis, no planning, there was simply the acceptance of the other person. Now whatever advantages this may or may not have had, this has been the American tradition for the last number of years.

Pastoral counseling, which is what you and I are for the most part engaged in, adds another dimension, the unfathomable region of grace, the world of the religious experience. There is in this area a rather curious development in the last twenty-five years. I think that twenty-five years ago it was unheard of for a religious superior to send a subject to a psychiatrist. I am almost of the impression that now we send many subjects to psychiatrists too quickly. I worked in a hospital in Montreal, and one of the common complaints among the psychiatrists with whom I worked was that many superiors were sending their subjects to the clinic for answers to questions of vocation, and to questions of spiritual direction. We have almost turned all the way around; whereas we were facing due east we are now facing almost due west. It is quite possible that in Protestant circles particularly, a fact that has been remarked by any number of authors, the traditional role of the minister has been forsaken for the role of the counselor, and that the individual pastor, be he priest, or minister, or rabbi, has tended in the last few years to substitute pastoral counseling for the traditional sacramental and ministerial role. On the other hand, one notices among many psychiatrists and psychologists a great fascination for religious experience. It is almost as though we had stood up, reversed our places and sat down again. The old antipathy that was so characteristic between the worlds of psychology and religion, the tendency to cast aspersion on the other group, the tendency toward reductionism, the tendency toward the very obvious type of name-calling, the psychiatrists and religionists, and vice versa, has given way to what now seems to me to be a very strained and self-conscious atmosphere of cooperation and even conciliation.

Now with that kind of background, let's get to some practical points. First, we are talking about the superior as counselor, and to avoid any confusion, let me first suggest that the superior is, of course, not always the counselor. This would be a prostitution of her role as superior. She is above all a superior; she is above all a spiritual leader, and she is an administrator. In talking about the superior as counselor there are certain conditions which must be met, and if they are met, the counseling binge which one detects in so many circles can be avoided. There is nothing more annoying for a person who comes in to ask for administrative direction than to be faced with a non-directive response. There is nothing more annoying for someone who comes in for spiritual advice than to be told, "What do you think?" There is a tendency for us to give over our traditional roles too readily. But when the time comes, that is, when the superior is asked in this person-centered ethic to be a counselor, she must respond.

I suggest that the elements of counseling for you and for me in dealing with religious personnel are these:

First of all, there must be an invitation; there must be a request in some way, either occult or overt. The individual subject must ask for the counseling; and there must be on the part of the superior the recognition of the moment when that counseling is to be effected, the time when the subject needs this. There are times when the subject does not need this, and to impose it upon her is again a very devious use of the precept of counseling.

The second element, after the invitation on the part of the subject and the recognition of that invitation on the part of the superior, the recognition that two worlds are involved. There is the world of the client, of the subject; what is her psychological frame of reference? what are her feelings? what are her worries? what is the history of those worries? This psychological-worry frame of reference of the individual subject who comes for this kind of help from you is the world that is usually emphasized in discussions about the various roles as counselor. How many times have you heard people urge superiors to be listeners, which means to be receptive to the world of the person who comes, to the psychological world, the emotional frame of reference of the other person? This is always emphasized. What is not always emphasized, and what I should like to emphasize is the other world, the world of the counselor, the psychological world of the superior. What are your feelings about this person? What are your feelings about this encounter? This, too, is part of the transaction involved between the two persons; there are two of us, and the world of the counselor is often de-emphasized in favor of stressing the world of the counselee.

Finally, of course, there is in the counseling relationship, the obvious interaction of these two psychological worlds, often two solitudes, two worlds distinct, apart; and again one must repeat the idea that the communication, which is basic to the process of therapy counseling, is both a sending and a receiving, and one must be open to the other world; in fact, both must be open to the other world.

There are some characteristics here. At one end, in one very clear extreme dimension, counseling is always involved in a world of mystery. There are no definite laws; one dips into the core of oneself, and of the other person where, for the most part, we meet fog. When you look deeply into yourself, there is a great world of uncertainty and mystery. This is why the use of labels and descriptions, the categorizing of people by types, by diagnoses, this kind of need for structure, can in many instances be very dangerous, because no one admits of labels this easily. It is too facile; it becomes very comfortable; the person is placed and therefore can be handled. In the counseling interaction, one of the basic ingredients, I think at least, for the effective therapist or counselor, is that he or she never lose the sense of the mystery of the other person. Once we lose the sense of the awe and mystery of the other person, there is great danger that we shall lose the other person. Because there is mystery always at the core of self the process of therapy is always a process of discovery. There is always more to know, more to meet in the other person and in oneself.

It is a rather curious thing that a number of priests involved in continuing sensitivity groups have remarked that they have never had a religious experience quite so profound as these sensitivity groups. But nothing of any specifically supernatural quality, nothing of any specifically sacramental or religious quality is ever mentioned in these groups. Why then a religious experience? It may be that in our pursuit of God we have looked in many different places.

Traditionally we have looked for a transcendent God who is somewhere out in the far beyond, and who has at least a passing interest in us; or, because this was not enormously satisfactory, we looked to an ethic of service for God, we found God in the service of the other person. And indeed this is probably a very effective way; God does come to us, as we know, through creatures. But we find in this pursuit of God in creatures considerable self-deception as well. There is a possibility that we may need the counselee far more than the counselee needs us, and therefore our pursuit of God is somewhat vitiated by this dynamic. It is quite possible, too, that we are coming now in this personalized world to search for God within ourselves, and it may be that the mystery that we find within ourselves in the pursuit of self-awareness is the image of God in us. So, that is the mysterious dimension of counseling.

On the other hand, to be very practical we must realize that when two people are engaged in this kind of a relationship, one of whom may be very desperate and the other of whom may be somewhat threatened and unsure, there is likely to be a great deal of mutual negotiation and manipulation. These are the practical sides of the counseling relationship. A therapist, a psychologist, from the University of Pittsburgh, whom I know rather well, facetiously describes psychotherapy as a process of the combination of two factors—oneupmanship and spontaneous remission. Whatever may be said of this description, there are always involved in a counseling relationship a host of intricate, subtle manipulations. We do a lot of this manipulation quite unconsciously. Erich Fromm calls it the substitution of anonymous authority for overt authority. Instead of telling the child, "If you do this thing, I shall punish you," we tell him, "If you do this thing, I shall be hurt," and the strictly punitive type of authority gives way to a very emphatic form of psychic manipulation. A. S. Neill in his description of the public school system, illustrates this by pointing out that when we give young people the impression that they are governing the school while we are pulling the strings behind the scenes, it is not self-government, it is not freedom, it is nothing but psychic manipulation.

A great deal of psychic manipulation of this sort goes on in the counseling relationship and it is to this that we must bring our skills. The openness has to do with the mystery of the other person, the skill has to do with the degree to which we can deal with the manipulative tendencies, conscious or unconscious, on the part of the other person. Beneath all this we must realize there are basic emotional transactions going on behind the very overt games that we play with each other. The games are obvious ones. There is the subject who patently lies to the superior in order to extort something she wants. This is a very obvious sort of game; there is nothing subtle about this. You recognize it; she recognizes it, and, because of the stress of the moment, is sometimes allowed to continue. The games may be somewhat more subtle, as for example, a kind of righteous observation on the part of the subject—"Mother, I really don't like to tell you this, but I feel that I must tell you that sister so-and-so is doing something. I must tell you this because I have deliberated about it a great deal, and I am quite sure that it is in her best interest, and in the best interest of the community that I bring this to your attention." What it really is is a very thinly disguised jealousy. As a counselor the superior must recognize this game. The game may be very subtle; the individual subject can appear to be exquisitely indifferent, with a carelessness that masks a great emotional need for your approval. It is to that emotional need, of course, that counseling tends.

Now let us look at the process of the counseling itself. First of all, it is not the relationship which fosters the dependence of the counselee. It is probably true that this sister, who is troubled, will need to lean on you, will need to ventilate, will need to depend for a while. It may be a very necessary part of the process, but it cannot be the term of the process; the term must be separation. The counseling relationship is also not custody; care which is essential to counseling is not custody. Care respects the independence of the other person; custody crushes his independence.

The process of counseling in this interpersonal transaction is, first of all, an action; it is something that is happening between you. There is a classic distinction in therapy between content and process. The content is what the individual says; the process is what is going on behind what she says. If you get caught up in the content, you are not likely to get into any counseling relationship. The content is the verbal report of the individual subject; the process is what is going on inside the psychological world of the other person which is only revealed by behavior or cues—an expression in the face, a movement of the body, a tonal quality of the speech, any of these can be indicators, indices of the process going on behind the content.

We are constantly faced with this in therapy. An illustration which is not immediately to the point but which I will use is the following. A woman comes in who is very depressed: she rambles on upon her family situation; recounts repeatedly the fact that her husband is a wonderful man; a great provider; and she keeps repeating and emphasizing this idea that he is an extraordinary man. What she really wants to say is that she hates him, but she can't allow the feeling of anger, this resentment against him for not attending to her to come out, so she covers it with this reaction formation, this protestation of the fact that he is an extraordinary man. If you listen to the content, you are going to miss the whole person.

Primarily, the interpersonal action, as I said, takes place on the level of emotion. Now there are two actions: there is the action in the counselee, the subject, the sister, the client; there is also the action in the counselor, the superior, the therapist, whoever it may be. These, broadly speaking, we speak of technically as the transference and the countertransference; these are on the emotional level. Now the action in the client, the individual subject, the sister who comes to you, may be aggressive, hostile, angry, or she may be very dependent. She may mask her dependency, but that is the underlying emotional action. She may be hungry for something; she may be testing us.

It is almost inevitable that in the early stage of any kind of counseling relationship the client, the counselee, the subject, whoever the person may be, will test us. There are various ways in which individuals can do this. The sister can come to you and say, "You are my last hope." If you respond to those words you are dead as a counselor, because from that point on you are eminently manipulative. You are no one's last hope, nor is the therapist, nor is the counselor; and once we exercise that somewhat divine prerogative of being someone's last hope, we have made the possibility of any counseling relationship virtually impossible. There is a great tendency on our part to bite at that and to say, "Oh yes, yes, I will help you since I am your last hope." At this point the individual has manipulated you into a position where you can never really create any sense of independence on her part.

Or the very opposite can happen. The individual will say to you, "You can't help me." I had someone say this to me the other day—a young priest referred to me by a psychiatrist—and he said, "You know you can't help me with your psychology and all this garbage. You can't help me at all." I represent a certain ethic of service, and what he expects from me is the reassuring response, "Oh, but I can help you." And what has he done? He has been able to ask me what he wants without saying it. What he really wanted to say was, "Please help me." But he couldn't bring himself to say it, so he said, "You can't help me," and in saying "You can't help me" he plays upon my sense of responsibility and I respond by saying, "Oh, but I can." Now the moment I have responded to his game—and that's what that is—I have stepped back from the counseling relationship. I have stepped away from the encounter of raw emotions where the person can say, "I need you at this moment," and come immediately to grips with the need. If he is successful in getting you to respond to that need without acknowledging it, he has successfully manipulated you.

In whatever way the individual tests, this is a crucial moment. The person is asking "Do you understand not what I say, but what I mean?" There are many ways of asking this: "Do you understand?"

And the moment of testing which usually comes in this form or something like it, is a little like what the jet flyers describe as those two moments of truth. Flying a jet, they say, is a matter of long hours of monotony, framed by two moments of stark terror, the beginning and the end. And this moment right here when the individual is testing you as the counselor to see what your response is going to be, to see how far she can manipulate you, and how you are going to yield to that manipulation, how threatened you can be—that's the moment of truth in the counseling relationship just as the moment of taking off and landing are the moments of truth in flying the jet. It is a little like getting into the breakers and out to the open water if you can manage it. So they are asking, "Do you understand not only what I say but also what I mean?" Usually this is "Can you help me?" You must then assess what this person is really asking. If you are doubtful, if you are confused, you can simply ask the sister, "What are you asking me? What do you really want? Look at yourself and see what your needs are, see the degree to which you are honest about them, or ask yourself whether you cloak them over with some mask."

Many people will present psychological problems as though they were spiritual ones because it is a lot nicer to have a spiritual problem. They are cleaner. It is a lot better to have a spiritual director than a psychiatrist and so the attempt will be to cleanse oneself of humanity by saying that this is really a spiritual problem. Perhaps it is, but there are many instances in which it is not, basically. And if you deal with it on the artificial level, a counseling relationship is almost impossible.

Then, of course, there is the whole world of transference, where the individual will transfer to the therapist feelings related to significant persons in the past. In this sense the therapist comes in as though entering the scene in the third act, when the first and second acts have already been played out. When any counseling gets to the level of transference, I would suggest that it should be referred to someone who is professionally competent. But there are feelings which the individual subject may have toward other people that are displaced upon the superior; this is a common enough experience. There may be the anger, the dependency, the feeling of omnipotence, the tendency to try to dominate, the manipulative tendency: all of these clusters of emotional residue which have been there for a long time can be displaced upon a superior.

What is really important is not here so much how the individual feels in himself or herself, but rather the point that we so often neglect in

the counseling relationship: how do I, as the counselor, feel about being here? What are my feelings, because if I am to be honest and present
to that person I must be honest and present to myself, and if I try to
cloud over the fact that I don't like this person—if I try to hide it and
act gracious and kind, if we get into any kind of level in which there
is any emotional transaction at all—this pretense will come out and the
counseling relationship cannot endure. So it seems to me that it is far
more important for us to ask ourselves what our feelings in the counseling relationship are, rather than all this focus on what the feelings
of the other person are.

Let us look at some of our own feelings. All of us who are involved
in any kind of therapy have to do this. There are feelings which all
of us commonly have experienced which I think are common to all
forms of counseling therapy. First of all, I have to admit my feeling of
power. I like it when somebody comes and says, "I want you to help
me." I feel potent, and if I try to deceive myself about that, my openness toward this person will be somewhat impeded. I, as a therapist,
look at myself in these respects and share experiences that I have shared
with other therapists. I like the feeling of power. I have a certain vo-
yeurism in my makeup. I am something of a "Peeping Tom," and I
think all of us, whether we are therapists professionally or not, must
acknowledge that in ourselves there is a little of the "Peeping Tom."
We like to pry; we feel gratified when someone divests his secrets to
us. I can't get over that feeling unless I acknowledge that it is there. On
the other hand, I am often annoyed; I am annoyed because I can't really
get through to the person when I want to; I am annoyed because I can't
accept my own limitations, or because I can't accept the limitations
of the other person. I am at times very comfortable with some and
very uncomfortable with others, and my own comfort has a lot to do
with the success of the relationship. If I am ill at ease in this relationship it will be known, it will be seen. I am often threatened; I can be
challenged; I can feel that some individuals are asking too much of me
and I am afraid to give. Maybe they are asking too much of me emotionally; maybe this person is emotionally overpowering and I don't
want to get involved. If this is so, I had better say it. I had best tell the
individual how I feel right now. These I think are countertransference feelings that are common to all therapists, and that we are frequently talking about in our own discussions among ourselves.

There are also feelings of countertransference that are especially
characteristic of religious priests and superiors. There is, first of all,

the feeling that I must help everyone, that I am a dedicated soul and therefore I must be of help to everyone in my community. Care and help are essential, but I am not the unique and universal dispenser of all care and all help, and I must begin by admitting to myself that I cannot help everyone. C. S. Lewis has a remarkably apt expression. Talking about a woman who, I presume, is in one of the helping professions— social work, psychology, one of these areas—he remarks that "she was an extraordinarily helpful woman. She helped many people. You could tell all the people she helped by their hunted expressions." There are times when, because of our specific religious background, we feel that we are the one to whom everyone must turn; we dispense help to everyone. This is impossible, and I think we all know this. But at least let us encounter that feeling within ourselves. It is kindred to another feeling that we ought to have as religious counselors. We feel an exaggerated responsibility for the other person. We feel that their failure becomes our failure, that we must take their burdens upon our shoulders, their worries upon ourselves. We are unwilling to let the person go, and we wear ourselves down trying to lift him up. This is more custodial than caring; this is what one psychologist has called "patientism"; it literally makes patients of people.

I also feel that many of us who are religious, because of our concept of the ethic of service, feel we must help in all problems. We do transfer people off, but sometimes we feel a little tinge of guilt when we refer the problem to someone else, or the person to someone else. I question the validity of this feeling. It seems to me there is some omnipotence involved. Sometimes we feel a great need to do something; and here our training is involved. We become ritualistic, we are immediately responsive to the person's demand that there is something we must do. Sacraments work *ex opere operato*, but counseling does not, and there is no magic, no ritual. One of the great American psychiatrists of the past, E. A. Strecker, was renowned because his therapy sessions were quite magical. The individual would come in, and Strecker would say, "My, you look a lot better today; you look wonderful." Through constant repetition of this, people did begin to feel better. Now there is very little that is traditionally therapeutic in this, but it is a kind of magic that sometimes works.

I must acknowledge in myself my own preferences; there are some sisters that I like more than others. I do not love them all alike; I do not like them all equally.

I may feel the need to be a great peacemaker, to keep peace in the community at all costs. There are some instances in which one must allow a certain amount of friction, some even negative emotions must be externalized. I would even suggest that some friction in the community is good, because if it is all suppressed it is going to reappear in some other form. If we feel that we have to be the peacemaker, to keep the peace, to be a kind of earthmother, then, of course, a good deal of this externalizing that should be going on, the willingness to show one's negative feelings in front of others, which is so important in the growth process, that willingness is suppressed. Keeping the peace then leads to a kind of ritualistic mechanical type of life. There are times when friction is necessary and the superior cannot and should not eliminate it entirely.

Again we must look at ourselves and say, "Do I care for this person," or do I want to take custody of this person? Often enough I do feel in myself a very strong tendency to follow someone out of my office, to go with him because I am afraid that he might not be able to make it himself. This tendency creates patientism. I have to let them go. A friend of mine who spent some time with an overweening religious leader said about her, "I couldn't stand it any longer, because I wanted to go to this very celebrated woman, this religious leader, and say, 'Would you please get your hands off my soul?' " The earthmother concept that I must take care of everyone, I must suckle everyone, can create this response on the part of many subjects. This is not conducive to growth.

On the other hand, if I look at myself I might find myself bound in by the tyranny of personal experience, and I might try to regulate other peoples' lives according to my experience, "This is what I did," or "This is what happened to me, and this is how I resolved it." Thus, "you should do the same." This is the kind of thing one finds in barber shops and beauty shops, but it is not appropriate to the counseling relationship. What is valid for me is not necessarily valid for someone else. In fact, this kind of advice can be very dangerous. Abraham Maslow, in talking about the tyranny of personal experience and the difficulty of trying to communicate my experience with somebody else, tells of a psychiatrist who had been making the same mistake for forty years and called it rich clinical experience. My experience is not relevant for someone else; it is relevant for me.

A final feeling within myself that we must encounter is our need for approval, our need to be liked. I am not saying this pejoratively in any sense. These are feelings that I encounter within myself. How do I feel, for example, when the individual subject comes to me and says, "You are the only one I have ever been able to say this to"?

You have all heard many discussions about the kind of counseling that a superior-subject relationship will involve. Usually I think it takes the form of discussion of the dynamics of the counselee's problem, a discussion of the importance of listening to the other person. I do not want to denigrate this; I think it is important too. But by way of a switch, I thought it more important to write here about how we feel. If we can come to grips with our own feelings we have overcome the greatest hurdle to a good counseling relationship for another person. We can only be open to others, and honest with others, if we are open and honest with ourselves.

The Tensions of the Middle-Aged Sister and the Role of the Superior

SISTER MARY EMIL, I.H.M.
President, Marygrove College
Detroit, Michigan

The woods seem to be full of prophets these days—so much so that I am greatly tempted to palm myself off as one too. The kind of knowledge you get from a real prophet, like that which you get from a real mystic, is both the best and the worst kind. It is the best, because if the prophet or the mystic has a genuine pipeline to truth, there is no better way to get truth, directly. It is the worst, because prophetic and mystical deliverances are seldom accompanied by a color photograph, enlarged, of the pipeline. So you should always ask the prophet, or the mystic, for her ID card. I will admit right away, that I do not have any, and if I slip into any predictions of where religious life in the United Sates is going, they are hunches—only that. Please evaluate them accordingly.

Besides prophets, the woods harbor experts. It is a little easier to check on them, but we don't do that as carefully as we should. The method here is to find out what they are expert *in,* and then say to yourself, "What can this kind of expertise tell me about what I need to know?"

I have been asked to write about tensions—the tensions of the middle-aged sister, to be specific. Now, there are all kinds of expertise from which we can draw conclusions about the tensions of middle-aged ladies. There is the expertise of the psychologist, of the psychiatrist, of the general medical practitioner, of the sociologist, of the anthropologist, of the political scientist (these are coming into their own in sisterdom), of the poet, playwright, or novelist, each with his special insight into the human condition. I do not have any of those kinds of expertness, and I am going to talk to you as though you already knew what these wise men and women have to tell you. If you do not know, then you will have to go back and do your homework. What I would insist upon, however, is that these specialized knowledges cannot of themselves say the last word about the tensions of religious, because as soon as you say the word "religious" you are in a different intellectual universe, the one we used to call "supernatural" until the new theologians got us nervous.

Symptomatic of our being nervous is that we don't quote St. Thomas any more, except when we really need him. One of the "in" quotes, however, is still the one about how "grace builds upon nature but does not destroy it." That has been an "in" quote for a long time now, but I wonder whether we have not focused too much on the "nature," and on the very true fact that nature is not to be destroyed. I wonder whether we have concentrated enough on the transcendent character of how grace builds, and the fact that although it does not destroy, it may go off in a completely contrary direction than nature would by itself. Grace is not just an elongation of nature, in other words. All of this could be amply proven from the Gospel.

I am belaboring this point because I think it is very important for us to remind ourselves that a theology of the spiritual life, and above all a theology of the religious life, cannot be deduced from the premises of psychology, sociology, anthropology, or political science. It cannot even be pulled out of my discipline, which is philosophy. All of these disciplines must be considered. They can tell us much about the nature which grace builds on, but they can tell us simply nothing about grace, or how or why or in what direction it builds, or what we should think of the tensions which occur in individual or group life when grace tries to build upon nature. For this we need the Gospel. We need the theory of how the Gospel principles are to be realized in the state called religious life, and we need the practical showing-forth of these principles in the history of religious life, the history of religious orders and the lives of the canonized religious—all of which manifest the workings of the Holy Spirit in men and women, and which are a very precious kind of salvation history for us.

So what I have to say will be on the plane of spiritual theology and salvation history—not proposed to you by an expert, but by someone who has read a little and observed a little, and who can illustrate the tensions as well as talk about them.

Let me define tension for our purposes, very simply. What we will mean by the word is "being pulled in two directions at once." Sometimes it is good to be pulled in two directions at once, because these pulls are like the ropes on tent-stakes, they keep the structure balanced. Sometimes these conflicting pulls are bad, because they threaten to pull us apart.

Our question is: what can the local superior do when the sisters are being pulled in two directions at once? Particularly, what can she do, when she is being pulled, too? The poor local superior is expected by general government to preserve the spirit of the order; by the school superintendent, the public and the parents to run a first class institution; by the sisters to make a home. She has to meld persons of different training, outlook, and perhaps even theology, into something called a community. We say, she has to do it—but she certainly cannot command it. In general, if the opposite pulls are making wholesome tensions, she should rejoice, try to implant the idea that the tension is wholesome, and above all do nothing to disturb the source of balance. If the tensions are bad, as so many are, she should try to change what she, as local superior, can change, and help the sister live with what cannot be changed. The age for preachments is gone forever. She can speak—but as *prima inter pares*. She can lead, but best by giving example. She should beware of even the suspicion that she is *using* the sisters to further her own ambitions and covering up the whole thing by pious moralizing.

All of this can be best illustrated if we take a few examples from the many, many tensions which challenge or bedevil sisters today.

Let me start with some ugly ones (like the day on sin in a retreat, which is such a relief to get past). There are the pulls between bad things.

The first set involves the pull between sloth and ambition. We don't need to be fussy about words, here, just honest. Instead of sloth you can say "the desire for comfort," "the wish for an easy schedule," "the determination not to work too hard or too long or to be held to any accountability." Instead of ambition say "the desire to get ahead," "to be somebody," "to be looked up to," "to dominate in some way," "to make a mark"—and so on. Now, the tension between comfort-seeking and getting-ahead-seeking is a very useful one for those of us who have responsibility for running any kind of educational or other enterprise. At least getting-ahead-seeking is useful in keeping down sloth. It keeps people on the job, and is in a way the equivalent of promotion and the paycheck for the lay worker. But what of the middle-aged religious?

Well, her physical energy isn't what it used to be. The pull of the easier and shorter schedule is stronger. She doesn't languish after ski togs or surf board any more, if she ever did—but a quilted robe and slippers, a rocking chair and an electric heater for her room look much better now than they did when she was generating her own steam. And into the lives of most of us middle-aged ones there comes the realization that, in a worldly way, we aren't going to get much of anywhere, any more. The sister in the ranks discovers that "they" are now picking superiors from classes younger than hers; the sixth-grade teacher realizes that twenty years hence she will probably still be a sixth-grade teacher doing business at the same stand. The college professor realizes that she is not going to be a renowned scholar, or a department head, or one of the people who get selected to go on junkets to Afghanistan.

There is a contrary development which could take place in middle age. By this time we can be accustomed to the deprivation of comfort, and sleep, and a "reasonable" schedule, and the drive to get ahead can take over. What I am saying is that sometimes one vice holds down another. Remove ambition, and sloth may come back full force. Kill sloth and you may get a cruel, hard, driving personality who burns up everything and everybody in her path. What does a local superior do when she notices this tension—or more dangerously, when she notices a slackening of the tension so that the vices don't cancel one another out any more? Administer a little contrary vice? Awaken some ambition to combat sloth? Suggest a little comfort-seeking to the sister who is trying to get ahead? It can be done, but this is to administer poison.

The local superior should know that what needs changing here is a whole motivational pattern, which requires to be lifted from the merely secular to the religious level. It needed that all along, of course, but the balance between vices kept the fact hidden, so that you seemed to have quite a good sister. The middle-aged disequilibrium is actually an opportunity. If the sister can be induced to take another look at what she really wants out of life and make a new choice—she is on the way to holiness. The task for the local superior is to attempt, ever so gently, without condescension, or homiletics, in a spirit of frankness and friendship—and with some degree of admission that this particular ugly tension and its middle-aged slackening have been experienced by us all—the task of the local superior is to get the sister to face *why* she has been doing things, and to make a reappraisal. If the local superior herself has never faced her own motivational pattern, she had better stay out of this completely. The odor of hypocrisy sometimes carries even further than the odor of sanctity. But a new motivational pattern isn't enough. If the middle-aged sister is to get in on an apostolate for the first time, there had better be an apostolate going on in her house. Here the local superior should learn everything there is to learn from the psychologist, the sociologist, the anthropologist, the political scientist, about building community and engendering enthusiasm for the common task; she should foster exchange and dialogue, but she should know that the common apostolate into which our middle-aged sister will be asked to fit as a member of the team is made into an apostolate only because of an orientation which at least some of the members have toward *God*. It is such an obvious question, but the local superior cannot ask it of herself too often. Is God the object of what we all are doing here together?

Another pair of pulls which may keep itself in uneasy equilibrium is that between coldness and selfishness in personal relations versus a sentimental, or *bon vivant* attitude which is just the conventual equivalent of the conviviality of the bridge table or the supermarket or the eternal telephone. This is perhaps more a problem of the young than it is for us, but for the young at least, religious discipline and public opinion operate to keep the tendencies somewhat equilibrated. The superior's eye can perhaps pull you out of your room during a community get-together, or dampen the hilarity of just food-and-noise parties, or discourage languishing exclusivities. By middle age, this tension slackens too, and there could be a temptation on the part of the superiors to try to interest the recluse in Sprite and Fanny Farmer, or to convince the sister who is writing verses to a companion or killing hours in confidential self-revelations that she could use her time in a manner which we describe as more "profitable." But, as it was with the first set of pulls, so it is here. You do not administer a contrary poison. The whole motivational pattern must be transcended.

In a religious house there can be good interpersonal relations—neither cold nor sentimental, neither harsh nor hail-fellow-well-met, neither selfish nor irresponsible—only if there is understanding of what our life is, and of how our relationships fit into it. This will not come about unless there is a spirit of prayer in the house, and a spirit of true friendship based at least in part on many strong individual friendships. What can the superior do here? Well, not preach, in any event. It will help if she prays. It will help if she does what a superior can to create an atmosphere conducive to prayer. It will be good if she is secure enough not to measure the "success" of her management of the house with a noise-meter. It will be very good if she has enough deep and true friendships of her own not to be threatened by other friendships around her, and it will help very much if she has learned from her own friendships that the good kind tend to multiply and to widen circles.

To put this in another way: if it be true, as it is, that the virgin is a sign to the whole Church that Christ, and Christ alone, fulfills—then it is a scandal when we seem to see a virgin who is not fulfilled— whether the sign of her nonfulfillment be a drying up like a persimmon, a coldness and a self-seeking that everyone knows instinctively will lead to nothing but disillusionment, or a seeking of self in a set of relations with others who bring her some kind of escape from her emptiness. The local superior, more than anyone else in the house, should know precisely where the scandal is. The scandal consists not in a sister's acting in a certain way; it consists in the fact that she is someone who has made a promise and to whom a promise has been made, and neither promise seems to have been carried out. If Christ does not fulfill her, it cannot be because Christ is not ready or because God is unfaithful. It is because our vows are not magic. Within the religious state, we are still free. Perhaps in a simpler age we thought of our vows as magic and our state as something which operated automatically. If this is an age in which we are called to confront our own freedom, we must perhaps face with new courage and new honesty what we did not quite face before, that even within our state we can miss a turn. When we miss a turn on the highway we swing around and retrace our way. In our life we cannot do that, but we can do something easier. We can turn to prayer, and Christ will always be waiting at the end of that road, which might be quite short. The superior would do well to know this, by experience.

Let us consider now a tension between a good pull and a bad one. If I would contrast faith and hope with a constellation of attitudes like cynicism, sadness and discouragement and call one good and one bad, you would surely think I was wasting your time laboring the obvious. We are living in times, however, which keep tempting us to be cynical, or sad, or discouraged, for good reasons. We hear of priests and religious leaving the Church, or abandoning their vows; we peruse one issue of the *National Catholic Reporter* and feel suicidal: we read that our orders are going to decline, that we have few postulants and will have fewer. And it seems legitimate to be sad and discouraged. So someone (and who better than the local superior) must remind us that it is faith and hope which are good. They *are* good. We *are* living in the age of the Resurrection, even though it looks to us like the hour after our Lord's crucifixion, in which the veil of the temple was rent.

We middle-aged, perhaps more than the young, feel this tension between a faith and hope which have to be rather blind these days, and a cynicism and sadness which seem to have so much reason. The young are more ebullient; they can possibly ride it out; they perhaps see this as a period in which they will rectify *our* errors. Then there is the fact that we middle-aged are now a kind of skipped generation. It was always true in religious life that the middle-aged period wasn't very long. You were young a long time, which meant that you weren't to be listened to, and when you were finally seasoned, they would listen to you, and they would call you "senior," not "old." So although you felt impatient about it, you knew your turn would come. But now, it is all turned around. Youth is listened to, and there still isn't much middle age, because now senility seems to start rather early. In any event it is our age group which before the council was too young to listen to, which now is too old to listen to. What comes through to us is that we are on the shelf. Well, even on the shelf, we can have faith and hope. Our whole atomic arsenal is on the shelf, isn't it, and it is a force to be reckoned with. I think it is the local superior who must convince us middle-aged sisters that we are still quite a credible deterrent to the forces of personified evil, and that, in any event, these are times in which we can perhaps be thankful that we weren't listened to! For the petulant, peevish, cantankerous spirit which stalks the land, at least they can't blame us, because we were the not-yet-responsible young ones. And whatever we are now, and more seriously, we know in Whom we have believed and we can hope in Him.

A third class of tension results from the pull between two good things. Here the resolution must come not by denying one or the other, or by moving to another plane, but by recognizing that we have a creative polarity and living with it joyfully. One such is certainly the tension between prayer and action in the lives of active religious. I do not mean now the action which is prayer, and which we have all discussed many times, but the prayer which is done on the knees, which takes remote and immediate preparation, and to which we give complete and unadulterated time. I cannot imagine a period in the foreseeable future when the wisest of major superiors' conferences, or mothers general, to say nothing of harassed superiors, will be able to arrange for us the kind of schedule in which the time for action and the time for prayer will not be making some kind of opposing demands on us that will create a tension. The only situation in which I could foresee even a diminution of the tension would be one in which our lives would be structured so completely and with such monastic finality that we had no decisions to make at all. As you know, every trend in modern religious life seems to be in the opposite direction—with fewer structures, fewer rules, fewer bells, more scope for responsibility. It is conceivable, but not likely, that the new freedoms will be used to cut down on action and to increase the amount of time devoted to prayer. It is obviously much more likely that we will find good reasons, excellent reasons, pious and praiseworthy reasons to leave God for God day after day and to cut down on the amount of time devoted to formal prayer until we end with not only an anemic spiritual life, but also the hollow shell of an apostolate. The tension between the demands of religious life and of action will always be with us. A few years ago there was a real need to hammer at superiors and sisters and all in any way concerned with the life of sisters, including the superintendents and pastors who should be hiring housekeepers for them, that the sisters had to have time for study and time for the personal contacts which were as much a part of the apostolate as actual teaching or nursing. Now we are in a different situation, where the tension is still with us, but the more urgent need perhaps is to insist on the inviolability of some assured prayer time. What can the local superior do?

A number of things. First of all, she can see to it that every sister really feels free and comfortable about *taking* the time she needs for prayer. None of us *has* the time any more, we *take* it, for what we feel is important. How do we make the sister feel free and comfortable in this way? Well, we may not succeed entirely, but we should do what we can. Obviously, the superior should take the time herself, and the sisters should know it. Then she should give some indication of what she thinks are the priorities. You know, in a situation in which all of us have much more to do than we possibly can do, it is very tempting, in fact it is necessary, to have recourse to the principle that we are not obliged to the impossible. Therefore if someone does not indicate the priorities, we can make our own choice of what the possible things are —and leave in or leave out of our list just about anything we want. This means the practical eclipse of the practice of obedience. The superior has this kind of cynicism coming if she tries to pretend that all the things she exhorts the sisters to are simultaneously possible although she knows they are not. She may think, for instance, that she can wring out the last ounce of effort by assigning too many things and not designating which ones should be done first. She may end by just frustrating the sister, who will let them all go—or worse, who will make the tragic choice of cheating on her prayer life.

Secondly, the superior has to believe herself, and then to make it somehow clear to the sisters that the religious community *owes* us an opportunity to *be* good. It does not owe us an opportunity to *look* good. If all we want and expect from the community is an opportunity to be good, then we know that we cannot be expected to do more than one thing at a time, and when we have used up all our time and strength according to the priorities obedience has indicated, then we can say of our daily sacrifice that it is indeed consummated, and there should be no frustration, no self-reproach. But if we expect that the community will somehow make itself responsible for us to look good on the job to which we are assigned (some of us will look good some of the time; all of us will look bad some of the time) there is limitless scope for frustration, self-pity, outrage, and feeling that we have been unjustly treated. Now either a sister can understand what I am saying or she cannot. If she does understand it, it must be on a more-than-natural level. This is where grace departs from nature. It does not destroy it, because it takes a naturally well-balanced person to have the interior calm to be able to understand this doctrine. Someone who does understand it and live with it will be a naturally better and more mature kind of person. But we are in the area of the tenth station of the cross.

Another kind of creative tension terribly needed in our day, and terribly in need of being maintained as a tension, is that between detachment and involvement. To use the language of Teilhard de Chardin, we must combine a passionate involvement in the things of the world with an absolute detachment. In our religious congregations today we are rapidly breaking down the old structures which prevented a passionate involvement in the needs and cares of our fellow-men— and this is good. It is not so clear to me what structures we are building to safeguard the detachment which will enable us to bring to the needs and problems of men the strength of our religious dedication. Some of this is going to be determined at the level of general chapters and general government, but many of these determinations will merely reflect what has been previously decided on the missions. And here the leadership, the intellectual leadership and spiritual leadership of the local superior, is invaluable. Of course the problem is difficult—exasperatingly so. Admittedly there are no books which contain all the answers. But the books actually do contain *more* answers than we get when we read them selectively. I think often of how Teilhard, who is certainly the prophet of involvement-spirituality, is also the author of some of the most moving passages written in our time on the diminishments which must occur if we are to move toward our own omega point. Certainly in his life, characterized by what Father de Lubac calls a fastidious attention to the least detail of his religious rule, and a detachment from his own will and his own success which are heroic by any standards, there are answers for his disciples who have learned only part of the lesson. Nor do we have to strike a fine balance between evaluating the exemplary life of Teilhard and assessing his controversial teaching, in order to get our answers on involvement and detachment. The Gospels are there; the section of salvation history which is the history of religious life is there; the conciliar documents which urge us to take to ourselves the problems of our fellows and to be faithful to the spirit and tradition of our orders, are there. We need to ponder them together, and no one is better able than the religious superior to see that we do.

So we have talked about the tension caused by the pull of opposing bad things—which must be transcended entirely; the tension caused by the opposition of good and bad, which we must resolve in favor of the good; the tension caused by the apparent, and only apparent, opposition of goods, which we must learn to make into a strengthening and purifying force rather than a weakening and debilitating one.

Finally, let me talk about the generalized tension brought about in us by our being caught between forces which we cannot identify as good or bad but which now seem inseparable from living in the Church of 1967, a Church whose boundaries we do not even know, a pilgrim Church whose destination is often dark to us. As the people of God go swirling around—apparently in all directions at once—it is hard for us to stay up on top of our mountain, giving them the splendid witness the council called for, when we are confused ourselves. I have been somewhat intimately connected with the affairs of sisterdom for a few years now, as you may know, and I must say that as I look out on what is happening in some of the religious orders I am tempted to despair. But I know equally well that there are many good sisters, more generous and more high-minded than I, who think that it is only the fears of such as I which are cause for despair. Who is right? Only God knows. Perhaps both are right, in the sense that both positions are permitted in order to balance out the other. Think of what Rahner says

about the three days' loss, where there was a real conflict between
Jesus' duty to obey His parents, and His duty to obey the Father.
Rahner observes that in life we may often have real conflicts with both
sides right, and only the unappealable freedom of God to decide.
Think of what Guardini says about St. Francis, working all his life for
the establishment of a way of life and a religious rule which the
Church refused to establish then and which has never been established.
Today perhaps we are seeing a comparable effort to cut down on le-
galism and live the pure Gospel. Perhaps we can resolve these difficulties in our day; perhaps we cannot.

Our problem today is to discuss how we can live with the tensions
which these uncertainties bring about, and how the local superior is to
assist us. First of all, we have to accept our times. These are the ones
God chose for us; He could have chosen any other. But we do not have
the actual graces to live in any other. We do have the grace, one day
at a time, one hour at a time, one minute at a time—as it is needed, not
before, and not after, but as it is needed—to meet the problem of the
moment. A religious priest—a scholar and a leader of our times, a man
of the world in the good sense—wrote me at Christmas in commenting
on the changes going on in some religious communities and their loss
of sisters from the formation period: "Now we know what it was like
to have lived at the time of the Protestant Reformation or the fall of
Rome." That sentence startled and appalled me—coming from a non-
traditionalist source as it did—but whether the parallel be accurate or
not, there were people who had to live out the Protestant revolt. We
are going to have to live out more revolts in the Church, and our question is, how can we avoid taking scandal, how can we strengthen our
brethren?

Obviously we should not retreat to some familiar holes like so many
frightened ostriches. We should think the problems out as they occur,
one at a time. We should take stands. We should take leadership if we
are called on for leadership, and local superiors are always called on for
leadership. We should be involved. On the other hand, we should be
willing to be pushed around; we should be content to be in darkness
if light is temporarily withdrawn from us; we will have to find strength
to watch good institutions break up around us if necessary.

All of this makes us feel tired, and very old. So this is just the time
when we should return to the Gospel and remember that even in the
post-conciliar age it is more true than ever that unless we become as
little children we shall not enter the kingdom of Heaven. There are

perhaps few groups who have as much cause to resent the advice to become as children, as we sisters, because often it has been real infantilism which was expected of us; but I think that in this crisis the spirit of the child as Father Voillaume holds it out to his followers in *Brothers of Men* is what we need.

The child is eager—ready to learn new things—willing to go to new places—to do things in new ways—to embark on new adventures. And with this he is willing to learn, willing to ask for and to receive direction. He is not mistrustful, not cynical. He relies upon his father. Our Father can take care of us in any period of history, even our own.

When I wrote this paper the first time, this was its end—an ending which fits our times, I guess.

But before I had it typed up I went back, for curiosity's sake, to another paper which I wrote on the same subject—"Tensions in Religious Life"—in 1958. 1958 now seems an eternity ago. So much has happened. We have changed in so many ways. Most of that paper would have to be radically altered today. But it struck me that one part would not, and that I should end with you where I ended before, because as we bear witness to change we should also bear witness to the unchanging, and I would like to close with a reference to what is for us the most timeless verity of all.

In closing with an audience of superiors at the College of St. Catherine, we had worked up to the idea of a hopeful, eager, buoyant spirit which should be brought to every aspect of our apostolate. "We can dream," we said, "and work toward multiplying our hospitals, our schools, our institutions, toward making the works of mercy more effective, toward forming our sisters, toward taking the leadership in social action." That is still true today—with vastly greater hopes and vastly greater hazards. But we went on, with something which is true today in exactly the same way, and I shall just quote it now.

"Somewhere, in all of this mighty effort which sisters will make in the Church of our day, there is a task for me, large or small, but mine." And here is the last tension.

"I give myself to this task. But I know that whatever I do for God I do in the mysterious framework of our Christian destiny. If I recapitulate the life of Christ, then I will indeed accomplish little or much for a while. God will cooperate, and the Palm Sundays you and I will have will be various. But the pattern of Christ's life will have to be repeated. God will seem not to cooperate all the way. Evil will seem to triumph. We will seem to be abandoned, and our work will go into eclipse. How this will come, when it will come, we do not know. But we do know that we must be ready, for the disciple is not above his Master. As a matter of fact, we have never deserved to accomplish at all, and it is abundantly clear what a limitation upon our usefulness as instruments is set by our imperfections. This Christian pattern is a hard one to accept—the symbol of it is on our persons and on our walls, and we make the sign upon us a hundred times a day. But we still hope that it will not have to be—or at least there is a tension in waiting. This revulsion from the cross all the time that we know we are walking toward it, and all the time that, please God, we try to will to walk toward it, this is the supreme tension. Our Lord bought for us the strength to endure it with a sweat of blood."